Rivers of Power

Rivers of Power

Creek Political Culture in the Native South, 1750–1815

BY STEVEN PEACH

UNIVERSITY OF OKLAHOMA PRESS : NORMAN

This book is published with the generous assistance of Tarleton State University.

Library of Congress Cataloging-in-Publication Data

Names: Peach, Steven, 1986– author.
Title: Rivers of power : Creek political culture in the Native south, 1750–1815 / by Steven Peach.
Description: Norman : University of Oklahoma Press [2024]. | Includes bibliographical references and index. | Summary: "Shows that Creek headmen came from matrilineal clans and small towns that counted on experienced leaders to address the dangers in the Native South from the mid-eighteenth century to the Redstick War. Headmen mitigated those dangers by forming coalitions within and across the provinces and communities. This created a riverine form of leadership which inspired coalition-building and guaranteed community influence in Creek affairs"—Provided by publisher.
Identifiers: LCCN 2023022315 | ISBN 978-0-8061-9326-7 (hardcover) | ISBN 978-0-8061-9327-4 (paperback)
Subjects: LCSH: Creek Indians—Politics and government—18th century. | Creek Indians—Politics and government—19th century. | Rivers—Political aspects—United States—History—18th century. | Rivers—Political aspects—United States—History—19th century.
Classification: LCC E99.C9 P43 2024 | DDC 975.004/97385—dc23/eng/20230526
LC record available at https://lccn.loc.gov/2023022315

The paper in this book meets the guidelines for permanence and durability of the Committee on Production Guidelines for Book Longevity of the Council on Library Resources, Inc. ∞

Copyright © 2024 by the University of Oklahoma Press. Published by the University of Oklahoma Press, Norman, Publishing Division of the University. Manufactured in the U.S.A.

All rights reserved. No part of this publication may be reproduced, stored in a retrieval system, or transmitted, in any form or by any means, electronic, mechanical, photocopying, recording, or otherwise—except as permitted under Section 107 or 108 of the United States Copyright Act—without the prior written permission of the University of Oklahoma Press. To request permission to reproduce selections from this book, write to Permissions, University of Oklahoma Press, 2800 Venture Drive, Norman OK 73069, or email rights.oupress@ou.edu.

To my partner, Aisha
To my parents, Alice and Steve
To my friend Greg

Contents

Acknowledgments | ix

Introduction: "The four rivers we have in our Country" | 1

Part I. Two Rivers: Abeikas and Tallapoosas, 1750–1776

1. "I am one of the Abehkas, & I speak for them & the Tallapoosas": A New Era of Peace | 21

2. "A Cloud that has been over us": The Creek-Choctaw War | 42

Part II. Three Rivers: The Cusseta Connection, 1777–1797

3. "Breath and Master of the Towns on the Three Rivers": Diplomacy and Revolution | 63

4. "The three rivers have talked, and wished for peace": American and Chickasaw Threats | 83

Part III. Four Rivers: Alabama Adumbration, 1798–1815

5. "No more Land . . . to White people": The Quest for Intertribal Union | 107

6. "The four rivers . . . is for us to Live upon": The Creek War and the Paradox of Riverine Leadership | 126

Conclusion: From Water to Sand | 146

Abbreviations | 149
Notes | 153
Bibliography | 203
Index | 213

Acknowledgments

In 2013 I traveled to New Orleans for the annual meeting of the American Society for Ethnohistory. I was scheduled to present my first paper on Creek history. My adviser, Greg O'Brien, had organized the panel and secured Joshua Piker for the comment. Among other things, my paper looked at an eighteenth-century Creek headman named Okfuskee Captain, who informed a British agent in 1759, "I am one of the Abehkas, & I speak for them, & the Tallapoosas."[1] I thought very little about Okfuskee Captain's words until Josh, sitting in the front row before the panel commenced, told me something like, "We're not used to seeing headmen talk that way." I cannot recall how I replied, but it was probably clumsily. In the following years, his remark frequently surfaced in my mind. I wondered why indeed it might be significant that a Creek headman invoked not a nation or a town but rather the Abeika and Tallapoosa provinces. This book is my answer to that question. I have worked on it for many years, in many academic institutions, and near many rivers. It has taken my wife and me from the Fox River in northern Illinois to the Ohio River in southern Indiana and, finally, to the Trinity River, one of whose branches flows outside our home in North Texas. Rivers define our world, we have come to learn, much as they did the Creeks'.

I would not have met the brilliant Josh Piker without becoming a student of the equally brilliant Greg O'Brien. Greg's careful mentorship at UNC Greensboro made me the historian I am today. He taught me how to be a good ethnohistorian, encouraged me to present and publish as often as possible, introduced me to the ethnohistorians (including Josh) who make up the collegial Native South crowd, and never hesitated to address my queries about research, job hunting, and academic culture. More than a few of our conversations unfolded over beers at Old Town across the street from the history department. Cheers, Greg! I am lucky that the PhD program included such wonderful peers as Brian

Lee, Sarah McCartney, Jamie Mize, Jason Stroud, Ginny Summey, and Monica Ward. All provided intellectual support as I worked on my dissertation. I must also thank Lauri, Dawn, and Kristie for their assistance in the front office. They kept me on track in ways big and small. As well, I am grateful for the Candace Bernard and Allen W. Trelease Dissertation Fellowships, which supplied crucial funds to complete the dissertation. I will always cherish the five formative years I spent at UNCG.

There are many others who contributed to the evolution of this project. Robbie Ethridge is one of them. She is an accomplished scholar who always lends a helping hand to junior scholars like myself. Throughout the years, she has provided insightful comments about my research. Thank you for being a wonderful person, Robbie. Joshua Haynes and Kevin Kokomoor deserve the utmost thanks for their careful reading of the manuscript. As my peer reviewers, they helped clarify my arguments and sharpen my contributions. The indomitable Bryan Rindfleisch merits special praise too. He has been a wonderful co-panelist on many occasions, and I appreciate his perspective on Native American and early American history. I model much of my academic profile after him. Likewise, I thank Kathryn Braund, Andrew Frank, Steven Hahn, Angela Hudson, Julie Reed, Kris Rey, Theda Perdue, and Greg Waselkov for giving advice that improved early versions of my chapters. I also want to thank two professors from my time at Northern Illinois University. Aaron Fogleman guided me when I was an undergrad and MA student. He introduced me to the world of early America and advised my first essay on the southern Indians. I will never forget his commitment to seeing me become a historian. Secondly, I cannot forget about Mark Nicholas, who shaped me at a crucial stage in my grad school career. He shared his insights on ethnohistory, introduced me to Greg O'Brien, and, more than anyone, taught me how to write.

I could not have completed my research without the guidance of archivists and librarians across the country. I extend my eternal thanks to the staff at the William L. Clements Library at the University of Michigan and at the Georgia Department of Archives and History. The good people there went above and beyond to fulfill my requests and permit me access to original manuscripts. Some even recommended sources whose existence was unknown to me. At Morrow I met the talented Hendry Miller, a former student of Andrew Frank, who talked me through some of my ideas about Creek leadership and guided my retrieval of many sources on the Creeks. I would also like to thank the staff at the Newberry Library, the UNCG Library, the University of West Florida

Library, and the Dick Smith Library at my academic home, Tarleton State University. Amy Castillo and other librarians at TSU made digital databases available to me and my students in the history program. Archives and libraries are more than repositories of old things; they are human institutions that animate many fields of study.

I wrote this book with the support of colleagues at two institutions, the first being Indiana University Southeast. When I was facing a future of contingent labor after graduation, Kelly Ryan took a chance and hired me as a visiting assistant professor. My wife and I soon moved to New Albany, just across the Ohio from Louisville, Kentucky. (For the uninitiated: It's pronounced *loovul*.) Kelly introduced me to the Kentucky Early American Seminar where I received invaluable feedback from its members, especially Brad Wood and Glenn Crothers. Thank you, Kelly, as well as Quinn, Elizabeth, and Yu, for my wonderful experience in Kentuckiana. Without their advisement, I may never have been prepared to earn a tenure-track offer from TSU. Since arriving in Texas, I have found nothing but good barbecue and even better colleagues in the history program. Every historian wishes they had colleagues (and friends) like them. Their impact on my identity as a teacher-scholar is immeasurable. They have helped me to see the value of academic labor and pushed me to write when I lost sight of the bigger picture. I must also thank the College of Liberal and Fine Arts (COLFA) for its intellectual and financial support.

I also want to thank the staff at the University of Oklahoma Press for shepherding my manuscript to completion. Foremost, I am indebted to Alessandra Tamulevich. As acquisitions editor, she long ago expressed interest in the dissertation that is now the book you are reading. She has been supportive and professional in walking me through the steps toward the completion of my first book. Peg Goldstein, my copy editor, polished the book and saved me from embarrassing mistakes. Thank you, Peg, for answering my many questions. Helen Robertson and Amy Hernandez also did their part to ease publication. All are reminders that authors are only as good as the support staff behind them.

Lastly, I could not have completed this book without my loved ones. I come from a working-class family whose hard work opened doors for me in the academic world. After I graduated high school in 2004, my parents told me, "You can either work full-time or go to school full-time." The decision was easy, and by fall I was enrolled in Elgin Community College. ECC introduced me to new ways of seeing the world. Thanks, Mom and Dad, for your loving support. The love of my life, Aisha, deserves the utmost praise. She and I met more than a decade ago when we were searching for love on the Internet. (Don't be mad at me for sharing this, honey!) We fell in love in downtown Chicago, near the river bearing that city's name, and embarked on an adventure that brought us to North Texas. Although this book robbed us of much time together, we have learned the value of companionate marriage and true love.

Introduction

"The four rivers we have in our Country"

In spring 1809, a Creek headman named Big Warrior was in a foul mood. The Cherokees had recently signed an agreement with the United States permitting American travel down the Coosa River, where many Creeks lived. Neither Big Warrior nor other Creek headmen had been consulted about the agreement, which accelerated the number of foreigners invading Creek lands and rivers in the nineteenth century. In a "talk," or written message, to Path Killer, one of the Cherokees involved in the affair, Big Warrior reminded him that the "small parcel of Lands, and the four rivers we have in our Country, is for us to Live upon. [I]t is our whole dependence." In defending the Creek realm, Big Warrior took the opportunity to lecture Path Killer on Creek space and power. By invoking "the four rivers," he called attention to the four watercourses that served as the political bedrock of the Creek world. Each one constituted a subregional political unit known as a province, which encompassed a unique grouping of towns (*italwa*) and matrilineal clans. Himself a member of the Tallapoosa province, he belonged to the town of Tuckabatchee and, possibly, the Eagle clan. The four constituent provinces formed, as he explained succinctly to Path Killer, his "Country."[1]

The political quartet articulated by Big Warrior is the conceptual basis of *Rivers of Power*. By tying community spaces to rivers, the Tallapoosa headman asserted an indigenous understanding of power that contributes to ongoing scholarly debates about politics and governance in Creek country and the wider Native South. Taking its cue from Big Warrior and other Creeks, this book examines the role of provinces in the fraught relationship between Creek leaders, on one hand, and towns, clans, and various individuals, on the other hand. Like Path Killer, we may learn from Big Warrior that a province was indigenous space, one of many 'Indian cores" spanning the entirety of Native North

America before 1815. Provinces were centers of power that Creek headmen used to cooperate with one another, elevate collective interests, and ease alliance-building with outsiders. By the same token, "the four rivers" acknowledged community interests and underscored the relevance of ground-level Creeks in political decision-making. What this book terms "riverine power" was therefore capacious and constrictive, flexible and inflexible. It created moments of visionary leadership that guided Creeks through wrenching change, but it also reined in headmen and tethered them to community interests. Headmen wielded riverine power to devise agendas and meet needs that put them into a dynamic, if fragile, relationship with those communities.[2]

Eighteenth-century Creeks conflated power with rivers for good reason. In his monumental *History of the American Indians* (1775), British deerskin trader James Adair introduced his chapter on "the Muskohge Nation, &c." with a naturalist's eye. "It is called the Creek country, on account of the great number of Creeks, or small bays, rivulets and swamps, it abounds with." Likewise, traders operating from British Charles Town earlier in the century noticed Creeks' affinity for rivers and bestowed the name Creek on Muscogean speakers living in small towns between the Oconee and Ocmulgee Rivers. By Adair's day, most Creeks nestled to the west along "four bold rivers," namely the Chattahoochee, Tallapoosa, Coosa, and Alabama, in present-day western Georgia and central Alabama. The Creek "towns are very commodiously and pleasantly situated, on [those] large, beautiful creeks, or rivers, where the lands are fertile, the water clear and well tasted, and the air extremely pure." Adair provided quantitative information as well, writing that the Creek country "extends 140 miles in breadth," reaching from the Coosa and Alabama on the "western boundary of their towns" to the Chattahoochee on the east. Experienced and capable traders like himself carried goods to the Creek towns along the "old trading path," or Creek Path, which began at Charles Town, Carolina, and intersected the many southward-flowing rivers drained by the Gulf of Mexico. While his account of "the Creek country" served Britain's ambitions in the area, as well as his own, it captured the bounty and beauty of a vast territory of Muscogee peoples nourished and bounded by watercourses. The Creeks needed the "four bold rivers" for crops, beverages, and physical well-being.[3]

Rivers were more than natural entities, however, for they underwrote traditional customs. Creeks practiced a daily ritual called "going to water," bathing in rivers or streams in the morning to cleanse their bodies. Mothers occasionally dipped newborns in the water to rid them of impurities and harden their constitutions. Freshwater also had sacred properties; Adair wrote that "the natives [enjoy] bathing and anointing themselves." These beliefs reached their zenith in the Green Corn Ceremony. European visitors called it the Busk because of its Muscogee name, *posketv*, meaning "to fast." This weeklong ceremony was held annually in late summer or early fall as the corn crop ripened. The townspeople assembled in and around the square ground, where they purified themselves by fasting, forgave one another's transgressions during the previous year, and thanked the Master of Breath for the new crop. When the Busk concluded, the people applied white clay to their bodies as an "emblem of purity" and walked "along in a very orderly solemn procession, to purify themselves in running water." The male square ground officiant led the "holy train" to the water, where women, children, and men "purified themselves, or washed away their sins." According to Adair, they emerged from the nearby river or stream with "joyful hearts." In Creek country, water carried cultural and spiritual significance for the community.[4]

Rivers also figured prominently in Creeks' sacred origin stories. One such account was recorded by the itinerant botanist and ethnographer William Bartram. In the 1770s, he traveled through Georgia and East Florida, querying Creeks, Seminoles, and other Native populations about their history and traditions. At one point, he learned that Creeks' ancestors had migrated from the west "beyond the Missisippi [sic], their original native country," and settled on the Ocmulgee River in present-day eastern Georgia. The inhabitants of this "first town or settlement" constructed earthworks on "rich low lands" and cultivated fields "up and down the river." By Bartram's time, this area was known as the Ocmulgee Old Fields. The still-visible mounds reminded Creeks of their ancestors' sacred journey, which according to archaeological evidence may have concluded by 1100 CE. In a related story, the sacred travelers originally lived "on the banks of a large & beautiful river called the Red River" in the lower Mississippi Valley. Environmental pressures had forced these early Creeks to abandon "relations & friends" who stayed behind, migrate across "the Great [Mississippi] River," and establish a new home in the Southeast. Other sources confirm that eighteenth-century Creeks believed that their forebears had migrated from the west, traversing bodies of water to found new communities in the riverine world of the Native South. For Creeks, then, waterways lay at the core of their history, identity, and cosmology.[5]

In addition to ethnographic reports, the Muscogee Creek language corroborates both the environmental and cultural dimensions of rivers. *Hvcce* (pronounced "hatchee") is the Creek term for "river" and is found in many names for Creek watercourses, such as Chattahoochee and Tallaseehatchee. A river's environmental features are highlighted by related nouns, such as *hvcce-onvpv* (riverbank), *hvcce-yoksv* (headwaters), and *hvccuce*, which means "small river" or "creek." Similarly, the word *ue-rakko* translates to "river" or, more precisely, a "great body of water." The prefix *ue-* is short for *uewv*, or "water," and generates many words emphasizing the malleability of water, ranging from terms for eddies, springs, and waterfalls to those for wetland bushes, water turtles, and the great Tie-Snake, a horned serpent whose transformative powers stoked fear. Clearly, then, Creek rivers teemed with plant, animal, and spiritual life that sustained human inhabitants along the gulf coastal plain. Finally, the root *ue-* suggests that Creeks linked the sacred properties of water with Christian newcomers in the region, for they named the Baptists Ue-Aksomkvlke, the Methodists Uewv-Ohkalvlke, and the Presbyterians Uewv-Ohfēskvlke. In their own tongue, Creeks saw rivers as the wellspring of life, animating the forces of this world and the next.[6]

If rivers supported Creek livelihood, they also nurtured subregional political enclaves called provinces. A Creek province imbued its towns and clan lineages with a common political identity that enabled Creeks to think and act beyond local spaces. Thus a Creek province did not operate in a vacuum; instead, it fostered collaboration with the other provinces, nearby indigenous polities, and colonial powers. Each one showed that rivers could be transnational and connective spaces that bridged humans in the pursuit of trade, diplomacy, war, and other exchanges. When British superintendent Edmond Atkin queried Long Lieutenant of Tallassee in 1759, "What River divides the Creek & Chactaw Country[?]," the headman educated his questioner plainly, "There is no such thing as a Division." He affirmed generally that no environmental boundaries divided the region's inhabitants and implied specifically that no rivers separated Creeks from other groups of people. This corner of North America brought Native and non-Native populations into regular contact with one another, providing Creeks with a riverine map with which they could organize and make sense of political space.[7]

Following this line of reasoning, my book intervenes in an ongoing debate about governance and politics in the Native South. There is consensus among historians and anthropologists that the eighteenth-century Creeks were thoroughly local. Clan lineages and towns governed their affairs autonomously, practiced rituals that enforced community identities, and shaped decision-making among Creek leaders beyond these localities. In this body of scholarship, political localism is considered the baseline from which other modes of governance sprang, ranging from multitown associationalism to coercive nationhood. *Rivers of Power* synthesizes these foci by arguing that Creeks invested in a provincial or, better, riverine format of governance that produced visionary leadership at the top and preserved autonomy on the ground. In this way, headmen formed partnerships and authored policies that reinforced cooperation among lineages and towns, but they rarely exercised top-down, centralized power consistent with political nationhood. Communities supervised aberrant headmen and forced them to course correct and promote community interests.[8]

A study of Creek provinces blazes a historiographical middle ground, then, because it clarifies how Creeks moved from local to extra-local patterns of governance. Both political concept and form, the province mediated between local communities, such as towns and lineages, and broader coalitions, policies, and treaties that constituted an extension of those local spaces. The fabric of Creek politics was, as Creeks articulated to each other and outsiders, cut from a provincial cloth. Accordingly, this book opens with two "rivers" implied by Big Warrior, namely the Abeikas and the Tallapoosas. These provinces are ripe for study because they shared common histories, circumstances, and agendas that encouraged unity among Abeika and Tallapoosa leaders. Moreover, like Big Warrior, Abeika and Tallapoosa headmen frequently called on the riverine contours of Creek country in talks to other Creeks; to the Cherokees, Choctaws, Chickasaws, and Seminoles; and to colonial powers like the British Empire and the United States. Some Abeika and Tallapoosa headmen spoke for all or most provinces in such phrases as "the four rivers" or 'the Three Rivers"; others highlighted specific provinces and the relationship between them, such as "the Abehkas … & the Tallapoosas"; and still others communicated on behalf of the "Upper Creeks." By following the Abeikas and Tallapoosas through time, finally, we may study how, why, and in what situations they partnered with the remaining two "rivers," namely the Lower Creeks and Alabamas. This approach provides an original and textured look at Creek leadership over time.[9]

"Upper Creeks" is a term that merits further discussion. While "rivers," "Abehkas," and "Tallapoosas" were unblemished Creek constructions of politics, "Upper Creeks" was an invention of both Creeks and British colonists. It originated from the Creek–British deerskin trade, for the Upper Creek towns resided at the northern leg of a trade path that originated in Charles Town and passed through the southern, or Lower Creek, towns at Coweta. Animal hides and trade goods moved back and forth on that multipolar trade path. On one hand, then, Upper Creek as well as Lower Creek peoples are defined in the historical record in their interface with Europeans. On the other hand, though, the term "Upper Creeks" reflects an indigenous perspective that confirms the subregional spaces at Creek country's heart. Moreover, its meaning changed over time. In its purest sense, it referred to the Abeikas in the upper reaches of Creek country. As the Abeikas partnered with the Tallapoosas more frequently, however, the term evolved to include the Tallapoosas. By the turn of the nineteenth century, "Upper Creeks" encapsulated the Alabamas, reflecting a closer relationship among those three provinces. Upper Creek political identity evolved over time, then, and reflected precise situations on the ground.[10]

The political shape of towns in Creek country must also be addressed. In 2004, Joshua Piker published an entire book on the Abeika town of Okfuskee, unpacking its political, diplomatic, and economic history. Just as British colonists framed their world through local spaces, he argued, so the Creek town was the principal social unit of Creek life because it offered a communal space for political discussion, bestowal of war titles, and religious practices. Town leaders included the *mico*, his advisers in the town council (*mikalgi*), and other titled men who debated town interests in domestic and foreign affairs. In particular, Piker argued that discrete towns formed the "building blocks of regional and national associations" in Creek country. To refine this construction metaphor, I argue instead that towns as well as clans were the foundation of Creek governance, the political cement that grounded the leadership in local interests. I argue, in turn, that the provinces were the architecture of Creek governance, the political columns and beams that held coalitions of towns and clans in place. Finally, Creek headmen who invoked provincial/riverine metaphors to characterize leadership resided atop the roof of this political edifice, one whose integrity remained fragile and swayed according to needs on the ground. By tracking these political rhythms, I seek to uncover another dimension of Creek history and political culture that is just beginning to receive sustained scholarly attention.[11]

To develop this analysis, *Rivers of Power* adopts the "ethno-ethnohistorical" approach of the late anthropologist Raymond D. Fogelson. Fogelson coined the term with a tongue in his cheek, but he seriously urged scholars to practice a blend of history and anthropology that foregrounds "native theories of history." An *ethno*-ethnohistorical method should root Native history in cosmology, in ritual, and "more generally in native philosophies and worldviews."

This constitutes ethnohistory in its purest form. Inspired by Fogelson and his students, this book traces Creek history from Creek political viewpoints. When Abeika and Tallapoosa headmen drew attention to the rivers shaping their world, they alerted outsiders then and today to a Native-centered epistemology of politics. That epistemology comes to life in a Creek archive that consists of headmen's talks; ethnographic observations of Creeks beyond the ken of political power; censuses and pictographs; and a Creek–English dictionary.[12]

Altogether these sources excavate a little-known pattern of provincial leadership that stalled Creek nationhood before 1815. Records from British, Spanish, and US colonial powers examined in this book are replete with words, phrases, and examples that capture the political salience of provinces as well as the towns and lineages enveloped by them. Acknowledging that Creek politics took shape from "the four rivers" addresses the call by Joshua Piker, Claudio Saunt, and others to dismantle tribal categories that unduly privilege nationhood at the expense of other modes of indigenous politics. When Creek headmen named the "Abekas" or "Tallapousses" or "Upper Creeks" in negotiations with outsiders, they cultivated a subregional form of politics that tapped into towns and lineages for strength, rendering nationhood unpopular and irrelevant. In many cases they ruled as Abeikas or Tallapoosas more than as Creeks. While it is clear that headmen affiliated with a political institution known as the National Council and spoke of "the Creek nation" to colonial and indigenous populations, Creek headmen were savvy politicians who masked internal divisions to project unity outward. "Nation" implied cohesion in a society rent by division. Headmen knew better and showed their hand. Even Big Warrior, an advocate of nation-building, carefully explained to Path Killer that "the Creek nation" was woven from four provinces, each one enlivened by distinct towns, webs of kinship, plants and animals, and spirits. Riverine leadership opened the door for community input and ensured that nation-building remained incomplete by the early 1800s.[13]

Consequently, a secondary argument running through this book is that Creeks removed from political office shaped the tone and trajectory of Creek politics. In various capacities and for various purposes, they supervised headmen who in turn revised existing agendas or created new ones to satisfy constituents. This book names those Creeks "local actors" or "local peoples," among whom were women, children, warriors, elders, and others whose identity is unknowable from the extant records. They left an extraordinary impact on the politics of Creek country as well as the geopolitics of the Native South. By recovering the myriad ways in which these people conditioned and contested the leadership, this book reconstructs the history of an indigenous population from the ground up. It is sensitive to the thoughts, needs, and actions of peoples who caused Creek governance to function the way it did and who changed the way it functioned over time. Terms such as "ordinary," "common," or "rank and file" hardly befit these peoples and, instead, dismiss their agency and legacy in Creek political life. These individuals were political actors who staked positions of influence alongside the leadership.[14]

Creek women were especially important owing to the practice of matrilineal kinship reckoning. They belonged to matrilineal clans denoted by a totem, such as an eagle, bear, or deer. Each clan consisted exclusively of the mother, her children, her brothers and sisters, and her maternal grandmother. No one from her husband's clan was considered kin because he belonged to his own mother's clan. This practice is called exogamy or interclan marriage, meaning that women and men from two separate clans married. Endogamy or intraclan marriage was deemed incestuous and taboo. In addition, women and their maternal relatives belonged to a specific matrilineage within the clan and, finally, to a specific household, or *huti*, within the lineage. Crucial members of the clan, women looked to protect kin from harm and to preserve kin interests in domestic and foreign affairs. Women exercised additional influence because of their productive capacities. According to Creek elder Jean Chaudhuri, who passed away recently, there are two "female principles" in the Creek cosmos: the earth spirit and the water spirit. Whereas the earth spirit takes the form of the "corn mother," the water spirit assumes materiality as "the rivers, lakes, streams, and the ocean." These two spirits are co-constitutive and work in tandem to sustain Creek life. As farmers, Creek women nourished clan members. They grew corn and other crops, gathered edible plants, and, by the late eighteenth century, tended herds of livestock. For these reasons, women exercised discretionary power over the matrilineage and, by extension, acted on male relatives who held formal political office. The nimblest headmen understood these familial logistics and ignored them at their peril.[15]

Creek kinship practice has been dissected by such historians as Joshua Piker, Michelle LeMaster, Natalie Inman, and Bryan Rindfleisch, who demonstrate that kinspeople shaped colonial expansion in the long eighteenth century. Yet scholarly conversations about clan and kin largely revolve around interactions between Indians and whites or between Indians and Blacks. Relationships *among* Indians deserve closer attention, however. Just as Creeks killed, traded with, and married white settlers, Black slaves, and free people of color, so Creek relations with other southern Indians proved equally fraught. The principal allies and enemies of the Abeikas and Tallapoosas were, in fact, other Native peoples. Abeikas and Tallapoosas became engulfed in wars with the Cherokees in the 1740s and early 1750s, the Choctaws in the 1760s and early 1770s, the Chickasaws in the late 1780s and early 1790s, and each other during the Creek War in the 1810s. On occasion, skirmishes with Euro-American settlers, traders, and other non-Indians accompanied these wars and further roiled Creek country. Each intertribal conflict—and in the case of the Creek War an intratribal one—was marked by headmen's relatives. When headmen launched peace negotiations, their kinspeople cooled or stoked the fires of war according to circumstances, agendas, and whims. In a word, Creek kin shaped the Native South's intertribal landscape.[16]

The term "kin" deserves closer inspection. Anthropologist Vernon James Knight has recently cautioned historians against the assumption that Creeks associated solely with their matrilineage and the larger clan to which it belonged. He theorizes instead that Creeks affiliated with "lineage aggregates," or amalgams of matrilineages drawn from multiple clans and from individuals who bore no biological relationship with those matrilineages but who still joined them as kin. He adds that these lineages probably "caucused together" in the town square ground to discuss and advance collective interests. The implications of Knight's argument are far-reaching and cannot be satisfactorily addressed in one book. Still, his revelation means that matrilineal clans blended together in a familial mishmash that mirrored the ethnic and linguistic diversity of Creek country, a "coalescent society" of diverse peoples. This insight, moreover, enhances understanding of how local peoples organized themselves and influenced the leadership to address shared concerns, such as accessing wares, pursuing retaliation, ending wars, and preserving land. Thus a more capacious understanding of kin widens the number of people who kept headmen in their sights. No wonder Creek leadership was hard work.[17]

Yet whether and how a local person shared kin ties with a headman must be approached with caution. Only when the records strongly suggest or outright prove that some local person (or persons) belonged to a headman's clan is "kin" or "relative" used to characterize that relationship. When possible, I discuss the specific clan and lineage to which that headman and local person (or persons) belonged. I follow Knight by considering the possibility that a headman's clan associated with others in town, but it is equally important to highlight specific clans and lineages from the archive. In other cases, evidence suggests that some local person (or persons) did not belong to a headman's clan but nonetheless acted on the behalf of their own. In those cases, clanship still imparted flavor to Creek politics. I seek, then, to locate and examine records that demonstrate the endurance of matrilineality among the eighteenth- and early nineteenth-century Creeks. While Knight's concept of lineage aggregates allows historians to peer more closely at the mechanics of kinship in the Native South, I also attempt to pinpoint who exactly conditioned the leadership, in what context, with what tools, and for what purpose.[18]

Based on Knight's work and the sources examined in this book, moreover, I suggest that the Creeks had begun to practice bilateral kinship reckoning by the eighteenth century. Paternal terms like "father" and "son" appear in the historical record so frequently that Creeks may have begun to repackage kinship to include the mother's and father's line and therefore to resemble that of Europeans and Americans. The ubiquity of paternal language in the extant sources does not suggest that the Creeks became patrilineal. Europeans and Americans were not even patrilineal; rather, they had a bilateral kinship form that traced descent through the mother and father. Admittedly, there is a problem with the evidence, since records about eighteenth- and early nineteenth-century Creek kinship derive from agents of empire. Still, these individuals were steeped in the cultures of the Native South. Bryan Rindfleisch has noted that Ulster-born deerskin trader George Galphin was the archetypal transatlantic patriarch on whom women, slaves, laborers, and Native people depended for patronage, goods, and influence. To open trade with Creek customers, Galphin married a woman from the Lower Creek town of Coweta and gathered information about Creek society. Similarly, British trader James Adair married a Chickasaw woman and spent many years in the region. The famed botanist William Bartram toured the Native South in the 1770s as he compiled one of the best ethnographies on the eighteenth-century Creeks. These figures were penetrating ethnographers on whom historians and other scholars continue to rely for insight on southern Indian culture. In short, the evidence raises the possibility that Creeks expanded the parameters of kinship as they navigated historical change.[19]

Like kinship, power in Creek country was fundamentally "relational." Anthropologist Eric Wolf has argued that power is not a bundle of "unitary and independent" forces wielded by lone rulers; instead, power takes shape within a dense web of "interpersonal" connections. These connections involve communities that guide, enhance, and frustrate rulers' objectives. Relational power is at the heart of what this book names "riverine power," a term that conveys Creek thought about leadership and governance. Sculpted by pristine rivers, the Abeika and Tallapoosa provinces functioned and shifted according to endless negotiations between headmen and local actors in the eighteenth and early nineteenth centuries. The Creek brand of relational power meant that only popular leaders offered demonstrable proof that they had gauged and obeyed local interests. By conceptualizing power as a fluid connection between rulers and ruled, then, we may bring the patterns of Creek and southern Indian leadership into sharp relief. No headman was an island. His local constituents established the parameters of his success and maneuvered in pursuit of their own goals.[20]

The political tie between Creek leaders and local actors merged with a vibrant culture of localism in the Native South. From the era of the Seven Years' War to the War of 1812, power relations between southern Indians and newcomers to the region remained, according to Gene Smith and Sylvia Hilton, "in political flux." Who held power in a region teeming with numerous populations, traditions, and settlements was always up for grabs. Likewise, David Andrew Nichols contends that Native hunters, warriors, community leaders, and other peoples interested in local concerns tended to "set the agenda" for Native diplomats, imperial agents, treaty commissioners, governors, presidents, and other regional authorities. Indeed, on-the-ground communities prized their management of local affairs. Bryan Rindfleisch's *George Galphin's Intimate Empire* runs with this idea as he argues that relationships gave life to the region's pattern of localism and ensured that colonial powers' relationships with indigenous people, especially the Creeks, were "negotiated." The basis of political leadership was always local, then, but as Daniel S. Dupre reminds us, this region was "at once global and local." European overseas empires wrought profound change in the Native South, as did the United States, but the rhythms of Creek politics heavily determined the scale and depth of that change.[21]

"The Abehkas ... & the Tallapoosas"

Those called "the Abehkas ... & the Tallapoosas" by a headman named Okfuskee Captain in 1759 emerged in the aftermath of the European invasion of the Native South more than two centuries earlier. Incursion began in 1539, when Spanish explorer Hernando de Soto landed at Tampa Bay with six hundred men under his command. Outfitted with horses, pigs, and guns aplenty, the Spaniards embarked on an *entrada*, or an armed reconnaissance of the area.

Until his death in 1542, de Soto led his men on a zigzag course in search of precious metals and new allies for Spain. He found neither. Instead he encountered a world of Mississippian chiefdoms whose rulers lived atop pyramidal earthworks and commanded tribute in the form of corn from surrounding villages and hamlets. De Soto clashed with various chiefdoms, took hostages, and raided corn stores; overall, the mission was an abysmal failure. Still, the impact of the entrada was devastating, for it introduced epidemic disease to immunologically vulnerable populations, upset the balance of power among the chiefdoms, and amplified a preexisting trade in Indian slaves. Anthropologist Robbie Ethridge refers to these vectors of change among the Mississippians as a "shatter zone." British and French overseas empire-building aggravated these shifts in the following century. The settlement of British Charles Town in 1670 and the arrival of the French in Louisiana in 1699 brought new waves of disease and tied the fate of all three empires to the ongoing Indian slave trade.[22]

Disease, enslavement, and political instability smashed the Mississippian chiefdoms, propelling numerous "displacements and migrations" of peoples across the Native South. The Mississippian era subsequently gave way to the colonial era, when a multicultural stew of indigenous, European, and African peoples jockeyed for position and marked a new phase in the Native South. During this epochal shift, a polyglot of refugees coalesced as the Abeika and Tallapoosa provinces. At the turn of the eighteenth century, they established towns along the floodplains of the Coosa and Tallapoosa Rivers. In these small communities, they sought refuge from slave raiders, formed mutual interests, and practiced a mixed economy of agriculture, hunting, and gathering. They spoke dialects of a common Eastern Muscogean language, which lent further coherence and unity to these provinces. By the early eighteenth century, the Abeikas and Tallapoosas had begun to carve out a sphere of influence in the region.[23]

Most Abeikas resided on the upper Coosa River in present-day north-central Alabama. They were descendants of the Coosa chiefdom, in what became northwestern Georgia, and inhabited several towns, including Aubecooche, whose name derives from "Aubecuh." Other Abeika polities emerged near the upper Tallapoosa River and its tributaries, including Okfuskee and Okchai. The Tallapoosa province contained an equal assortment of migrants and towns. There Abeika refugees mixed with peoples indigenous to the area to form polities along the middle and lower Tallapoosa River near present-day Montgomery, Alabama. Tallapoosa *talwas* of note included Tuckabatchee and Tallassee. The

Detail from Emanuel Bowen, *A New Map of Georgia, with Part of Carolina, Florida and Louisiana*, 1748
By dividing Upper Creek country into the "Upper" and "Middle" Creeks, Bowen revealed the cascade of provinces that gave shape to this riverine world. Part-time allies of the Abeikas and Tallapoosas, the Alabama towns lie between each province in an uneasy tension. Rivers and footpaths created opportunities for trade, war, and diplomacy involving Creek and non-Creek peoples. Courtesy of Georgia Archives, Historic Map File, hmf0117.

Coosa–Tallapoosa nexus hosted a dense Native population by mid-century. Of thirteen thousand Creeks, more than half called the Abeika and Tallapoosa provinces home, and according to a British census of Creek country, no less than nineteen of thirty-five towns belonged to the Abeika and Tallapoosa provinces.[24]

The kaleidoscope of Abeika and Tallapoosa communities appears on a 1748 map produced by British cartographer Emanuel Bowen. In *A New Map of Georgia, with Part of Carolina, Florida and Louisiana*, he divided the northern sphere of Creek country into "Upper Creeks" and "Middle Creeks." The former were Abeikas of "Cousa" (Coosa), "Abacouse" (Aubecooche), "Ockoi" (Okchai), and "Great Oukiuskee" (Okfuskee), while the Middle Creeks or Tallapoosas nestled in "Tooakabatche" (Tuckabatchee), "Talasee" (Tallassee), and other towns. At the southern limit of the Middle Creek towns lay "Chauoklyhatche," a village offshoot (*talofa*) of Tallassee. Bowen also depicted the Abeikas' and Tallapoosas' part-time ally, the Alabamas, in uneasy tension between the two provinces. Alabama towns on the upper Alabama River included "Cussate" (Koasati or Coosada), "Taskeechi" (Tuskegee), and "Puckney" (Puckana). Lending coherence to this hub of indigenous communities were rivers and trade paths on which Natives and newcomers traveled, directing flows of goods, livestock, war captives and slaves, microbes, and numerous other items. At its center were the Abeikas and Tallapoosas (in Bowen's formulation, Upper and Middle Creeks). Albeit an artifact of European imperialism, Bowen's map echoes the riverine divisions of Creek country.[25]

This book is organized into six chapters that follow the Abeikas and Tallapoosas through the late colonial, revolutionary, and early republic eras. Based on Native theories of history-writing, as explored in Raymond Fogelson's corpus and Peter Nabokov's *Forest of Time*, the chapters weave an indigenous narrative that reflects the Abeikas' and Tallapoosas' mind-set. By allowing their experiences to drive the storyline, parts I–III unpack the interrelated themes of war and diplomacy. From the mid-eighteenth century to the early nineteenth, these Creeks struggled to maintain peace with outsiders and, ultimately, among themselves. The best way to track how Creek governance and leadership functioned and evolved, then, is to situate the Abeikas and Tallapoosas in a wider regional context. Their story is necessarily both Creek *and* Native southern. They belonged to a vast cultural web that caught the South's diverse peoples in patterns of violence and peace. In this way, the Abeikas and Tallapoosas star in a production whose supporting cast includes other Creeks, namely the Alabamas and Lower Creeks; other indigenous populations, namely the Cherokees, Chickasaws, Choctaws, and Seminoles; and governors, traders, travelers, settlers, and other agents of empire.[26]

Part I, "Two Rivers: Abeikas and Tallapoosas, 1750–1776," tracks the vectors of intertribal war and British incursion in the era of the Seven Years' War. After experiencing relative stability since their formation earlier in the century, the Abeika and Tallapoosa provinces became embroiled in war with the Cherokees. The Creek-Cherokee War not only jeopardized the security of Upper Creeks but also highlighted their dependence on trade goods. To protect themselves from the Cherokees, Upper Creeks demanded that the leadership access weapons and ammunition from British traders. Reinforcing trade dependence was leaders' recognition that commerce required good relations with the British. When violence erupted between Creeks and settlers, then, leaders sought to keep wares flowing into their communities. Chapter 1 examines these imperatives and argues that Abeika and Tallapoosa headmen's attempts to preserve peace with Indians and colonists alike depended on local actors, especially kin. Additionally, this chapter interprets Creek relations with Europeans as an extension of intertribal relations. The methods and purpose of peace-making during the Creek-Cherokee War influenced Creek–British relations during and after the Seven Years' War. In both cases, relatives kept a close watch on the leadership; women and men decided who was legitimate and how diplomacy should be conducted with Native and non-Native peoples alike.

Local actors remained vital to the agendas and legitimacy of the leadership when war with the Choctaws erupted in 1766. The Creek-Choctaw War, the subject of chapter 2, originated from the Treaty of Paris. The Paris Peace ended the Seven Years' War in Britain's victory over France and Spain, but it worsened Creek reliance on British wares and produced economic competition between Creeks and Choctaws. Initial raids gave way to a vicious cycle of attack and counterattack. While Abeika and Tallapoosa diplomats made joint peace arrangements with Alabama assistance, many Upper Creeks went about their business. Some renewed war by retaliating against their enemies, and others performed ceremonies to assuage the grief-stricken and to bring about peace. This chapter advances the discussion about the local textures of Creek history by highlighting moments when warriors and other local peoples dragged high-profile diplomats into fresh rounds of violence with the Choctaws. Furthermore, it sheds light on Upper Creeks' cultural creativity during the bloodshed. Abeika and Tallapoosa peoples invented and practiced local ceremonies meant to reestablish peace and console affected communities. In short, the Creek-Choctaw War evolved according to peoples on the ground.

Part II, "Three Rivers: The Cusseta Connection, 1777–1797," transitions to the revolutionary era, when new dangers menaced Abeika and Tallapoosa communities. The rise of the United States to the east and the eruption of war with Chickasaws to the west embroiled Upper Creek communities in familiar patterns of violence and crisis. The context had shifted from the late colonial period, however, for the scale of US expansion was far larger than Britain's, and the Chickasaws were a far deadlier enemy than the Choctaws. This section drives home the argument that the revolutionary years witnessed extensive cooperation among the Abeikas, Tallapoosas, and Lower Creeks. The Upper Creeks allied with the Lower Creek town of Cusseta, in particular, and confronted new threats.

Chapter 3 is about one Tallapoosa headman who attempted to pacify revolutionary Georgia. Named Tame King, he promoted neutrality with all of Britain's enemies, including Georgia, and believed that a Creek–Georgian alliance was the only hope to preserve land and access trade during the American War for Independence. In pursuit of this task, he forged a coalition with the Abeika town of Okfuskee and the Lower Creek town of Cusseta. By constructing his leadership along the lines of cooperation and partnership, he stood in marked contrast to his rival, Alexander McGillivray of Little Tallassee, around whom scholarship on Creek governance and nationhood in the late eighteenth century has revolved. While shedding new light on Creek governance, Tame King also illuminates the relationship between headmen and local peoples during the revolutionary tumult. Foremost, he accepted the guidance of the Tallassee mico, his relative and elder, who understood what made European empires tick and who could therefore steer Creek country away from danger. In the 1770s and 1780s, Tame King spoke for this person during peacekeeping missions with Georgia authorities and gained experience in diplomatic affairs based on training from the elder man. The localist currents of Creek governance remained strong in the revolutionary era.

Chapter 4 centers on the postwar years, when US expansion intensified and trapped the Creeks in warfare with Americans and Chickasaws alike. Creek–American skirmishes and the Creek-Chickasaw War were manifestations of a Native South awash in violence by the 1790s. To mollify US and indigenous enemies, Abeika and Tallapoosa headmen deployed Tame King's approach to Creek politics. Specifically, headmen located in Okfuskee (Abeika) and Tuckabatchee (Tallapoosa) collaborated with Bird Tail King of Cusseta (Lower Creek) to frame an inter-provincial policy on behalf of three Creek provinces. Capturing their outlook, this chapter refers to the agreement as the Three Rivers Resolution and argues that the 1790s constituted the golden age of riverine power in Creek country. It contends that the leadership created not a national policy but one premised on riverine divisions. In acknowledging community interests, however, the Three Rivers Resolution failed to curb violence between Creeks and outsiders. For years, local actors killed settler and Indian foes alike, worsening regional trends in warfare, raiding, and theft. Only in 1797 did women, children, and men demand that Upper Creek leaders put an end to the Creek-Chickasaw War. As the eighteenth century waned, political relations fluctuated wildly and guaranteed increased room for maneuver by local peoples.

Part III, "Four Rivers: Alabama Adumbration, 1798–1815," studies the Alabamas' ascent in Upper Creek politics at the turn of the nineteenth century. Constituting the fourth and final province, the Alabamas were led by Singer of Hickory Ground. His proximity to the Upper Creeks' erstwhile Chickasaw enemies made him an ideal diplomat. Chapter 5 retrieves his chiefly rise, conditioned as it was by the Tuckabatchee headman Mad Dog. Mad Dog underpinned Singer's efforts to charter an intertribal resolution meant to cultivate indigenous unity and halt American expansion. Unlike Alabamas who responded to the US menace by hiving off Creek country and migrating to Spanish-held territories, Singer and his kin faced the United States head-on. Yet Singer caved to the demands of southern Indian leadership. To maintain the Creeks' financial solvency, he succumbed to pressure by US agent Benjamin Hawkins to cede land to the young republic in exchange for forgiveness of trade debts. Outraged, Creek warriors killed Singer. His demise was a turning point in Creek history because it legitimized political violence and paved the way for the Creek War. As a new century dawned, tensions between authorities and communities in Upper Creek country exploded into civil conflict.

Rivers of Power concludes with the Creek War. Following Singer's death, a growing chorus of Alabamas, Abeikas, and Tallapoosas criticized American interference in Creek affairs. Known as Redsticks, they pinned the source of land loss and other Creek woes on Agent Hawkins. He appeared to corrupt otherwise popular leaders like Singer and championed the federal government's "plan of civilization," which called on the southern Indians to abandon their customs and adopt those of white Americans. Many Redsticks rallied around the indomitable Tame King, who opposed headmen in the National Council. Through this institution, headmen like Big Warrior had supported the civilization plan, at the expense of clans and towns, to preserve good relations with Agent Hawkins. Tame King believed that Big Warrior and other council headmen were co-opted sellouts who suppressed community autonomy. Still, evidence indicates that Big Warrior, like his rival, exhibited leadership that echoed the concerns of local peoples. He took steps to secure a future for southern Indian children, attempted to work with clans as he fulfilled American demands, and criticized Hawkins's role in the controversial Treaty of Fort Jackson.

By 1815, Creek country lay in ashes. US invasion had crushed the Redsticks and caused a refugee crisis. An indigenous-centered interpretation of the historical record indicates that until that point, both Creek leaders and local actors took their cue from the provinces. Abeika and Tallapoosa headmen freely advanced agendas, but a host of on-the-ground Creeks were always close by. They demanded a voice in decision-making, departed from peace agreements, and devised alternative courses of action that made them leaders in their own ways. Over time, the Abeikas and Tallapoosas partnered with the Cussetas and Alabamas to achieve collective interests; then, as before, local concerns both mattered and took a multitude of shapes. It is to this world of flowing power that we now turn.

Part I

Two Rivers: Abeikas and Tallapoosas, 1750–1776

Chapter 1

"I am one of the Abehkas, & I speak for them, & the Tallapoosas"

A New Era of Peace

On July 7, 1759, a delegation of eighty Abeikas and Tallapoosas greeted a newcomer. Named Edmond Atkin, he was the new superintendent for the Southern Indian Department in British North America and tasked with managing affairs between Indians and colonists in the region. Days earlier he had arrived on the outskirts of the Upper Creek towns to survey attitudes toward the British and their inveterate French enemies. Atkin's hosts knew that both European empires were competing for southern Indian allies in the ongoing Seven Years' War, known in North America as the French and Indian War. They knew specifically that he had come with a demand that Upper Creeks sever trade ties with the French and buy goods exclusively from the British. Since Atkin jeopardized the security and livelihood of their provinces, they approached the superintendent with caution and convened with him at an encampment far from the nearest cluster of towns. To convince him that they enjoyed the fruits of British trade, the Abeika and Tallapoosa delegates practiced rituals of diplomacy meant to satisfy Atkin. Several "painted" warriors sang and danced before him, stroked his face with "Eagle tails," and presented him with a "Pipe."[1]

Following these gestures, an Abeika headman named Okfuskee Captain introduced himself to Atkin and stated, "I am one of the Abehkas, & I speak for them, & the Tallapoosas. We are come to receive you in the best manner we can." The joint Abeika–Tallapoosa delegation subsequently escorted the official to the Upper Creek towns, where he later shared his aggressive trade policy with headmen, women, and children. The superintendent so offended his hosts, however, that they heckled British authorities for his dismissal; by year's end, he was sent packing. A disgraced Atkin fell victim to Okfuskee Captain and other headmen who eliminated threats to eighteenth-century Upper Creek society by casting themselves as riverine leaders. The Okfuskee headman voiced Abeikas' and Tallapoosas' wish to make peace with Atkin and, when the time came, excise him from the region. In doing so, he spoke not for a nation, a political concept gaining traction among some Lower Creeks, but for provinces woven from communities of kin and town in Upper Creek country. In his relationship with the superintendent and the British Empire more generally, Okfuskee Captain set the parameters for effective leadership among the Abeikas and Tallapoosas.[2]

While Okfuskee Captain's leadership tempered British colonial expansion, it originated in response to a formidable indigenous enemy: the Cherokees. The Creek-Cherokee War had begun earlier in the century after warriors from the Lower Cherokee town of Tugalo, possibly under the influence of alcohol, massacred a visiting delegation of Lower Creeks. By the 1740s, the war had spread to Okfuskee, Okchai, and other Upper Creek towns, whose inhabitants became embroiled in a cycle of raids with the Cherokees. Beginning in 1750, nine years before the Upper Creeks' encounter with Atkin, Okfuskee Captain participated in an Abeika–Tallapoosa coalition that ended the war and advanced peace with the Cherokees. The conclusion of the Creek-Cherokee War spawned new political developments in Upper Creek country. Most immediately, the coalition of which Okfuskee Captain was a part served both to halt an intertribal war and to unify the Abeika and Tallapoosa provinces when Superintendent Atkin appeared on their doorstep. As well, leaders like Okfuskee Captain secured peace with the Cherokees by devising and implementing diplomatic measures that could be redeployed in negotiations with the British in the 1750s and 1760s. Creek–British diplomacy was altogether an extension of diplomacy with other southern Indians. More broadly, Abeika and Tallapoosa collaboration popularized the riverine mode of leadership in Upper Creek country for the remainder of the century.[3]

This book opens, then, with the twinned crises of intertribal war and colonial expansion that marked a new era in Creek history. While the region had been beset by wars and rebellions since the early eighteenth century, the Abeikas and Tallapoosas were spared the worst effects of the chaos. Their autonomy remained intact following the Yamasee War (1715–1718), which abolished the Indian slave trade; the Stono Rebellion of 1739, which rocked the plantation system in South Carolina; and the War of the Austrian Succession (1739–1748), which was a mere prelude to the Seven Years' War. At mid-century, however, the balance of power among the region's Native, European, and African peoples began to shift, and the Upper Creeks felt it. The Creek-Cherokee War caught up to the inhabitants of the Coosa and Tallapoosa Rivers just as the British Empire renewed its expansion into the region. By 1750 Cherokees and Britons had created a palpable sense of alarm for the Upper Creeks.[4]

In response, Abeika and Tallapoosa leaders ushered in an era of peace by negotiating with the Cherokees and smoothing over tensions with their British trading partners. Headmen from both provinces led diplomacy with Indian and non-Indian groups to mitigate the dangers that emanated from Cherokee country, the British colonies, and the wider Anglo-Atlantic basin. Along the way, networks of local peoples approved, revised, and thwarted Upper Creek headmen's diplomatic agendas. Diplomacy across the Native South was a messy process that involved headmen's constituents, especially kin, but those same peoples did not concern themselves with indigenous–European relations alone. They also participated routinely in intertribal exchanges, negotiations, and agreements. They helped to ensure that the peace-making strategies formatted for the Creek-Cherokee War could be reformatted for the Seven Years' War and increasing British aggression.[5]

"The whole Body of the Upper Creeks"

After years of intermittent raiding between Cherokee and Lower Creek towns, the Creek-Cherokee War reached the Upper Creeks in the 1740s. In 1745, according to British trader James Adair's *History of the American Indians*, the Abeika town of Okchai tortured and "burned" to death a young Cherokee captive, suggesting that conflict had erupted between the Cherokees and Okchais before that date. What happened next is unclear, but South Carolina deerskin trader George Galphin reported that in late 1749, Lower Creeks went "out to War against the Cherokees" and that in the following spring, some four hundred Lower Creeks attacked the Cherokees, killing nearly forty. These Lower Creek raids sparked counterattacks that ensnared the Upper Creeks in renewed rounds of violence with the Cherokees. Beginning in 1750, headmen from the Coosa and Tallapoosa Rivers expressed outrage over the bloodshed and launched a joint effort to deescalate the war. The available records illuminate the centrality of riverine leadership in a successful, if gradual, attempt by Upper Creeks to make peace with their foes.[6]

The Upper Creek peace initiative originated with the Abeikas. Their towns bore the brunt of Cherokee raids in Upper Creek country because of their location on the upper Coosa and upper Tallapoosa Rivers. These communities were nearer the Cherokees, specifically those from the Lower Cherokee towns, than were the Tallapoosa towns, whose location on the middle and lower Tallapoosa largely shielded them from Cherokee raids. Additionally, cultural significance thrust Abeikas into the diplomatic spotlight, for Okchai was deemed the town where "Matters" of conflict resolution were "determined." For these reasons, Gun Merchant of Okchai spoke for the Abeikas in diplomacy with Cherokee leaders. In October 1750, a British trader stationed in Okchai learned from Gun Merchant that the "Upper Creeks," or Abeikas, desired peace. The headman explained that "if the Lower Creeks and Lower Cherokees are for War," he and other "Upper Creeks" wanted "Nothing to do with it." By October 20, Gun Merchant had set off with twenty Okchais to meet with Lower Cherokees "to settle Matters and make a lasting Peace."[7]

Other Abeika towns and leaders became involved in Gun Merchant's initial extension of peace with the Cherokees. In summer 1751, only months after the Okchai leader traveled to Cherokee country, the Abeika town of Aubecooche hosted Shawnee Indian emissaries on the upper Coosa River. Part-time intermediaries for the southern Indians, the Shawnees arrived from Cherokee country with a "Peace Talk." They told Aubecooche leaders that Cherokees intended to visit the "out Towns" of northern Upper Creek country, namely Aubecooche, Coosa, and Breed Camp. Face-to-face diplomacy signaled a firmer commitment to peace. According to a British trader familiar with the situation, the anticipated Cherokee delegation wished to finish its tour in Okchai "to conclude a firm Peace" with Gun Merchant. Whether Cherokee diplomats visited these Abeika towns is uncertain, but the trader did report that some Abeika headmen prepared their own embassy to Cherokee country. Furthermore, Gun Merchant "expected a Party of Cherokees" in Okchai by late July 1751.[8]

Although Abeika leaders had begun to coordinate diplomacy with Okchai, Abeika–Cherokee relations remained fragile and soon collapsed. British trader Lachlan McGillivray reported that Cherokee warriors killed "some Okfusskee Men" in summer 1751, when Abeika and Cherokee leaders were pursuing terms of peace. By December, unidentified Upper Creeks, possibly warriors from the Abeika town of Okfuskee, had retaliated by killing "seven or eight" Cherokees. In the same month, The Raven, a Cherokee headman of

Hiwassee, addressed a talk to South Carolina governor James Glen. In it he explained that two of his townspeople had been killed by "the Upper Creek." The assailants were members of the Abeika town of Nauchee. Months later, in April 1752, Galphin informed Governor Glen that peace negotiations in the Abeika towns of Okfuskee and Coosa had stalled when one "Man" was killed in each polity. Galphin's report suggests that both victims were Cherokee and that at least one survivor "made the best of his Way back" to Cherokee country to report the treachery.[9]

These violent reprisals were the product of an entrenched custom in the Native South known as the "international law" of retaliation. When a Cherokee killed a Creek, for example, any Creek bore a legal and social obligation to kill any Cherokee in response. This group-to-group custom, according to legal historian John Phillip Reid, was the main cause of war between southern Indians in the colonial era. Yet some evidence suggests that those most affected by an individual's death were surviving kin, who demanded retaliation against the enemy. Thus retaliation could meet kinship as well as legal obligations. The trader James Adair explained that a person slain by an outside group fell into a state of "crying blood." This meant that the blood of the decedent cried out for retaliation by the offended clan and the lineages within it. Until clanspeople reacted appropriately, the ghost of the departed haunted the community, awaiting entrance into the afterlife. To quiet crying blood, kinswomen wailed publicly for the dead and exhorted all able-bodied male kin to avenge the dead by killing an equal number from the offending society. Killings rarely went unavenged. Adair claimed, "I have known the Indians to go a thousand miles, for the purpose of revenge." Once the men carried out what Adair called their "kindred duty," the ghost traveled to the spirit world and normalcy returned. By exacting retaliation, then, clans rendered justice, met kin needs, and spared the community from further harm.[10]

Retaliation continued to fuel Abeika–Cherokee animosity. In spring 1752, in response to the killing of Cherokees in Okfuskee and Coosa, Cherokee warriors ambushed and attacked a party of twelve "Oakfusskees" en route to Georgia on the Lower Trade Path. Only "one Man" survived. The death of eleven people from Upper Creek country was catastrophic because it deprived clans of important sources of leadership, knowledge and labor. In the wake of the Cherokees' animosity, the Okfuskees felt sadness and even resignation. Okfuskee Captain expressed these sentiments months later in a talk to Governor Glen, who, like the headman, wished to see a peaceful outcome between the combatants. There "is no Appearence of their concluding a Peace with us," Okfuskee Captain lamented, as the Cherokees "[keep] killing us every Day under Pretence of making a Peace with us." Cherokee assaults produced death and agony among the Abeika towns, especially Okfuskee Captain's.[11]

There was a silver lining, however, for the renewal of conflict spurred a bolder round of peace talks that featured both Abeikas and Tallapoosas. As Okfuskee Captain told Governor Glen, "The whole Body of the Upper Creeks are to [soon] meet at the Oakfuskees" and discuss measures to end the violence. Interpreting his meaning is tricky, but by adding "whole Body" to "the Upper Creeks," Okfuskee Captain suggested that the Abeikas had partnered with the Tallapoosas for conflict resolution. Since recent Cherokee aggression threatened to engulf the Tallapoosa towns, leaders from both provinces took steps to coauthor a peace initiative with their Cherokee enemies. This partnership bloomed in spring 1753 when numerous Upper Creek headmen and warriors traveled to Charles Town to draft Governor Glen as an intermediary between the Creeks and Cherokees. Nearly seventy, or about two-thirds, of the ninety-nine delegates were Abeikas and Tallapoosas. They represented at least four Abeika towns, ranging from Okfuskee and Pucantallahassee to Upper Eufaula and Nauchee, and seven Tallapoosa towns, including Tallassee, Tuckabatchee, Autossee, Cooloome, Sawanogi, Muccolossus, and Little Tallassee. Among the most prominent of the attendees were Okfuskee Captain and Wolf, who lived in the Tallapoosa town of Muccolossus and who claimed power over "eight Towns" in the Tallapoosa district. Gun Merchant remained at home in Okchai, busying himself with "confirming a Peace with the Cherokees." A British trader later reported that the headman had dissuaded several "Head Warriours" from attacking the Cherokees. Across the region, then, Upper Creek leaders worked to taper the bloodshed.[12]

Other Upper Creek leaders participated in this flurry of diplomacy. Soon after headmen disbanded from the Charles Town meeting, the Okfuskee leader Red Coat King addressed a talk to Governor Glen, pledging that the Upper Creeks would soon "shake Hands" with the Cherokees "and make every Thing firm and strong" with them. He expected a show of good faith from the Cherokees, however, so he asked them via Glen to send gifts of "two Northern India[n] Slaves" to the Upper Creeks. Warring groups throughout the region normally smoothed over tensions by exchanging Native slaves, who tended to be Iroquoian or Algonquian peoples. The Okfuskee headman confessed that such gifts might "make a good Peace between us and the Cherokees." Buttressing the collaboration among Abeika and Tallapoosa leaders, Red Coat King closed his message by telling the governor that "All the Head Men of the Upper Creeks are to meet" in fall 1753 to confirm peace with the Cherokees.[13]

Whether Upper Creek headmen received slaves from the Cherokees is unclear, but they convened in Okfuskee according to plan. Peace materialized over the following months. By November 1753, Gun Merchant had learned from a Coweta headman named Malatchi, whose townspeople had been at war with the Cherokees for decades, that "a firm Peace was agreed on" between the Creeks and Cherokees. Similarly, Red Coat King believed "the Peace is strong." In early 1754, a prominent Okchai war leader named Mortar tag-teamed with fellow townsman Gun Merchant and other leaders by going to Cherokee country "to confirm a Peace." Mortar also planned to escort Cherokee delegates back to Okchai "to conclude a general Peace" with them. By spring, no new bouts of conflict had erupted.[14]

These diplomatic maneuvers not only prevented further conflict but also established a military alliance between the former combatants. For one, Deval's Landlord of the Abeika town of Pucantallahassee "joined" several "Cherroekees" who arrived in the Upper Creek towns in August 1754. The joint war party intended to raid the Choctaws, who lived along the Pearl River in present-day Mississippi. Deval's Landlord had sought but failed to obtain "Satisfaction" against the Choctaws earlier in the year, which suggests that he planned to attack them for a second time, only now in the company of newfound Cherokee allies. While tensions with the Choctaws simmered, the peoples of the Coosa and Tallapoosa Valleys had turned a corner by mid-1754. Upper Creek leaders like Deval's Landlord had cooperated with one another for months to cultivate ties with their Cherokee neighbors.[15]

As the Creek-Cherokee War closed, a new era of stability dawned. The peace effort the Abeikas launched in 1750 and that transitioned into a collaborative relationship with their Tallapoosa neighbors, introduced a new chapter in Creek history. The Upper Creeks labored within and across the provinces to end a conflict that began early in the century. Creeks who called the Coosa and Tallapoosa Rivers home could breathe a sigh of relief. Moreover, they won new allies among the Cherokees, whose geopolitical power proved useful in the coming decades. In the process of negotiating for peace with Cherokee diplomats, countless headmen, ranging from Gun Merchant and Mortar to Okfuskee Captain and Wolf, exercised their political muscle and gained invaluable experiences in the international arena. In all, the Creek-Cherokee War was a proving ground for the Upper Creek leadership.

Headmen's Relatives: Warriors and "their Women and Children"

Upper Creek leaders who negotiated with the Cherokees in the early 1750s devised techniques for diplomacy in conjunction with relatives. As the beating pulse of the Abeika and Tallapoosa provinces, these relatives influenced the process and outcome of diplomacy with Cherokee emissaries and British authorities. They attended high-profile negotiations, traveled with or on behalf of headmen, demanded trade goods from colonial leaders, and altogether ensured that headmen ruled for their benefit. They helped blur the line between Creek–Cherokee and Creek–British relations, thereby demonstrating their centrality to Upper Creek politics and diplomacy in the mid-eighteenth century.

Among those relatives who partook in diplomacy were nephews. According to the southern Indian matrilineal tradition, young men learned the traits of proper leadership from their mother's brothers. Through this familial apprenticeship, nephews embarked on the path from boyhood to manhood. Once they came of age, they accompanied their uncles on the hunt and in battle. They became men after they stalked and killed their first animal and took their first human life during a raid or skirmish. They earned war titles and held political office after additional demonstrations of prowess in hunting and warfare. In addition, uncles trained nephews in the methods of diplomacy. A British report based on testimony from a Creek war leader explained that a "Nephew" of Mortar, the Okchai headman instrumental in the Creek–Cherokee peace, "always" accompanied his uncle on diplomatic circuits in the region, traveling "every where with him." Named Okeelysa, the young man "hears all his [uncle's] Talks." Uncles modeled the arts of oratory and persuasion for their nephews, who learned how to ease tensions, recruit allies, and cultivate relationships with peoples around the Native South.[16]

Good leadership also depended on headmen's sons, at least during the Creek-Cherokee War. Okfuskee's licensed trader, George Johnston, reported to Governor Glen that the son of Red Coat King assisted Okfuskee headmen as the Upper Creeks sought peace with the Cherokees "some Months after" the Charles Town meeting in spring 1753. According to Johnston, three Cherokee diplomats spent "a considerable Time" in Okfuskee "to confirm and strengthen the Peace" then taking shape between the combatants. The Cherokee delegates returned home after the Okfuskee visit with "ten Creek Warriours of note, among whom were the Red Coat King's Son, the Indian called the Handsom[e] Fellow," who "made some Stay among the Cherokees." Cherokee leaders subsequently held "Conferences and Talks" with their visitors, who became convinced that the Cherokees were "sincere and hearty in the Peace." Whether Handsome Fellow gained the skills of oratory and diplomacy from his father or uncle is uncertain; still, he shared a kin tie with Red Coat King and assisted his prestigious relative in the ongoing Creek–Cherokee peace talks. When he and other Okfuskees returned home from Cherokee country, for instance, they were escorted by "fourteen to fifteen Cherokees," some of whom were "principal Head Men." Negotiations got under way for a second time in Okfuskee, where Cherokee and Upper Creek headmen, including Gun Merchant of Okchai, exchanged words of peace. Clearly, then, headmen's relatives laid the basis for Creek–Cherokee amity.[17]

Other young kin, including warriors under the authority of Okfuskee Captain, criticized the Creek–Cherokee settlement. He and eleven of his men attended negotiations in Charles Town, where his Upper Creek colleagues recruited Governor Glen as a go-between for them and the Cherokees. Okfuskee Captain signaled his intention to support the governor in that capacity by explaining that he had recently advanced "Peace with the Cherokees." Despite losing "many of our Friends" to Cherokee attacks, he had kept "my Warriours at Home." By directing these men to forgo raids on the enemy, he prevented them from earning war titles and amassing power. In the interest of peace, moreover, he suppressed the custom of retaliation meant to release spirits to the afterlife and strengthen the affected clan or clans. Okfuskee Captain revealed to Glen that he incurred "the ill Will of many of my People" for this risky decision. The trade-off between tradition and diplomacy was steep, and it undermined his legitimacy as a war leader.[18]

During the Charles Town conference, Okfuskee Captain announced to Governor Glen that the Okfuskee warriors so resented his diplomacy with the Cherokees that they forced him to return his "Commission" to the governor. Like other European empires, the British granted commissions to influential headmen to establish peace and stability with the recipient's society. A condition of Okfuskee Captain's commission was, according to the headman, to "discharge the Trust reposed in me" by maintaining peace among his people, the British, and any British allies, including the Cherokees. By choosing to side with the governor and remove all obstacles to peace with the Cherokees, Okfuskee Captain committed a grave error. As a result, his men made him forfeit his peace commission. Defeated, Okfuskee Captain requested Glen "to appoint some other in my Place who may be more deserving and may have better Success." The headman was caught in an impossible position and found his power curtailed.[19]

The eleven warriors who joined Okfuskee Captain in Charles Town affirmed their commitment to securing war honors and exacting retaliation against enemy populations. They expected leaders to recognize those needs and critiqued headmen like Okfuskee Captain who ignored them. Even so, the Creek-Cherokee War highlighted Upper Creek dependence on British trade goods and the consequent need for diplomacy with British authorities. Upper Creeks had been trading with multiple empires since the early eighteenth century, but by mid-century they had developed a closer relationship with the British to procure muskets, ammunition, shot, and other goods meant to protect themselves from Cherokee warriors and satisfy consumer tastes. More than French and Spanish traders, British ones provided a reliable store of inexpensive goods to the Upper Creeks, making diplomacy with British officialdom essential. How Upper Creek leaders might procure British wares to comfort relatives without conceding ground to an expanding empire was an extraordinarily complicated problem that headmen tackled for the remaining decade.[20]

In one attempt to resolve the deepening trade crisis, the Abeika–Tallapoosa partnership originally formed to mitigate conflict with the Cherokees resurfaced. At the Charles Town conference, Abeika and Tallapoosa delegates requested from Governor Glen everything from guns and blankets to "Shirts and Boots." Since they were beholden to their relatives, leaders desired for "their Women and Children" countless products, such as "Pewther Basons, Gartering, Cadiz, Bobs, Beads, and some other Triffles." Some relatives altered the trade discussions to their benefit, just as they had left their mark on Creek-Cherokee diplomacy. The brother of Wolf expected goods, as did the few women who attended, including "a Relation of Deval's Landlord," the Pucantallahassee headman who would later make common cause with Cherokee warriors. The governor approved these requests from headmen and kin alike. This delighted many, including Okfuskee Captain's eleven warriors, who permitted their war leader to reacquire his commission. In doing so, the warriors decided that gifts of trade goods constituted an adequate substitute for retaliation and other martial traditions. Okfuskee Captain was now in the clear. "I therefore take back my Commission," he told the governor, "and shall continue a true Friend to the British until the Day of my Death." Hungry for goods, the Upper Creeks closed ranks in Charles Town.[21]

During the 1750s, the quest for British trade dovetailed with the closure of the Creek-Cherokee War. The same headmen who negotiated for peace with Cherokee emissaries advanced commercial relations with British authorities, especially Governor Glen. Relatives were there every step of the way, guiding and thwarting the male leadership as they saw fit. They voiced their interests and actively participated in diplomatic situations with both Native and colonial powers. Yet change was afoot. As the Cherokee military threat receded, the commercial might of the British Empire beckoned. The British supplied manufactured wares more plentifully than other colonial powers and caught Upper Creek communities in a thickening web of trade dependence. Okfuskee Captain is a case in point. His warriors consented to his reinstatement as a commissioned headman only because he offered proof that his relationship with a colonial governor could produce tangible results for them.

"Prevailing on the Relations of the kill'd"

As the Creek-Cherokee War gave way to a tighter connection with the British Empire, headmen's kin clashed with British settlers along the southern frontier. Emboldened by the French and Indian War, which erupted in 1754, thousands of settlers hunted animals and built homes in the corridor between the Ogeechee and Oconee Rivers. The newcomers blatantly defied a treaty that Lower Creeks had signed with the colony of Georgia years earlier, in 1739, establishing the Ogeechee as the boundary between Creek country and Georgia. This area teemed with white-tailed deer and other animals hunted by the Upper and Lower Creeks, Cherokees, and other Native peoples. Men hunted to provide themselves and relatives with meat, oil, and the raw materials for clothing. They also purchased British wares with the products of the hunt, including skins and hides. Thus British settlers who moved into eastern Creek country and western Georgia threatened Native hunters' livelihood.[22]

This emergency intensified as Creeks perished in armed clashes with settlers. Just as custom obligated Creeks to take revenge on indigenous groups, so Creeks exercised a similar obligation to attack settler communities who killed Creeks. Although Creeks could accept gifts to smooth over tensions, they usually elected for retaliation. Attacking colonial powers raised the stakes, however, for British colonists tended to interpret isolated Creek raids as a declaration of war by all Creeks. Settlers then organized into militia units and targeted individuals or whole communities in Creek country with indiscriminate force. Upper Creeks who hunted and camped in the contested zone between the Ogeechee and Oconee Rivers were often targets of settler violence, as is illustrated by what became known as the Ogeechee Incident.[23]

In September 1756, seven Tallapoosa Creek men stole blankets, horses, and other items from a British settlement illicitly located west of the Ogeechee. These men practiced theft to contest illegal settlements along the Creek–Georgia boundary and to warn squatters to turn back. Settlers from the affected community responded by tracking the Tallapoosas and opening fire on their encampment, killing two. In the wake, the Lower Creeks, whose towns rested in the immediate path of Georgia's expansion, scrambled to prevent the violence from spiraling. Days after the attack, Lower Creek headmen met in Coweta and addressed a peace talk to Georgia governor John Reynolds. They assured him that warriors from the grief-stricken clan or clans in Upper Creek country would not attack the colony. They alleged that two colonists as well as two Tallapoosas had died in the Ogeechee confrontation, which implied that the parity of deaths would preclude the Tallapoosas' call for retaliation. The colony and its governor, they suggested, had nothing to fear.[24]

To keep peace between Georgia and Creek country, however, Coweta leaders may have embellished the casualties of the Ogeechee Incident. No evidence corroborates the death of two Ogeechee settlers; plus, British agent Daniel Pepper believed that the Tallapoosa deaths remained unrequited. In a letter to William Henry Lyttelton, governor of South Carolina, Agent Pepper averred that he "shall meet with the greatest Difficulty in prevailing on the Relations of the kill'd, to be satisfy'd with Presents alone, but shall do the utmost in my Power." He was skeptical that British presents alone might mend fences. No fewer than two British deaths would set things right and reestablish peace between the affected clan or clans and the British. Furthermore, the Cowetas were in no position to render judgement; matters of crime and punishment fell strictly to relatives.[25]

The influential Wolf of Muccolossus was a "Relation to one" of the dead. Although expected to get revenge against the British, Wolf was a cautious headman who favored peace with his trade partners. He had worked with Abeika headmen to reduce the spate of killings between Upper Creeks and Cherokees earlier in the decade. Moreover, he kept the British close to ensure goods and security for his family and town. It is no surprise, then, that this diplomat informed Agent Pepper that "the White People [British colonists] were not to be blamed" for the Tallapoosa deaths. He also endorsed a Muccolossus colleague who claimed that the British assailants had acted in "self Defence." Although Wolf looked to avoid war with the British, he ignored an important kin ritual.

Whether he believed that the Ogeechee settlers had justifiably killed the Tallapoosa thieves was irrelevant because Creeks disregarded homicidal intent and excused no killer (or killers) for lethal action. Absent satisfactory gifts from the British, Wolf's relatives were supposed to retaliate in response to the killings.[26]

Like Okfuskee Captain, Wolf restrained his kin from pursuing retaliation on an outside group. Both headmen had witnessed the perils of unchecked violence in the late Creek-Cherokee War and preferred peace to escalation. By holding the deceased Tallapoosas culpable and exonerating the Ogeechee settlers, Wolf charted a course of alliance-building during the French and Indian War. He expressed his diplomatic stance in other ways too. In 1757 Wolf stopped several Creek headmen "in the French interest" from attacking British settlements and later bragged about his decision to British officials. Finally, Wolf participated in negotiations that convinced Georgia that the Tallapoosas would forgo retaliation on the British southern colonies. In late October 1757, he joined more than one hundred Upper and Lower Creeks in the Georgia capital of Savannah, where they parleyed with the governor. The resulting Treaty of Savannah resolved the Ogeechee Incident. Article 2 acknowledged Wolf's kin and suggested that prior "Grievances & dissatisfactions of every kind shall be forgiven & forgot as thoroughly as if they never had happened." Wolf put his mark to the treaty and closed the conference by urging the Creek delegates to honor all "antient Treaties with the English."[27]

Yet the Ogeechee Incident festered among some Creeks. Nearly a year later, British agent Joseph Wright recorded a conversation with men in the Lower Creek town of Chehaw, who complained that the two Tallapoosa deaths "some time ago" were still unavenged. He responded gingerly to a query about the assailants' fate by saying that all were "yet alive" except for one, who had died in custody in the Savannah jail. The death of one colonist under British jurisdiction hardly consoled the afflicted relatives, since they, not Europeans, were obligated to apprehend and execute colonists. The Treaty of Savannah prohibited them from conducting the requisite executions. By calling for peace, Wolf so lost the confidence of his people that they stripped him of power. In 1759, three years after the Ogeechee Incident, the new British superintendent of the Southern Indian Department, Edmond Atkin, wrote about his attempt to "restore the Wolf to his lost Credit." Thus kin who shaped the course and outcome of the Creek-Cherokee War exerted similar influence as tensions with encroaching colonists turned bloody. Caught in the crosshairs of kin who objected to diplomacy, Wolf found that his people neither forgave the Ogeechee settlers nor endorsed the treaty erasing past offences "as thoroughly as if they never had happened."²⁸

In the end, Wolf's removal from power was temporary. Like Okfuskee Captain, Wolf was a capable riverine leader, for he regained the trust of his relatives by upholding the trade. With British authorities in the late 1750s and early 1760s, he endorsed agreements and signed treaties that maintained his alliance with British governors, traders, and other colonial agents. By swapping retaliation for trade, however, Wolf demonstrated a menacing dependence on goods manufactured and supplied by a distant colonial power. He calculated that a reprisal against British settlers was far riskier than keeping Upper Creek towns and clans well provisioned. His relatives who carefully observed his leadership in Creek–British affairs eventually accepted this position.²⁹

"Every Town in the Upper Crick Country"

The Upper Creeks continued to trade and advance diplomacy with the British during the French and Indian War. Yet a minority of them opposed the Creek–British alliance. This included Mortar, the prominent Okchai war leader who had assisted other Upper Creek leaders in negotiations ending the Creek-Cherokee War. In 1759 he and the Lower Cherokees allied with the French Empire in a bid to expel British settlers from the region and torch British forts. Alarmed, Superintendent Atkin toured the Upper Creek towns in summer and early fall 1759 and threatened to revoke trade with towns that supported France and its alliance with Mortar. In response to Atkin's demand, Abeika and Tallapoosa leaders repudiated Mortar's agenda and tried to persuade the superintendent that their trading relationship with the British trumped that with the French. It was a Herculean task, but the dire need for trade forged a remarkable expression of intra- and inter-provincial unity.³⁰

On July 3, 1759, a war leader named Wolf Warrior welcomed Superintendent Atkin and his retinue to Upper Creek country. Hailing from the Tallapoosa town of Fusihatchee, located upriver from Wolf's town of Muccolossus, Wolf Warrior was joined by several warriors who had intercepted Atkin's westward travel from the Lower Creek towns. The Tallapoosa welcome party appeared to deem Atkin a threat because it consigned him to a rural encampment called the Springs, ten miles from the closest Tallapoosa town and far removed from Tallapoosa communities. Although Atkin was a powerful British authority, the Tallapoosas reminded him that he lacked control over diplomatic engagement with the Upper Creeks. The Springs was Tallapoosa space and under Tallapoosa sway.³¹

Wolf Warrior received the foreign visitor but stalled negotiations to buy time, explaining, "There are but few of us here you see." The small delegation constituted neither a majority of headmen nor a consensus about how best to respond to the superintendent's policy. Wolf Warrior implied that the Upper Creeks had to confer with one another to develop a strategy for dealing with Atkin. The headman encouraged Atkin in the meantime to contact "all" the Abeika and Tallapoosa "Towns [so] that they may know" British demands. Wolf Warrior also indicated that there were no "old People among us." In the absence of elders and their wise counsel, the superintendent had to wait for a proper meeting with the Abeika and Tallapoosa headmen, young and old, charged with evaluating his trade policy. Wolf Warrior's instructions to Atkin established leverage and formed the basis for a workable, if tense, relationship with the agent. Wolf Warrior assured Atkin that all headmen and 'the old People" would give the Briton a fair audience. Wolf Warrior eased relations with Atkin to no avail, however. Loyalty mattered foremost to the superintendent, who said that "The Great King," George II, had sent "me to see who are his Friends among the red People." If Upper Creeks "love the French better," Atkin warned Wolf Warrior, "let them take care of you."[32]

Atkin's threat roused a political call to arms. Four days later, on July 7, some eighty Tallapoosa and Abeika war leaders and warriors launched a second round of discussions with Atkin. They greeted the superintendent at a new camp along Cedar Creek, seven miles from the easternmost Tallapoosa towns. This larger delegation featured the seasoned and elder headmen whom Wolf Warrior's delegation had lacked; one of them was Okfuskee Captain. By now an experienced diplomat in the good graces of his relatives following the Creek-Cherokee War, Okfuskee Captain matched wits with Atkin. While the superintendent spoke for the British Empire, Okfuskee Captain announced, "I am one of the Abehkas, & I speak for them, & the Tallapoosas." He identified with his province and spoke for the neighboring Tallapoosa province in the presence of Tallapoosa leaders, who doubtless endorsed him. Likewise, he defended those provinces from Atkin's trade policy, which jeopardized all Upper Creeks' access to trade wares, not merely access for his own family or town. As a speaker for two provinces, he gave Atkin the green light to convene with the Upper Creeks, saying that "Headmen from every Town in the Upper Crick Country are met, & ready to receive you." Confident and masterful, Okfuskee Captain augmented Wolf Warrior's diplomacy in the hopes of restraining a foe.[33]

While Okfuskee Captain and Wolf Warrior established the diplomatic contours of a relationship with Atkin, headmen from the Tallapoosa town of Tuckabatchee hosted the superintendent. Tuckabatchee, whose headmen admitted the superintendent after his conversation with Okfuskee Captain, was emerging as a popular meeting ground in Creek country. It was equidistant from the Abeika towns on the upper Coosa River to the northwest and the Lower Creek towns on the middle Chattahoochee River to the southeast. Wolf of Muccolossus opined that it "is the properest place" for conferences, "as it is the most Central" in Creek country. In addition to its geopolitical edge, Tuckabatchee housed some famed copper and brass plates that were sacred to the Creeks. During each Busk, spiritual leaders took out the objects from a hidden location, cleaned them in the Tallapoosa's purifying waters, and displayed them for the duration of the weeklong ceremony. Lastly, Tuckabatchee was a "red" town. In what anthropologists call the moiety system, red designated war and underscored the town's military leadership, which included Tuckabatchee Half Breed and a young warrior and rising political star named Mad Dog. For these reasons, Tuckabatchee was the ideal location for Upper Creek leaders to confer with the brash superintendent.[34]

Throughout summer and early fall 1759, Tuckabatchee leaders met with the superintendent and invited other Upper Creeks to attend. Those who did were war leaders such as Okfuskee Captain, young men seeking war accolades, and in one case "20 women." These men and women sensed the aggression behind Atkin's zero-sum trade policy and sought to protect Upper Creek families, towns, and lands by dealing with a bellicose outsider. On September 28, Upper Creeks and a smattering of Alabamas and Lower Creeks convened in Tuckabatchee with the British superintendent. War leaders and warriors from nearly all Abeika and Tallapoosa towns identified in the British records throughout the 1750s, including Wolf Warrior and Okfuskee Captain, turned out for this early fall meeting on the Tallapoosa. Like other councils in Creek country, this one took place in the town's central square ground, where wooden cabins surrounded a firepit. Everyone sat in the cabins according to age and rank. Per custom, the superintendent took his seat as a guest in the area reserved for the town mico. After exchanging pleasantries with his hosts, Atkin stood up and issued his ultimatum, warning them that they must trade exclusively or forfeit trade with the British Empire altogether. Unbeknownst to him, a Lower Creek warrior named Tathlabegey had plotted his assassination. As Atkin harangued the Creeks, the warrior leaped up and struck Atkin four times with a pipe hatchet. Atkin suffered two blows to his skull, one to his right hand, and one to his right shoulder; the attack nearly killed him. The assembly disbanded in a furor.[35]

While no evidence confirms that the Upper Creeks knew about Tathlabegey's plan, they succeeded in isolating the superintendent. Following what Atkin amusingly named the Hatchet Affair, most Upper Creek headmen refused to grant him a second audience and retired to their homes. This was diplomacy by rejection. The few who remained in Tuckabatchee, including Wolf of Muccolossus, allowed the maimed Atkin to finish his speech the next day in the "Yard" of a headman's residence, beyond the public square ground, where headmen normally conducted official business with colonial and indigenous guests. When Atkin closed his talk, the Upper Creeks "had *no Answer to make.*" Since most warriors and other attendees had gone home, neither Wolf nor the few others who stayed behind exercised legitimacy to speak for them. The Ckchai headman Gun Merchant later remarked that Atkin's scathing words and general unpleasantness had "*daunted*" and "*confounded*" the headmen. After learning this unpleasant news, British authorities in London relieved Atkin, who left Upper Creek country in mid-December.[36]

Britain's superintendent for the Southern Indian Department had first arrived on Upper Creek lands in early July 1759, two months before the Hatchet Affair. During his rocky tenure, the Abeikas and Tallapoosas coordinated a sophisticated diplomatic response to him. When they realized he could not be reasoned with, they shunned him and hastened his removal from their communities. In doing so, they both preserved commercial ties with their main trading partner and exhibited intra- and inter-provincial cohesion drawn from war leaders, warriors, women, and other Upper Creeks. To neutralize Atkin, headmen like Wolf Warrior, Okfuskee Captain, and Wolf mobilized the Upper Creeks in a time of duress. While Upper Creek headmen like Mortar never attended a council with the superintendent and adopted a militant stance toward the British, the Upper Creeks believed that preserving trading ties with the British outweighed going to war against them.[37]

At the height of the French and Indian War, the Upper Creeks averted disaster. While the Cherokees descended into war with the British, the Upper Creeks adopted a program of diplomacy that involved numerous peoples. Okfuskee Captain positioned himself at the center of Upper Creek–British peace. By using his diplomatic experience with the Cherokees, he led the charge to rout a pesky agent of empire and accomplished that task through a partnership with Abeika and Tallapoosa men and women. He typified the prevailing style of leadership in Upper Creek country because he spoke for the "Abehkas . . . & the Tallapoosas." At the center of these provinces were warriors, women, and other local peoples who expected wise decision-making from the leadership. They decided that diplomacy was the wisest course of action.[38]

"He and his Family are Masters of all the Land"

Upper Creeks kept diplomacy alive as the French and Indian War entered its final phase. In fall 1759, the British army captured the French Canadian capital of Quebec City, and one year later the governor-general of the colony relinquished control of Montreal to the British. More than two years elapsed before the British and French assembled in Paris to negotiate a treaty. Signed in February 1763, the Treaty of Paris transferred to Britain the North American colonies of France and Spain, which had entered the war on France's side late in the conflict. No Native American delegates had been invited to the treaty table in Paris, however, prompting widespread indignation among the southern Indians. Mortar, the avowed critic of Britain, conveyed disbelief that colonial powers could redraw the map of North America absent indigenous input. He opposed Britain's attempt to seize "all the Lands which they [the Creeks] lent the French and Spaniards." Creeks were permanent owners of these lands and had merely leased them to European occupants. In addition, Mortar was alarmed by a new wave of Georgia colonists illegally "settling all round them."[39]

As the Treaty of Paris reshuffled the geopolitics of the Native South, Mortar led the Upper Creek peace agenda with the victors. He recognized that his fellow Creeks preferred diplomacy and trade to aggression and bloodshed in relations with the British. His alliance with the French had vanished, he understood, so a new one with the British must be forged. Although Mortar had his finger on the pulse of popular opinion, kinship also spurred his diplomatic position. He belonged to the prestigious Bear clan, grouped under a kinship moiety known as the Hathagalgi, or "white people." White was the color of peace in the Creek world, and according to early twentieth-century ethnographer John R. Swanton, the Hathagalgi bore responsibility for promoting peace throughout the Creek realm. Armed with a clan-inspired mandate, Mortar defended Upper Creek lands from the British through diplomacy, not war. His leadership in the postwar era therefore reflected those Upper Creek relatives who had been guiding diplomacy since the Creek-Cherokee War.[40]

Mortar invoked his clan and specifically his lineage in a talk criticizing the Paris Peace. He addressed it to Georgia governor James Wright, charging that "he and his Family are Masters of all the Land, and they own [recognize] no Masters but the Master of their Breath." No treaty negotiated in faraway Paris could disguise the truth that Mortar and his kin owned Upper Creek lands. As he defended his relatives to the governor, Mortar invoked the Creek world of spirits. When he spoke of Hisagita misi, rendered in English as the Master of Breath, he called upon a gender-neutral deity that sustained life and held ultimate control over the land. He also informed Wright that Bears were custodians of the resources that provided kin with sustenance, including the "Wood [that] is our Fire, and the Grass [that] is our Bed [a]nd our Physic [sacred medicine] when we are sick." Thus Upper Creeks "love" their "Lands a great deal" and, as ancient landowners, had a stronger claim to them than the British. As peacekeepers, then, Bear kin protected their lands from Georgia settlers and other intruders.[41]

Anchored in the white moiety, Mortar communicated the Upper Creeks' staunch refusal to part with land. This put him at odds with the Lower Creeks. In November 1763, just months after Mortar's talk, Lower Creek headmen signed a treaty in Augusta, Georgia, with the new British superintendent, John Stuart. The Treaty of Augusta authorized a land cession to Georgia in return for a guarantee of the remaining Lower Creek lands. Although Mortar declined to attend the Augusta negotiations, he developed a cautious relationship with Superintendent Stuart. To communicate with Stuart, Mortar partnered with Emistisiguo of Little Tallassee, a prominent war leader who lived at the confluence of the Tallapoosa, Coosa, and Alabama Rivers. In April 1764, Emistisiguo sent a talk to the superintendent, explaining his and his colleague's land policy. "As to the Lands Granted you by the Lower Creeks," the headman said, "we agree to that, providing that you keep your Slaves and Cattle within that Bounds." In exchange, Emistisiguo instructed Stuart to cease requests that Upper Creeks permit the British to build forts among their communities as part of Britain's postwar expansion. He stated firmly, "You will have no thought of Erecting any Fort" on Upper Creek lands. Forts would attract unwanted soldiers and settlers and inflame tensions that neither Upper Creeks nor Stuart desired.[42]

Mortar reiterated this position months later. He told Stuart that "no settlements may be made on this [the east] side of the [Alabama] River . . . as [Upper Creeks] are determined to keep free Possession of all that and other Lands they have Enjoyed for Many Years" before the Paris Peace. To offer proof that he was willing to cooperate with the British, Mortar spoke like a diplomat. He had "buried all Red Talks, [a]nd desires none but white Talks," he had discarded his war title (Yahahtustunnogy), and he had accepted peace with the British. He was no stranger to diplomacy. During the Creek-Cherokee War, he assisted the Abeikas and Tallapoosas by negotiating with Cherokee emissaries to halt a conflict that had wrought devastation in Upper Creek communities. He drew on those experiences to implement a vision of peace designed to maintain Upper Creek lands and security. He promised to do his part to keep the young warriors in check and reduce the likelihood of flare-ups between warriors and colonists. Still, British authorities like Stuart would need to meet him halfway. Mortar warned that British stragglers who trespassed onto Upper Creek territories would "certainly Occasion disturbances" and spark retaliation from warriors beyond his control. Emistisiguo moved to convince Stuart of Mortar's sincerity, informing the superintendent that the headman promised to labor diligently to establish "a firm Peace." With years of diplomatic experience under his belt, Mortar advanced good relations with the British Empire.[43]

Yet Mortar's peacekeeping duties failed to sate Britain's desire for more land. Although Stuart had won Upper Creek approval for the Treaty of Augusta, he and West Florida governor George Johnstone wanted to expand the colony to accommodate incoming immigrants. Accordingly, Stuart and Johnstone invited Upper Creek leaders to assemble in the colonial capital of Pensacola to discuss a land cession. In late May and early June 1765, Mortar and Emistisiguo joined other Upper Creek treaty delegates in the port city. After two days of tiresome negotiations with Stuart, they consented to the Treaty of Pensacola, which authorized the sale of land south of a boundary extending from Pensacola northwestward to the Alabama River. In return, Stuart pledged a reduction in trade prices. A table listing fixed rates was appended to the treaty and meant for both Upper and Lower Creek customers. Although Mortar uncharacteristically approved a cession, his about-face stemmed from his recognition that the Upper Creeks were more dependent on British trade than ever before. Without France or Spain as trade alternates, the Upper Creeks made their peace with Britain.[44]

Mortar explained to Superintendent Stuart, however, that the Treaty of Pensacola required approval from his Bear kin. During the closing ceremonies at Pensacola, he informed Stuart that "I am a King of the Ancient Bear family" and must "return to my Nation, in order to speak to my people whom I have left behind." Mortar's hands were tied. For the moment, the treaty was a temporary agreement between British and Creek authorities, not a binding document on two constituent parties. Moreover, the Bear spokesperson was teaching Superintendent Stuart how kin guided political leadership, especially in treaty councils, whose results affected more than the signers. Since the Bear clan was "Ancient" and respected, any input offered by its members carried weight and decided the legality of all treaties. The Pensacola Cession demanded careful attention from relatives who stood to lose access to hunting grounds, natural resources, and sacred places.⁴⁵

Although no evidence confirms his relatives' decision, Mortar averred that a foolish headman ceded land absent deliberation with them. They had the final say. A headman's legitimacy flowed upward from family members, and any misstep lowered his approval rating. Female relatives were especially vocal. Mortar learned this the hard way during the French and Indian War, when Superintendent Atkin reported that Mortar's alliance with the Cherokees had raised a "Clamour" among the Okchais, particularly the "Women of that Town." Doubtless they included his female kin, who had "forced [him] to quit" his militancy against the British. This scrap of evidence suggests that Mortar lacked a mandate to do as he pleased years later when he arrived in Pensacola to treat with Superintendent Stuart. Leashed by the Bear clan and especially its clanswomen, he had no choice but to tell Stuart that treaties were provisional documents in the absence of kin. Mortar's whole program to fasten ties with the British after 1763 was the product of careful maneuvering with these relatives.⁴⁶

The Treaty of Pensacola was the culmination of more than a decade of Upper Creek diplomacy with Native and non-Native peoples. Abeika and Tallapoosa headmen ended the Creek-Cherokee War, removed Superintendent Atkin from Upper Creek country, and maintained fruitful trade relations with the British. To advance peace on multiple fronts, these headmen adapted the diplomatic experiences gained from negotiations with the Cherokees in relations with British superintendents, governors, traders, and other colonists. In this way, the entanglement of intertribal and Indian–European relations creates new ways of telling the history of the eighteenth-century Creeks. One fed into the other. Yet the Upper Creeks' diplomatic successes depended heavily on the intricate mechanisms of indigenous politics in the region. The riverine form of governance motivated high-profile leaders among the Upper Creeks to imagine and enact solutions to regional dangers, but it also tethered them to local peoples, and especially kin, who determined their standing. Women, warriors, and other local actors imagined their own solutions to the problems that beset Upper Creek country. These realities persisted as an old enemy to the west loomed.

Chapter 2

"A Cloud that has been over us"

The Creek-Choctaw War

The Choctaws of present-day central Mississippi had been the target of Creek animosity since the early eighteenth century. For decades, Upper Creek warriors raided the Choctaws for captives and blocked Choctaw attempts to access British goods. Upper Creeks held the advantage in these encounters and confined the Choctaws to trade with the woefully under-provisioned French and Spanish. By mid-century, the Upper Creeks were more worried about securing peace with Cherokees and Britons than with Choctaws, who posed little threat to the Upper Creeks' livelihood. All that changed after the controversial Treaty of Paris ejected the French and Spanish from North America and made Britain the sole trade supplier to the southern Indians, including the Choctaws. Vying for British products, Choctaw and Upper Creek hunters clashed on many of the same lands to obtain animal skins for British trade. In 1766 a brutal war erupted between the Upper Creeks and the Choctaws, specifically the Choctaws of the Western Division towns. While the Creek-Choctaw War resulted from international and regional circumstances, it progressed according to the political rhythms of Native Southerners. In all, the Upper Creeks entered a heart-rending era of death.[1]

The scale, intensity, and duration of the Creek-Choctaw War set it apart from the Creek-Cherokee War and created a sharper discord between high-profile diplomacy and local needs. On one hand, Abeika and Tallapoosa leaders forwarded peace talks to like-minded Choctaw leaders in an attempt to lift the "Cloud [of war] that has been over us." These leaders spoke for the Upper Creek provinces, including on occasion the Alabama towns, drafting both British and other indigenous authorities to serve as go-betweens for the combatants. On the other hand, local peoples took actions that erased diplomatic gains. As young men took vengeance against Choctaws, they unleashed seemingly endless cycles of violence. Grief-stricken kin urged warriors to respond to Choctaw aggression and set things right among the surviving relatives. This custom merged with warriors' decisions to secure war honors and booty, dragging the peace-minded leadership into raids against the very people with whom they sought peace. Warriors dictated the ebb and flow of war, not diplomats. To preserve legitimacy among constituents, Upper Creek leaders reassumed positions of war leadership and struck the Choctaws in the company of warriors. Those skirmishes caused more fatal conflict in turn.[2]

Ground-level actors in Upper Creek country should not be blamed for the violence, however, but they should be recognized for their political and diplomatic impact on the leadership. Nor did all Upper Creeks call for war or seek to topple headmen's diplomacy. Many went about their own business to resolve problems beyond the scope of negotiations between Upper Creek and Choctaw emissaries. This is revealed by British authorities, travelers, and other colonists who visited Upper Creek communities touched by war. These communities devised and practiced a repertoire of dances, songs, and other customs meant to mourn the dead and assuage the living. They embodied the flexibility of kinship systems in the Native South and assisted the Upper Creeks in the search for peace with their enemies. As an intertribal war engulfed Upper Creek country yet again, local peoples seized the reins and shaped the pace of violence with Choctaws.[3]

The Creek-Choctaw War was neither the first nor the last intertribal war to involve the Abeikas and Tallapoosas. Still, it was a significant episode in Upper Creek history. These peoples reeled from violence on a larger scale than during the Creek-Cherokee War or in flare-ups with British colonists. The Choctaws' newfound access to British goods, including weapons and ammunition, prolonged a war that claimed many lives on both sides. Furthermore, this war carried the Upper Creeks into the revolutionary era. The Creek-Choctaw War was not a narrative blip but a chronological bridge linking the Seven Years' War with the American War for Independence, which erupted in the region as the Creek-Choctaw War came to a dramatic close. Just as British colonists resisted parliamentary law and authority on the Atlantic Seaboard, so local peoples among the Upper Creeks critiqued their own officialdom. The Creek-Choctaw War amplified leaders' dependence on local peoples, including kin, who cast a long shadow over the political arena following the war. In short, the Creek-Choctaw War tells scholars a great deal about Upper Creek political culture during a pivotal moment in the region.[4]

"The Abekas [and] Tallipoussas" at Wartime

Since the early eighteenth century, the Upper Creeks had exercised military dominance in affairs with the Choctaws and protected lucrative relations with British traders by obstructing their adversaries from establishing similar ties with the British. Upper Creeks held the Choctaws to French and Spanish traders, who were outcompeted by British traders peddling abundant, inexpensive, and durable goods. The underlying cause of the Creek-Choctaw War was decades of friction between the two parties, then, but the proximate cause was the Treaty of Paris. The 1763 settlement redrew the map of empire across the globe and emboldened British commercial expansion in the late colonial era. Once the Paris Peace removed Britain's competitors from the region, British authorities devised a policy of free trade with all southern Indians eager for goods. While the Upper Creeks remained an old trading partner, the Choctaws clamored for a new one. They happily forged relations with the British, whose supply of trade goods was more plentiful and cheaper than those of the outgoing French and Spanish. After 1763 the Abeikas and Tallapoosas watched with trepidation as the Choctaws gained a new source of weapons, ammunition, and other goods.[5]

The Upper Creeks launched a series of assaults on Choctaw country to cut off Choctaws from British traders. They killed more than twenty Choctaws in the three-year span between 1763 and 1766. These Upper Creek assaults were the opening salvo of the Creek-Choctaw War. Around fall 1766, the Choctaws struck back, killing two aggressors. Those seeking retaliation of their own counterattacked, slaying an equal number of Choctaws as of January 1767. The violence spiraled as reprisal begat reprisal. For instance, another two Upper Creeks lay dead in early 1767 after a Choctaw warrior responded to his foes' counterattack. The Upper Creeks and Choctaws dug in for war. According to a British report from March 1767, there was "perpetual apprehension on both sides." Locked in a nasty cycle of retaliation, each group remained wary of the other. By 1767 the Upper Creeks were facing a confident and well-supplied enemy.[6]

Intertribal escalation alarmed both Upper Creek and Choctaw headmen, for they recognized that sales of British arms threatened all Native peoples. They chastised British authorities for putting profit ahead of Native customers' well-being and contended that the British ought to take steps to promote peace between the warring groups. Emistisiguo, headman of the Tallapoosa town of

Little Tallassee, captured this outlook in a talk addressed to Superintendent Stuart in 1768. He expressed frustration that the Choctaws were "killing our People and Burning our Towns" with British arms. To limit Choctaw access to British goods, especially weapons, he proposed that the superintendent "draw the Traders out from among the Chactaws" and restrict the Choctaw–British trade to Mobile, far from the Choctaw towns. Protecting colonial interests, Stuart declined Emistisiguo's self-serving request.[7]

Emistisiguo's talk to Stuart exposed not only the geopolitical stakes of intertribal warfare but also the wartime experiences of "our Towns," especially those belonging to "the Abekas [and] Tallipoussas." Choctaw warriors raided many of these towns and set them ablaze, destroying property and killing people. On occasion, the Choctaws taunted their foes by deliberately apprising them of plans to sack towns, such as the "Wolf Kings [Tallapoosa] Town" of Muccolossus and the Abeika town of Pucantallahassee. Evidence suggests that Choctaws acted on that threat and killed members of these towns. In other cases, the Choctaws weakened the Upper Creek towns piecemeal by skirmishing with foes in the no-man's-land between the Alabama and Tombigbee Rivers. There they killed two Creeks hailing from the Tallapoosa town of Hoithlewaulee, located on the lower Tallapoosa River near Emistisiguo's town. Equipped with British arms, the Choctaws took the fight to their ancient enemies. One British official learned that the Choctaws were so committed to battling Upper Creeks that they stationed "100 men to lye between Pensacola & the upper Creeks to kill all they can find."[8]

As in other conflicts between southern Indians, the war party was the main organizational unit of the Creek-Choctaw War. Its strength was to enable the participation of warriors as well as women and children in violent situations. Able-bodied men formed small mobile war parties designed to surprise the enemy, inflict maximum damage, and retreat with minimal casualties. The Choctaws who "Burn[ed]" Upper Creek towns, as indicated in the talk from Emistisiguo, were examples of brutal, successful war parties. Furthermore, effective war parties mastered the proper spiritual powers to protect themselves from harm and return home with captives as evidence of supremacy over the enemy. Warriors presented captives to relatives, especially women and children, who decided their fate. Male captives were subjected to ritual torture followed by death, both to expiate collective grief and to emasculate the helpless captive. Female captives were usually spared, adopted into the lineage, and exploited for their labor. Captives in the Creek-Choctaw War met with similar fates. One Upper Creek war party captured a "Principal Leader" of the Choctaws and marched him home, where he was "Fles'd... alive, and Tortured... most inhumanly." By contrast, a war party from the Tallapoosa town of Tuckabatchee captured the niece of a Choctaw headman; evidence suggests that town members adopted her. Male war parties worked in tandem with women and children to power the Creek-Choctaw War.[9]

The threats, raids, and killings that marked this war constituted more than physical aggression. Although the southern Indians enacted bodily harm, they also communicated violence to one another using a rich trove of metaphor, symbolism, and material culture. Violence was as much cultural as corporeal, then, encoded in objects and intimated in messages conveying bad blood. The Upper Creeks understood as much when they sent "black wings" to Choctaw headmen in the war's early stages. Since black was the color of death, the bird wings portended Choctaw suffering. The darkened wings also symbolized a breach in Creek–Choctaw relations and anticipated many years of violence between the groups. Four years into this war, in 1770, Upper Creek headmen spoke about "a Cloud" hanging over their people and the Choctaws. That cloud and the black wings were metaphors for a dark era in intertribal relations.[10]

The Creek-Choctaw War heralded another chapter in the history of the Upper Creeks. Smoldering tensions between them and the Choctaws gave way to full-blown war after the 1763 Treaty of Paris restructured North American colonialism and paved the way for British commercial dominance in the region. The British policy of free trade birthed an Anglo–Choctaw alliance, put the Upper Creeks on the defensive, and set the two indigenous populations on a collision course. The deep-rooted custom of retaliation spawned vicious cycles of raids and counterraids between the combatants. By the late 1760s, dozens on both sides lay dead, victims of clan reprisals, shock-and-awe raids, skirmishes in rural areas, and ritual torture. Whether Upper Creek and Choctaw headmen might achieve peace remained to be seen.

"The Heads of the Abekas & Tallipouses" Sue for Peace

Beginning in the early months of 1770, Upper Creek headmen spearheaded a peace initiative with the Choctaws. While earlier attempts at diplomacy had been premature, headmen from both sides appeared more willing to negotiate a settlement as casualties mounted. In concert with Choctaw headmen, a cadre of prominent Abeika and Tallapoosa headmen coauthored a peace settlement with their adversaries. Emistisiguo "assure[d]" the Choctaws that the resolution was "from the Heads of the Abekas & Tallipouses," especially himself and his Abeika colleague Mortar. These two headmen additionally provided diplomatic assistance to the nearby Alabamas, who became involved in the war and clamored for peace with the Choctaws. After several years of violence between Creek and Choctaw countries, Emistisiguo and Mortar decided the time for peace was ripe.[11]

The two leaders' diplomatic résumé was illustrious. In the 1760s British authorities named them "great medal chiefs" to cultivate good relations between Creek country and the British Empire. Only three other Upper Creek headmen held that honor. The honorific also recognized each headman's political weight. Emistisiguo had a personal relationship with the cousin duo Superintendent John Stuart and Deputy Superintendent Charles Stuart, from whom he received gifts of trade goods. The Tallapoosas referred to him as "Chief Man of the upper Creeks" because of his privileged access to the Stuarts and the British trade wares they funneled to Tallapoosa communities. During the Creek-Choctaw War, Emistisiguo appointed the Stuarts as mediators for the combatants. The cousins obliged him because they feared the war's possible spillover into the British backcountry. For his part, Mortar had served on behalf of his Bear clan to promote peace with the British. When the Creek-Choctaw War threatened his kin and the Abeikas more generally, Mortar adapted like the political chameleon he was and pursued negotiations with the Choctaws. Experienced and well connected, Emistisiguo and Mortar were poised to reopen talks with the Choctaws in 1770.[12]

In March, Emistisiguo contacted the Choctaws in a "peace talk" dispatched by Deputy Stuart. Months later, negotiations proceeded apace. From Pensacola, Deputy Stuart wrote Superintendent Stuart on June 17 that Emistisiguo had recently visited him to inquire about the effect of his talk. During his conversation with the headman, Deputy Stuart presented him with "a talk" of the Choctaws' own, promising to cease hostilities with the Upper Creeks. Along with the talk, Choctaw headmen forwarded "three strings of white beads" and "pipes and tobacco" that Emistisiguo "received with great Joy." These items symbolized peace. The southern Indians identified white as the color of peace and smoked tobacco from pipes as part of a ritual designed to establish good relations between parties. Furthermore, white beaded strings were regularly crafted and deployed by southern Indians to signal peace between the interested parties. In a word, the objects transmitted by the Choctaws were the antithesis of the black wings the Upper Creeks had sent their foes early in the war.

For the first time during the Creek-Choctaw War, peace seemed likely. Both Emistisiguo and Mortar confirmed as much by having Deputy Stuart transmit a similar message and objects to the Choctaws. Emistisiguo presented the deputy with two "white wings and some tobacco" so that the Choctaws may "wipe away all bad talks."[13]

Upper Creek negotiations with the Choctaws culminated around September with a creative flourish. According to Deputy Stuart, the Upper Creeks designed a "Belt of Whampum" to be forwarded to the Choctaws. Wampum were small beads, originally rendered from the quahog clam (*Mercenaria mercenaria*) of southern New England, woven into a strap or belt of animal sinew to create an elaborate object that communicated a message from author to recipient. The tradition of wampum belt diplomacy belongs to the Iroquois Confederacy and other Iroquoian speakers of the Northeast. The origins and ubiquity of this practice in the Native South are unclear, but Deputy Stuart's correspondence with his cousin and the Upper Creeks suggests that southern Indian leaders had been creating belts in the Iroquoian fashion by the time of the Creek-Choctaw War. Since the Upper Creeks and Choctaws exchanged beaded strings during peace negotiations, it would not have been a stretch for Upper Creeks to design a wampum belt in the pursuit of peace. Desperate times called for desperate measures. The main difference between Iroquoian belts and those of the Upper Creeks was that the latter were probably made from glass beads obtained through British trade.[14]

Together, then, Emistisiguo and Mortar incorporated Iroquoian diplomatic tradition into southern Indian diplomatic practices to meet the needs of the Abeikas and Tallapoosas. Emistisiguo requested Deputy Stuart to forward the belt of wampum to the Choctaws with the message that "this Belt is Sent by the Consent of the Whole Nation[, namely the] Tallapousses & Abekas[,] and that they have Sent this as a Token of their Sincerity." Mortar added in a similar message that this initiative "came from the Abekas & Tallipousses," who wished for nothing but peace with the Choctaws. Both headmen spoke for the peoples of the Coosa and Tallapoosa Rivers even as they borrowed diplomatic techniques from the distant Iroquois. Additionally, the Upper Creek wampum belt trafficked in color symbolism. Woven into one end of the belt was a "black ring" that represented war with the Choctaws. At the opposite end was a "white bead," gesturing toward a bright, peaceful future with the Choctaws. In short, Upper Creek headmen sought to erase a past rife with violence and chart a new course with their westward neighbors.[15]

To actualize peace, however, they needed to build trust with the Choctaw recipients. The wampum belt visualized a way forward. Emistisiguo informed Deputy Stuart that the center of the belt was a metaphor for Upper Creeks and Choctaws walking together on a "Clear Path." Those who walked on this path, which fostered exchange and alliance between the two peoples, were Emistisiguo and a Choctaw headman named Holaghtaobaye, also known as Holacta Hopayi. The shape of each leader clasped hands in the middle of the belt, signifying the major persons responsible for bringing about peace. Once Emistisiguo closed his interpretation of the belt to Deputy Stuart, he instructed the British official to present it to Choctaw emissaries, including Holacta Hopayi. He expressed hope that they would "take Great Care of the . . . Great Beloved Belt." Freighted with meaning, the wampum belt was an elaborate code for peace between adversaries.[16]

Upper Creek leaders bolstered this agenda in late 1770 by forwarding to the Choctaws supplemental "Tokens of Peace," including a string of white beads. Emistisiguo explained that the beaded string depicted the "Alabama Fort" or Fort Toulouse, formerly occupied by the French Empire at the confluence of the Coosa, Tallapoosa, and Alabama Rivers. In Emistisiguo's day, the fort remained intact among the Alabamas, with whom the French had had peaceful relations until the Paris Peace evicted that colonial power from North America. The French were gone, Emistisiguo admitted, but their colonial legacy endured. He reminded the Choctaws that the French had kept the path between indigenous southerners "always white & Clean" and that they "had peace among us." The French were expert path makers. Emistisiguo invoked the memory of the easygoing French to pressure the Choctaws into laying down their weapons and joining hands in peace. Like the wampum belt, the string of beads drew upon the metaphor of paths to curb intertribal antagonism.[17]

Emistisiguo invoked Fort Toulouse to acknowledge the Alabamas as much as the French. The French Empire had erected it in the early eighteenth century for purposes of trade and alliance with the Alabamas. By 1770 the inhabitants of at least four Alabama towns had fallen in with the Choctaws. In September, Deputy Stuart reported to his cousin that the "Chief of the Cusados" killed two Choctaws and took their "Scalps." Emistisiguo confirmed this report, saying that men from the Alabama town of Coosada "were going to War" against the Choctaws. Later in the year, however, the Coosadas shifted course and joined Emistisiguo and Mortar in peace negotiations. Relying on Deputy Stuart as the mediator, they forwarded beads and tobacco to the Choctaws "as a Sign of peace." Alabama participation in these talks was crucial, if subordinate, to Abeika and Tallapoosa headmen. Deputy Stuart accepted these items of peace not from Coosada leaders but from Mortar, who presented them to the Briton on the Coosadas' behalf. The political arrangement between Mortar and the Alabamas was one of disparity. Mortar and his Tallapoosa ally continued to take charge of the peace settlement with the Choctaws.[18]

Upper Creek diplomacy in 1770 typified the creativity of riverine leadership. Led by Mortar and Emistisiguo, it blended Iroquoian and Muscogean traditions to create a "Belt of Whampum" illustrating an end to hostilities with the Choctaws. Woven into this belt were shapes and patterns whose meaning communicated peace and alliance-building between Upper Creek and Choctaw headmen. The belt's cultural complexity was matched only by its rarity in southern Indian diplomacy; the Upper Creeks were pulling out all stops to halt the war. Emistisiguo and Mortar deployed additional ritual objects, such as tobacco, white wings, and beaded strings, to affirm the peaceful intentions of the Upper Creek as well as Alabama towns. To protect British settlements from possible violence, Deputy Charles Stuart mediated intertribal negotiations by ferrying messages and gifts between the Upper Creeks and Choctaws.[19]

Peace Falters on "these Rivers"

The Upper Creeks' diplomatic tokens were, as Emistisiguo and Mortar put it, "sent by all the Headmen of these Rivers" to the Choctaws. This language captured the riverine conception of governance that the Abeikas and Tallapoosas continued to practice at wartime. Although Upper Creek headmen exercised a wide latitude in diplomacy, warriors and other local actors kept them on a short leash. Exerting their own influence in Upper Creek affairs, they decided whether the peace settlement crafted by Upper Creek headmen in 1770 served local interests. When Upper Creeks perished after a fresh round of Choctaw attacks late in the year, they removed peace from the table. New rounds of war with the Choctaws soon disrupted the hard work of diplomacy. Furthermore, warriors expected headmen like Emistisiguo and Mortar to fall in line. None escaped the clutches of localism.[20]

The turning point came in December, when Upper Creek headmen traveled to Mobile to visit Deputy Stuart. He had scheduled this meeting months earlier to offer a neutral space for the combatants to meet face to face, advance negotiations, and "confirm" peace. At the helm of the Upper Creek delegation was Emistisiguo, anxious to clasp hands with Choctaw emissaries. The stakes were high, and peace seemed just around the corner. En route to Mobile, however, Emistisiguo learned that Choctaw warriors had recently killed "4 or 5" Upper Creeks. The parley dashed, he and his companions returned home. Emistisiguo told Deputy Stuart with regret that "it would be to no purpose to make the peace today and [make] war tomorrow." The reason that renewed war seemed likely, he continued, was that "they that had lost their friends [relatives] in that action [and] would surely seek revenge." Choctaw headmen expecting to greet Emistisiguo in Mobile felt the same and told Deputy Stuart that they "were sorely disappointed and wanted much to have peace" with the Upper Creeks. Lamenting this development, each side braced for renewed war.[21]

Whether the Upper Creeks retaliated as Emistisiguo assumed is unknown, but they balked at diplomacy with the Choctaws. Thomas Gage, lieutenant general of the British army, wrote his superior in January 1771 that "the Creek nation does not seem unanimous in the desire of peace" with their foes, indicating that some Upper Creeks clamored for war. Gage's is one of few British reports about Creek–Choctaw relations in 1771. Since British authorities busied themselves with the growing imperial crisis on the Eastern Seaboard, few British records track Creek activities at this time. Fortunately, a Dutch surveyor, cartographer, and botanist named Bernard Romans wrote a travel account that offsets the paucity of British correspondence on the Creeks. His account demonstrates that the Creek-Choctaw War had resumed by fall, several months after the abortive Mobile congress.[22]

Employed by Superintendent Stuart, Romans led a surveying party through Choctaw lands adjacent to the British colony of West Florida. On September 30, he and his team crossed Buckatunna Creek in present-day southeastern Mississippi. They traveled for nearly twelve miles through "pine land" and encamped at a place called Noisy Owl. There, on Choctaw hunting grounds, they encountered a "hieroglyphick painting" or "a painting in the Creek taste." According to Romans, "ten of that nation of the Stag family came in three canoes into their enemies country." Of that ten, six warriors "near this place, which was at *Oopah Ullah* [Noisy Owl], a brook so called on the road to the Chactaws, had met two men, and two women with a dog." The six warriors "lay in ambush for them, killed them, and . . . all went home with the four scalps." Romans concluded that "the scalp in the stag's foot implies the honour of . . . the whole family." His interpretation indicates that Creeks and Choctaws had once again plunged into war. Creek warriors who belonged to the "Stag family," or Deer clan, slayed unsuspecting Choctaws and took scalps as an emblem of mastery over their

Creek Pictograph, Reproduced on Copperplate by Dutch Traveler Bernard Romans, ca. 1770

The Dutch surveyor Bernard Romans discovered this rare Creek "painting" during his travels through Choctaw country in fall 1771. The animal at the top represents the Deer, or Stag, clan as it holds a Choctaw scalp and symbolizes the Creek warriors' victory over their enemies. The original artists conveyed both the importance of clanship and the fragility of diplomacy during the Creek-Choctaw War. Public domain; from Romans, *A Concise Natural History of East and West Florida*, 74, 150 (figure 14).

enemies. Before rowing home, they memorialized the Choctaws' defeat in a painting likely made on deerskins, a popular medium of communication in the Native South. Choctaws in isolated areas of the region had become sitting ducks for Creek war parties.[23]

The "hieroglyphick painting" is more than a depiction of Creek aggression against the Choctaws. It is a rare source crafted by indigenous artists linking warfare with local circumstances in a specific era. Put differently, the artists drew a correlation between taking life and serving warriors' needs during the Creek-Choctaw War. These artists were probably the Deer warriors themselves. They conveyed their relatives' military "honour" by means of a clan totem clutching a slain Choctaw's scalp. Below the totem are the victors, representing the clan's efficacy in battle. The strength of the Deer clan and the prowess of its warriors are as evident as the humiliation of the Choctaw victims. Whether these warriors hailed from the Upper Creek towns is inconclusive, as Romans was in no position to know. Yet the Deer clan was prevalent among Upper Creeks, who remained the principal enemies of the Choctaws in the 1770s. That strongly suggests that the Deer warriors featured in the hieroglyphic were Upper Creeks. Thanks to an Upper Creek clan, intertribal war had returned to the region.[24]

The hieroglyphic source also reveals the warriors' political impact on the second phase of the war. These men determined whether leaders' diplomatic ventures would succeed or collapse. If they spared the unsuspecting Choctaws, they would ease the achievement of peace for which the Upper Creek headmen strove. If they killed their targets, however, diplomacy would topple and cause the Choctaws to respond with raids. The choice was stark, but as Romans discovered, the Deer clan warriors chose violence. The timing could not have been worse. By killing Choctaws, the Upper Creeks dissented from the peace settlement carefully built by Emistisiguo and Mortar, sending the region spiraling. This phase of the Creek-Choctaw War was especially aggressive. British authorities concerned about the safety of colonial settlements wrote reports that prove or suggest that Upper Creeks and Choctaws killed one another in 1772, 1773, 1774, and 1775. The "Cloud" of war reappeared.[25]

These outbursts of violence blindsided Emistisiguo and Mortar. They commanded power and respect in Upper Creek country so long as they heeded local constituents. Young men seeking war honors, retaliation, and other objectives were among those constituents. They demanded that the headmen reassume positions of war leadership and lead them into battle against Choctaws. Left with no choice, the headmen abandoned peace and accepted the likelihood of more conflict with the same group with whom they had been negotiating via Deputy Stuart. The evidence is clear and damning. In October 1772, a British agent named David Taitt reported to Superintendent Stuart that Emistisiguo departed Upper Creek country with "a large Party" to hunt along the Escambia River and "to War [against the Choctaws] before they Return to their Towns." A month later, Taitt wrote Stuart that Mortar and his warriors had "gone Over the Coosa River to [wage] War," presumably on the Choctaws. Taitt confirmed his earlier report about Emistisiguo as well, writing that the headman had embarked for Pensacola "to Hunt and afterwards to War against the Chactaws." Assuming a political mantle, Upper Creek warriors forced Emistisiguo and

Mortar into a compromising position. While these leaders had been "daily striving to maintain peace and good order" in Creek–Choctaw relations, warriors had other ideas for them.[26]

As intertribal hostilities reemerged in the 1770s, the Upper Creek peace agenda that had originated with Emistisiguo and Mortar collapsed. Local actors on the Coosa and Tallapoosa Rivers reignited war with the Choctaws by securing war honors, exacting retaliation, and otherwise asserting local needs in Upper Creeks affairs. They expected leaders like Emistisiguo and Mortar to fulfill those needs by heading up war parties against the Choctaws. Consequently, the very leadership that had advanced peace with Choctaw emissaries could no longer pursue diplomatic resolution. Commitment to peoples on the ground outweighed all else.

The Search for Peace through Ceremony

The war's second phase devastated the Upper Creeks. According to Agent Taitt, the "burden lays upon the Frontier Towns in the upper Creeks," namely the Abeika towns along the upper Coosa River, where the Choctaws raided with frightening regularity in the 1770s. Taitt and other colonial observers wrote similarly about the Tallapoosa communities farther from Choctaw country. Amid the violence, Upper Creek women and men devised ceremonies to alleviate collective suffering. In particular, the ceremonies consisted of dances and songs that brought townspeople together and supplied a creative outlet for grief. The Tallapoosa towns of Tuckabatchee and Muccolossus capture this trend. Chance visits to these towns by British colonists resulted in uniquely nuanced records that demonstrate that ceremonialism was yet another way in which local peoples exerted influence in Upper Creek affairs. Just as they forced headmen into raids, so they expected headmen to participate in ceremonies that offered respite from the ongoing violence. As a result, they led their towns on a spiritual journey that helped lay the groundwork for peace.[27]

In Tuckabatchee, one ceremony aimed to restore the life of a townsperson captured, "skinned" alive, and killed by the Choctaws in late 1771. He was the town's fire maker, a ritual specialist who lit the sacred fire and performed other tasks during the community's annual Busk. The fire maker's death sent shock waves through the town. Our source for this is Agent Taitt, who visited the town months later, in April 1772, during a tour of Upper Creek country to drum up support for a land cession. On April 6, he recorded that the by-then experienced leader Mad Dog was "very busy preparing physick and causing the people to dance every night on purpose to bring back to life their firemaker." Mad Dog crafted physic, a sacred medicine that generated spiritual power, to energize the dancing townspeople and to resurrect the late fire maker. He first entered the British records in 1759 as a noted warrior; over time he gained the proper spiritual training to serve the town as a trusted ritual leader. Consequently, he would have been a colleague of the late fire maker and known him quite well. Mad Dog was more than aware that the town's upcoming Busk was in peril absent an experienced person to oversee the lighting of the town fire. Only the proper medicine could revive a holy man slain by Choctaws.[28]

Mad Dog's leadership depended heavily on his sister. She had been married to the decedent and, as a widow, assumed importance in ceremonial activities resulting from his demise. She was in no position to call for retaliation since she, like other southern Indians, had married outside her clan. Securing retaliation lay with her late husband's clan, not hers. Still, she was being haunted by the unavenged ghost, about which she alerted the townspeople. According to Taitt, she "persuaded the people that he comes to her sometimes in the night and that he keeps about the square" and other town spaces. Tuckabatchee was in crisis, and Mad Dog's sister was at the center of it. Since the fire maker's ghost jeopardized the town's safety as well as her own, she convinced the townspeople that they had to follow her brother's ritual prescriptions. Agent Taitt learned that the deceased "will soon make his appearance in public if they make the physick strong enough and take proper care." The community was under strong pressure to follow the guidelines initiated by the haunted widow. Although she relied on her brother's religious expertise, she was the host and organizer of a ceremony meant to stem the town's present crisis.[29]

Siblings had an unusually intimate relationship in matrilineal societies. A woman maintained good relations with her brother into adulthood and counted on him to raise her sons. Moreover, women were important lineage members and exerted influence on their brothers and other male relatives. Mad Dog's sister was one among many indigenous women who ensured that men were attentive to kin needs as the ghosts of the Creek-Choctaw War came home. For these reasons, Mad Dog committed himself to preparing medicine and leading the community in dance. Taitt reported that the Tuckabatchees danced for several consecutive days because of uncertainty as to "the time when the firemaker would come." On behalf of his sister, he "ordered them all to attend" the vigorous dance schedule "until [the fire maker] came' and returned to life as a Busk officiant. In sum, the strong attachment between siblings in Tuckabatchee helped the community weather Choctaw raids in the 1770s. Ceremony was an extension of that kinship connection.[30]

The tie between Mad Dog and his sister was so strong that it interfered with his diplomatic schedule. Agent Taitt had previously invited him to attend a meeting with Abeika and Tallapoosa leaders in Okchai, upriver from Tuckabatchee. The agent wished to ascertain whether Upper Creek headmen supported another land cession to the British southern colonies. That meeting had been set for mid-April, just as the Tuckabatchees danced for their fire maker. On April 18, when Taitt opened the convention with Upper Creek leaders in Okchai, Mad Dog was noticeably absent. He had remained at home, "being afraid to leave his women," not least his sister. Abandoning them not only imperiled the success of the community ceremony but also invited an unwanted backlash against his leadership. Since his power rested on their needs and approval, his hands were tied. To serve his female relatives, he limited his availability in Upper Creek politics and annoyed the agent to boot.[31]

The ceremony that led Mad Dog to decline Taitt's meeting was novel. The Creeks and other southern Indians normally staged dances to commune with spirits and guide deceased relatives to the afterlife. Few dances aimed to resurrect the dead, however, suggesting that the Tuckabatchee dance observed by Taitt was a singular product of the Creek-Choctaw War. The loss of a ritual functionary was immeasurable to the Tuckabatchees, who relied on Mad Dog and "his women" to bring this person back to life. There was no replacement for a trained and trusted fire maker. In coordination with his sister and other kinswomen, then, Mad Dog strove to regenerate a cherished community member.[32]

Like the Tuckabatchees, the people of Muccolossus grew weary of war in the 1770s. The traveling botanist William Bartram visited the town in 1775, noting the "sighs and tears" of its inhabitants reeling from conflict with the Choctaws. At the center of Muccolossus–Choctaw animosity was Wolf, the Muccolossus headman who had participated in peace negotiations with the Cherokees and British at mid-century. Whether Wolf led raids into Choctaw country is unclear, but one of his brothers had attacked the Choctaws early in the war. By the time Bartram arrived on the Tallapoosa watershed, Wolf and other Muccolossus denizens had had enough. The townspeople sought peace with their enemies by breathing life into the community's ceremonial practices. In particular, they sang songs of Choctaw derivation that resembled what Bartram called "elegies." This music equipped the people of Muccolossus with new ways to ease the pain of war and, more broadly, to chart a course of peace with their foes. On the Tallapoosa River, people sang for peace.[33]

Songs in the eighteenth-century Native South came in all shapes and sizes. Some celebrated the Busk, others mourned the dead, and still others warded off disease. All encouraged communal unity and lent a voice to those high and low, female and male, old and young. In many cases, southern Indians borrowed songs from each other. In Bartram's opinion, some of the Creeks' "most favorite songs" hailed "from their enemy, the Chactaw." This was especially the case in Muccolossus. During Bartram's stay there in late 1775, the townspeople held a ceremony to sing "new songs" based on the musical traditions of their foes. Everyone sang "with harmony and eclat [éclat]." Bartram quoted the chorus of one song in particular: "All men must surely die, Tho' no one knows how soon, Yet when the time shall come, The event may be joyful." This song captured the inevitability of death in wartime and encouraged future victims of Choctaw raids to prepare for a glorious entrance into the afterlife. This and other songs in Muccolossus were the spiritual product of the Creek-Choctaw War. They allowed community members to make sense of the violence and cultivate inner peace. Bartram understood the sacrality of these songs, calling them "religious lectures" and "solemn address[es]" to the spirit world.[34]

The Choctaw songs enjoyed by Muccolossus resulted from a strategic marriage between a Muccolossus woman and a Choctaw man who had traveled to the town with Bartram. Bartram referred to the Choctaw as a "Mustee" because of his mixed ancestry and remarked that this individual was proficient in Choctaw culture, especially "music and poetry." As for the Muccolossus woman, Bartram wrote that she was the "daughter of the chief," meaning Wolf. His belief that a woman's father played a role in her marital decisions should not be dismissed outright. Bartram toured the Native South in the 1770s, absorbing much knowledge about the cultural traditions of the area's indigenous peoples. Plus, Wolf was a prominent headman, well-known among Creeks and Britons and by 1775 desperate to end the Creek-Choctaw War. It is thus probable that he shaped conversation on the Muccolossus–Choctaw union, but he was neither so powerful nor so foolish as to override female opinion on the matter. Creek women chose marriage partners following the approval of mothers and aunts, who vetted suitors to ensure that they would not diminish the clan's reputation and resources. The decision by the daughter to marry a Choctaw outsider should be considered too. She asserted herself in the arena of diplomacy and attempted to restore peace to her war-torn community. As a result of her agency, the newlyweds threw a large "festival," where her husband taught new music to the townspeople of Muccolossus. Song, marriage, and diplomacy went hand in hand.[35]

Like the revival dance invented by the Tuckabatchees, the Choctaw songs served a people weakened by war. Muccolossus inhabitants gladly accepted the gift of songs from their Choctaw guest to find peace, mourn the departed, and otherwise strengthen ties across their community. By singing songs that originated in Choctaw country, moreover, they endorsed peace between Choctaws and Upper Creeks. None called for violence, and everyone sought reconciliation. The time for peace between two bitter enemies had arrived. Complemented by Wolf, female actors played a leading role in that development.[36]

The innovative ceremonialism in Muccolossus and Tuckabatchee helped to create lasting peace with the Choctaws. In October 1776, mere months after Bartram's stay in Muccolossus, Upper Creek and Choctaw headmen convened in Pensacola, where Superintendent Stuart brokered the negotiations from his house. The timing of his participation was no accident. Since the British Empire had recently become embroiled in the American War for Independence, colonial authorities like him needed all the Native allies they could get. According to his record of the Pensacola meeting, the Upper Creek and Choctaw delegations assembled "about 300 yards" from one another, standing on the street in front of Stuart's house. As each side held "a white Flagg as an Emblem of Peace," political leaders in each party echoed Muccolossus by "singing the Peace Song." Headmen then "advance[d] slowly when at a Signal given a Number of young men sallied out from each party and made a sham fight in the Space between them." This bloodless battle was yet another overture of peace. Finally, "both parties met, and after saluting each other," they "joined hands" in Stuart's presence. The men subsequently entered Stuart's "house, and delivered into my hands two War Clubs painted Red as the last Ceremony of laying down their Arms; which I promised to burry very deep in the Earth." These negotiations ended the Creek-Choctaw War once and for all, and they flowed from the ceremonies of dance and song pioneered by Upper Creek communities. The "Cloud" of war dissipated.[37]

The Creek-Choctaw War was an important chapter in the Upper Creeks' history. For those who lived on the Coosa and Tallapoosa Rivers, it rivaled the previous conflict with the Cherokees in scale and duration. Countless Upper

Creeks perished in cycles of raids and counterraids that locked the region in continual death. Although Upper Creek leaders momentarily reversed the damage by promoting peace with Choctaw emissaries, the riverine texture of Creek governance seldom kept headmen and local people on the same page for long. Women, warriors, and other people beyond political office drew the leadership into renewed acts of war against the Choctaws. Indeed, war became a means of strengthening local actors' influence. By calling for retaliation, displaying scalps, balking at diplomacy, and practicing ceremony, the Upper Creeks left an imprint on their leaders more than ever before. It was these on-the-ground actors who helped bridge the late colonial and revolutionary eras. How the Abeikas and Tallapoosas might navigate the war of rebellion that sizzled on the Atlantic Coast, however, demanded coordination with Creeks to the eastward. The Chattahoochee River beckoned.

Part II
Three Rivers: The Cusseta Connection, 1777–1797

Chapter 3

"Breath and Master of the Towns on the Three Rivers"

Diplomacy and Revolution

In response to American Independence, the Upper Creeks forged a remarkable partnership with their counterparts on the Chattahoochee, especially the Lower Creek town of Cusseta. Instrumental to it was an aspiring headman named Tame King, who belonged to the Tallapoosa town of Tallassee, east of present-day Montgomery, Alabama. Styling himself the head of "Three Rivers," he stitched together a provincial trifecta that included his natal Tallapoosa town, Cusseta, and the Abeika town of Okfuskee. As a result, he expanded the riverine dimension of Creek governance and set the political tenor of Creek country for years to come. This partnership also gave him and his supporters the political tools to manage affairs with Georgia rebels, who claimed Creek lands along the Oconee River, as well as other participants in the War for Independence. The alliance among Tallassee, Okfuskee, and Cusseta therefore sought to keep Georgia at arm's length and retain the Creeks' own independence. These Creeks promoted collaboration on a riverine scale to protect their world from colonial rebellion.[1]

Okfuskee and Cusseta were a strong fit for a project meant to defend Creeks from the American rebels. Okfuskee leaders had served the Upper Creeks as prominent negotiators for a long time; likewise, the Cussetas were peace advocates owing to their unique political status. They lived in one of a few "peace towns" in Creek country, which meant that its leaders sought to maintain order and peace within the Creek realm. In addition, a peace town offered sanctuary to criminals and provided other services to the Creeks. One observer confirmed Cusseta's political importance in the eighteenth century, writing that it was the "great mother town" of the Creeks. The Cussetas were also noted diplomats. Since mid-century, they had mediated disputes between Upper Creeks and neighboring populations in the region, including other Indians and British colonists. Most recently, Cusseta leaders had helped broker an effective peace between Upper Creeks and Choctaws in Superintendent John Stuart's presence in 1776. Cusseta and its Abeika counterpart were more than prepared to assist Tame King with peacekeeping duties.[2]

Leaders from Cusseta, Okfuskee, and Tallassee sewed themselves into a revolutionary fabric that involved far more than the British and the American rebels. French participation on the American side altered the pace and outcome of the War for Independence, but so too did the Spanish Empire, which made a triumphant return to the Southeast beginning in 1779. Spanish generals, sailors, and soldiers recaptured the Floridas from the British after besieging such outposts as Manchac, Baton Rouge, Natchez, Mobile, and Pensacola. Along with the French, the Spanish provided crucial financial and military support to the American rebels, thereby weakening the British military and hastening Britain's defeat at Yorktown, Virginia, in fall 1781. In addition to Europeans, enslaved Africans and other southern Indians fought in this war for their own reasons and helped launch the Age of Atlantic Revolutions. In short, the War for Independence in the Native South differed from that in the Mid-Atlantic and New England. A kaleidoscope of peoples and powers ranging from the Spanish, Americans, and British to the Chickasaws, loyalists, and slaves presented political leaders like Tame King with opportunities to build alliances and maximize opportunities for maneuver.[3]

A regular node of alliance-building was rebel Georgia. By advancing peace with Georgia's authorities, he presented an alternative to Alexander McGillivray, a popular subject of historical inquiry. Scholars have spilled much ink on this Creek patriot who allied with the British Empire to oppose Georgia's economic and territorial expansion into Creek country. To unite Creeks around the British, McGillivray envisaged an agenda that subordinated clans and towns to a cadre of leaders like himself who would speak for a Creek "nation" and the National Council. In his view, the nationalists would be the official voice of all Creeks and deny any requests for Creek land by Georgia. Only centralized leadership, he argued, would save the Creeks from peril. If McGillivray believed that Creek survival depended upon nationhood, Tame King invested in a partnership among towns affiliated with, in his words, "Three Rivers." The Tallapoosa leader constructed a power base from three provinces and objected to national rulers, such as McGillivray, who sought to suppress the autonomy traditionally exercised by clans and towns within the provinces.

Tame King was as much a patriot as McGillivray. Yet his brand of patriotism differed markedly from his rival's by sprouting from the riverine contours of Creek country.[4]

Like his political ancestors, Tame King was enmeshed in a world of localism. People on the ground were as invested as the leadership in the consequences of a revolution that spawned a new colonial entity: the United States. In addition to working with other high-profile leaders in Creek country, he rendered decisions in concert with a Tallassee person whose life can be gleaned from a handful of records. Tame King called him "Father" in speeches recorded by deerskin trader and patriarch George Galphin, who sympathized with the rebel cause. While matrilineal tradition suggests that this individual was Tame King's uncle, the frequency with which Tame King invoked a paternal relationship with him precludes absolute certainty. More certain is that Tame King believed the two men shared a kin tie, that the Tallassee man had been Tallassee's mico and held the title Tallassee King after retirement, and that Tallassee King was considerably older than Tame King. According to this line of reasoning, then, Tame King was possibly a son or a grandson of Tallassee King. Furthermore, age defined this kin connection. As a wise elder, Tallassee King brought years of diplomatic experience to the table. He continually advised the young Tame King to chart a course of peace, trade, and security in revolutionary Creek country. Tame King heeded his relative's input as he traveled about the region cultivating alliances with rebel Georgians like Galphin and European powers like the Spanish. Local actors accounted for the decisions, tactics, and gambles of Tame King during his parleys with the revolution's many participants.[5]

"Three Rivers"

Several factors contributed to Tame King's appearance on the international stage in the 1770s. His name was not a personal moniker but a political title that suggests that he was gentle, meek, and affable. Those characteristics suited him for leadership both in Tallassee and across the Native South. "King" derived from eighteenth-century British commentators who mistook southern Indian leaders like him for miniature kings with absolute authority over their towns. But in keeping with Creek norms, Tame King would instead have been one among many Tallassee leaders who led by cooperation and persuasion. Moreover, he was well connected in Upper Creek patronage networks that included Tallassee King. The older man had been a town leader in the colonial era and served in that capacity by attending councils with other Native and European authorities.

By the early 1780s, Tallassee King had grown too "weak" to maintain his political responsibilities, so he relinquished power to the ambitious and capable Tame King. Being tied to a prominent but retired headman in Tallassee, Tame King inherited his elder's contacts, including the noted Okfuskee headman Handsome Fellow, "son" of Red Coat King. More experienced in the realm of diplomacy than Tame King, Handsome Fellow participated in early negotiations with Georgia and lent diplomatic expertise to the Tallassee neophyte.[6]

Tame King's ascent stemmed from the political geography of Creek country, too. His hometown belonged to the Tallapoosa province, known occasionally among Creeks and colonial observers as the Middle Creeks. The map of the Native South produced by Emanuel Bowen earlier in the century features the Middle Creek towns, including "Talasse." These towns inhabited a strategic location between the Abeikas to the northwest and the Lower Creeks to the southeast. Tame King recognized the Tallapoosas' political center of gravity when he migrated to a village offshoot or talofa of Tallassee no later than the 1770s. Called Halfway House, this small community hosted two hundred people on Chavacleyhatchie Creek near the Tallapoosa River. Records pinpoint Halfway House some twenty-five miles east of the main town. Tame King lived quite literally halfway between the Lower Creeks and the Abeikas. By moving closer to the Lower Creek towns, including Cusseta, he scouted political opportunities there while preserving neighborly ties with the Abeikas.[7]

His perch at Halfway House established, Tame King opened talks with Georgia in June 1777. He assembled on the Ogeechee River with the longtime deerskin trader George Galphin and other rebel commissioners to pursue two objectives. First, he came to pledge peace with the Americans to minimize the likelihood of armed clashes between Creeks and Georgians in coming years. Equally important, he carried a mandate from Tallassee King to pursue trade with Galphin, a trusted businessperson among the Creeks. His relative in Tallassee had previously contacted Galphin to explore this possibility. Tame King was no lone actor, then, for he possessed clear instructions in advance. The conference opened on June 17 when Galphin and his colleagues promised to supply the Creeks with "Goods in Abundance" on the condition that Creeks protect rebel traders who vended their wares to Creek customers. Tame King approved the arrangement the following day and underscored his role in the incipient Creek–Georgian alliance. "This, Friends and Brethren is the first Time I ever came to see the beloved men here," he explained. Acknowledging his inexperience as a diplomat, he confessed that he was a "young man" who "may do wrong in the World." Despite being wet behind the ears, Tame King wisely remarked that "he [who] grows in Days ... will grow in Experience."⁸

Tame King privileged trade with his new allies. The War for Independence sharpened Creek dependence on manufactured wares because it interrupted regional and transatlantic trade routes, rendering Creeks desperate for the goods to which they had been long accustomed. In addition, the war created food shortages among the Creeks. Just as Tame King prepared to meet Galphin and other rebels in mid-1777, John Stuart reported that there was "such a scarcity of Provisions in the Creek Nation as borders upon a Famine." While Tame King looked to curb these problems with manufactured wares and supplies of food from Georgia, authorities there failed to satisfy Creek requests. When Tame King requested from the commissioners on the Ogeechee five packhorses "loaded with Goods," for example, he returned home with large "quantities of Rum," securing no useful commodities or calories. Evidence also suggests that Georgian authorities save for Galphin and a few others were less interested in Creek consumers than in Creek lands. Tame King nonetheless attempted to make Georgia a useful ally for himself and his Creek supporters.⁹

He identified those supporters during the Ogeechee congress and in doing so laid bare his vision of Creek leadership. To the commissioners, he declared, "I am the Breath and Master of the Towns on the Three Rivers." This statement merits careful analysis. While it is tempting to assume that Tame King asserted power over all Creeks, he championed the riverine form of Creek politics in place since mid-century. He was the speaker ("Breath") and leader ("Master") of select Creek "Towns" that endorsed his alliance with rebel Georgia and accompanied him to the Ogeechee negotiations. Those towns included Okfuskee and a handful of Lower Creek towns, especially Cusseta, the "greatest part" of which joined Tame King on the Ogeechee. Headmen from these towns believed that a Creek–Georgian alliance presented an alternative to the British. They gave their full support to Tame King, who revealed as much when he informed the commissioners that "I am appointed to Speak for them." He was the head of precise towns on three rivers (provinces)—not all towns and certainly not those of the Alabama province where his rival Alexander McGillivray lived. A skilled architect of provincial coalitions, Tame King engaged the rebels with a popular mandate.¹⁰

Tame King served three Creek rivers during a pivotal moment in the Native South. When he invoked these rivers in 1777, he meant to defend Creek land under threat from westward-moving Americans, who craved it for the expansion of commercial farming, chattel slavery, and a nascent country that deemed indigenous people "merciless Indian Savages" in its founding charter, the Declaration of Independence. Rebels in nearby Georgia readily clamored for access to the fertile river valleys along which Creeks had lived for centuries. Those less than willing to supply trade wares to the Creeks even began to call for the expulsion of southern Indians from their lands. Tame King strove to counter these alarming trends through diplomacy. He and his supporters in Creek country argued that the Creek–Georgian alliance promised to taper the rebels' thirst for indigenous lands and to convince them that indigenous southerners should be equal partners in the region. As a result, he named three rivers explicitly in his address to the commissioners: the "Tallapussee, Coosahatchee and Otchsatchee." He defended the political and territorial integrity of Creek country and encouraged Georgia to do the same.[11]

Tame King's leadership on the Ogeechee captured three Creek provinces in miniature. The delegation for which he spoke consisted of Abeikas from Okfuskee, Tallapoosas from Tallassee, and Lower Creeks from Cusseta. On behalf of this political triad, Tame King presented the commissioners with a "white Pouch" of tobacco, whose smoke "will ascend white" and "make the path white and plain" between Creeks and Georgia. He gave a "String of Beads" as another gift to double down on peace with Georgia, explaining that this object was a "Token" of peace from Okfuskee, Tallassee, and Cusseta, who were assembled as the "Three Towns." In the midst of these gestures, Tame King called on Cusseta and Okfuskee for political assistance. He referred to Cusseta as the "largest Town" in Creek country and intimated that it would play a central role in Creek–Georgian relations. Then he yielded the floor to Handsome Fellow, who closed talks by inviting the commissioners to keep the trade "Path" between Georgia and Creeks "straight and open." Although Tame King was the speaker for Okfuskee and Cusseta, then, he was no self-centered headman; rather he favored a politics of riverine partnership.[12]

The peace struck on the Ogeechee in summer 1777 evolved from a network of Creek towns and a triad of Creek provinces. As the "Breath and Master" of "Three Rivers," Tame King advocated a riverine style of leadership that featured Okfuskee, Cusseta, and his town of Tallassee. This triumvirate worked together to promote peace and commerce with the rebels, although Georgia was unable and unwilling to meet its obligations. At the center of the Tame King–led coalition were local actors who steered headmen in ways beneficial to towns, clans, and other local entities. For example, Tame King was dependent on a wise patron, who authorized the young leader to rule in his stead and lent a helping hand in diplomacy with Georgia. This townsperson mattered immensely when Tame King courted allies from the rebel colonies.[13]

"Old Tallassee King"

Tame King experienced a setback in the following months, causing him to shift course and secure new adherents. It all began when Handsome Fellow died while returning home from a fall 1777 parley with rebel authorities in Charleston, South Carolina. Foul play may have been the cause of his demise. His nephew White Lieutenant held that view when he succeeded Handsome Fellow as an Okfuskee leader and courted the British. Evidence also suggests that some Cussetas and Tallassees reopened ties with Superintendent Stuart in the pursuit of goods. While Tame King had his work cut out for him, all was not lost. Like other Upper Creek headmen, he responded to the shifting winds. Foremost, he won fresh allies by seeking diplomatic alternatives to Georgia, including the rebels' newfound French allies in 1778, as well as other colonial powers jockeying for position in the region. The impetus of this ambitious diplomatic program was none other than "the old Tallassee King," who continued to steer the young headman in foreign affairs.[14]

Tame King shared his elder's agenda during a second meeting between Creeks and Georgia on the Ogeechee River in December 1778. He assembled with a familiar face, George Galphin, along with other state commissioners intent on swaying Creeks to the rebel side. The young headman launched the gathering by expressing pleasure to see "old friends" and pledged to "stand by" the "one white path" binding Creeks and Americans in a mutual relationship of peace and exchange. Goods from Georgia had been woefully inadequate in months past, however, so he shifted tone to emphasize the Creeks' available options for trading partners. "Formerly," Tame King explained, the Creeks "were frinds with three Mothers. the British, French and Spaniards," and he expected that they "will be" the Creeks' friends in the future. "I will still hold them three fast by the hand," no matter the outcome of the War for Independence. He had a backup plan should relations with Georgia turn sour.[15]

Tame King made these remarks to encourage Georgia to copy a model of European imperialism that acknowledged Creek needs. In particular, he underlined the conduct of the French and Spanish Empires. While the British had invaded Creek lands and undercut Creek independence, "the French and Spaniards [had remained] at the end of our land," making fewer claims on Creek territories than the expansionist British. He welcomed the return of the French and Spanish to the region, "hop[ing] they may soon come back to their former places" at a safe distance from Creek country but within grasp of Creek headmen, such as Tame King. A trustworthy ally both respected Creek lands and traded with Creek peoples. If Georgia fumbled, he warned, other powers might fill the void. Tame King preferred to keep all options on the table, allowing him to move between allies as necessary.[16]

During the second Ogeechee meeting, Tame King admitted to the commissioners that "the talk that I give is not of my own making"; instead "tis from the ol^d Tallassee King." As the Tallassee mico in the mid-eighteenth century, he had witnessed the effects of trade dependence firsthand, learning that the Creeks needed multiple allies to avoid reliance on one colonial power for goods that they lacked the technology to produce. He had learned too that the British exploited that dependence to intimidate the Creeks. British superintendent Edmond Atkin's threat to end British trade in Creek towns that remained open to French traders exemplified the ways in which British authorities abused their commercial influence. Tallassee King defied Atkin by staying "at home" in Tallassee after the superintendent had invited Creek leaders to a conference in neighboring Tuckabatchee, a mere stone's throw from Tallassee. Tallassee King applied this real-world experience to the War for Independence when he formulated the idea of engaging Georgia commissioners and lawmakers without abandoning opportunities to form alliances with other colonial powers. He believed that peace and trade with multiple entities was the best route for meeting Creek needs, and he encouraged his advisee to adopt this outlook.[17]

Tame King readily complied because doing so not only benefited the Creeks but also guaranteed him political dividends. His power base had slipped as Creeks turned away from Georgia to contact the British for supplies and allies. To restore his reputation, he traded on the influence of Tallassee King, who had been "as great as any" Creek headman earlier in the century. Tallassee King became the conduit through which Tame King recaptured power as the Creeks' "Breath and Master." During the second Ogeechee meeting, for instance, Tame King outlined his elder's strategy in the presence of other Creek delegates, such as a Cusseta leader named Fat King and "the headmen of four other [Lower Creek] Towns." These leaders "say they hold by the above Talk," thereby confirming Tame King as their spokesperson, "and have nothing farther to Say." The four Lower Creek towns were Apalachicola ("Parachuckles"), Hitchiti ("Hitchatas"), Yuchi Town, and Sauwoogelo. In this way, Tame King renewed his partnership with Cusseta via Fat King and won new adherents among Lower Creek polities beyond Cusseta. Fat King was especially crucial because his town was the gateway to other Lower Creek towns where Tame King cultivated a following. Upper Creeks attended the Ogeechee meeting too, including Tallapoosas from the town of Autossee and Abeikas from the town of Kialijee ("Killigees"). They designated Tame King to speak to Georgia on their behalf. Thanks to Tallassee King, Tame King once again led a coalition of three rivers.[18]

To ascertain the motives of Tame King's new supporters is difficult, but developments beyond Creek country must have persuaded them that he and his elder relative had the right idea about multilateral diplomacy. Mere months before the Ogeechee meeting of 1778, rebel emissaries in Paris signed a treaty of alliance and a treaty of amity and commerce with the French. These agreements beckoned new sources of goods and hastened France's return to the region, thereby validating Tallassee King's agenda that Tame King announced in front of the Creek delegation on the Ogeechee. In the same vein, however, French intervention on the side of the Americans threatened to embolden rebel settlers and other interlopers who espied Creek lands and resources. The Creeks recognized that a new phase in the War for Independence brought both opportunity and peril to their world. Still, Tame King and his patron offered a way forward.[19]

The Lower Creeks particularly feared rebel designs on Creek territory. They lived in towns directly in the path of Georgia's expansion in the late 1770s and for that reason empowered Tame King to lead negotiations with Georgia. For example, the towns of "Tomathlies" and Miccosukee ("Meckasukey") dispatched a "Twist of Tobacco" to Tame King, who in turn presented it to Galphin. The Tallapoosa leader informed his recipient that the objects symbolized the towns' "friendship towards the white people." By seeking peace with the Americans, the peoples of the Chattahoochee attempted to protect their lands and communities from danger. Other Lower Creeks who granted Tame King the authority to speak for them aimed to defend sacred lands from the "white people." These Creeks lived at the Ocmulgee Old Fields, Mississippian-era mounds that lie on the Ocmulgee River in present-day Macon, Georgia. The earthworks are as visible now as they were in the eighteenth century, when Lower Creeks considered them "Ruins of their Camp & first Settlement" in the ancient past. The Ocmulgee mounds were sacred space, convulsing with history and tradition. The peoples who inhabited this area during the War for Independence looked to safeguard the Ocmulgee watershed by partnering with Tame King and, by extension, Tallassee King. In short, the Lower Creeks made a linkage between peace and the integrity of their landholdings.[20]

The concerns of his supporters in mind, Tame King expanded his diplomacy with Georgia by contacting European powers that supported the rebels. He revealed as much in a talk delivered to Commissioner Galphin at the latter's plantation in Silver Bluff, South Carolina. In November 1779, the headman apprised Galphin that "his Father [Tallassee King] has sent him Down and hopes that goods may be Sent" to Creek "headmen and warriors [who] ware verry poor." To mark the occasion, Tame King presented Galphin with a "white wing" as a token of "Friendship." Yet Galphin was merely one of Tame King's contacts, for the leader shared with Galphin that "he has Delivered this Day" a white wing and beaded string "to the French and Spaniards at St. Marks at East [Florida]." By this Tame King had developed a backchannel with his relative's preferred choice of empires, the French and Spanish, who entered the war on the rebels' side. Shortly before Tame King convened with Galphin, Spanish forces commanded by Bernard de Gálvez besieged British forts and other British-controlled areas on the Gulf Coast. Spanish as well as French intervention in the War for Independence boded well for Tame King and Tallassee King. Both men pursued new allies for the Creeks and used that diplomacy to coax Georgia into offering goods for trade. Alarmed by the possibility of losing his Creek friends, Galphin assured Tame King that "I will [do] Every thing in my power to Get goods for you."[21]

Tame King wrung few trade goods from Galphin and other Georgians in the late 1770s, however, which proved that the rebels were unreliable allies. Yet his communications with Galphin were bound up in a larger agenda that sought trade partners from other sources. Dialogue with the French and Spanish promised multiple avenues of trade, while routine meetings with Georgia massaged relations with American rebels bent on territorial conquest. This complex arrangement garnered Tame King new adherents, especially from the Cussetas, who acted as a broker between him and other Lower Creeks. Similarly, local peoples like Tallassee King guided Tame King through successive negotiations with Georgia commissioners and European powers. Aged and experienced, he supplied the diplomatic expertise necessary for Tame King's leadership and, more broadly, Creek survival.

"Peace & qui[e]tness in the Land"
The diplomatic landscape of the Native South shifted in October 1781 when allied American and French forces defeated the British Empire at Yorktown, Virginia. Despite retaining his commitment to multilateralism, Tame King

focused his diplomacy on the newly independent and aggressively expansionist United States. To protect Creeks from the US, he sought "Peace & qui[e]tness in the [Creek] Land." If he could "but live to see this brought about," he announced in the postwar era, he "Shall be happy and sleep in quiet." He pursued this goal in a coalition with Fat King and other Lower Creek headmen who gave him the green light to represent their interests in talks with the United States, especially Georgia. His leadership style differed markedly from that of his opponent Alexander McGillivray, who held that negotiations with outside powers must be restricted to Creek national leaders. No nationalist, Tame King labored diligently with like-minded headmen to ensure Creek independence following the war.[22]

Tame King met with Georgia authorities in the 1780s to implement peace throughout Creek country. One of his first postwar conferences with them came in spring 1782. Flanked by other "Head Men of the Tallasee" town, he addressed Georgia authorities in the state capital of Augusta. He expressed a wish that both sides might "speak the truth and [renew] the Friendship" he had established with allies like Galphin, who had passed away two years earlier, in 1780. He argued that placing honesty and friendship above mistrust and antagonism ought to be the basis of Creek–Georgian relations going forward. This relationship hinged on the preliminary articles of peace that US and British diplomats were drawing up in Paris thousands of miles from Creek country. Unlike the 1763 Paris Peace, any settlement struck between diplomats in faraway Europe had to be vetted by Creeks and other Native peoples. Consulting with indigenous leaders on terms of peace augured a future in which "our Children [may] eat out of one Dish that is one with a Red Hand and the other with white." By speaking about "Red" and "white" children living in harmony, Tame King envisioned his own treaty for the Creeks and complemented negotiations in the French metropole.[23]

In case the Creek–Georgian peace faltered, however, Tame King hedged his bets by treating with European powers. He informed the officials in Augusta that "the French have heard his Speech and that he has seen them, as also the Spaniards have heard his Talk, likewise also the Dutch." Inspired by his elder patron, Tame King burnished his preexisting relationship with the French and Spanish and forged a new one with the United Provinces, all of whom had committed resources to the American rebels. To what degree he believed these Europeans might intervene as necessary in affairs between the Creeks and Georgia is impossible to know. Yet he remained dedicated to exhausting all diplomatic options, for Tallassee King had taught him that many allies were better than one. Furthermore, Tame King reminded authorities in Georgia that both Creeks and Georgians once counted these European empires as allies. The Americans had vanquished the British in union with "the French [and] the Spaniards" as well as "the Dutch." Had not Georgia allied with these powers "to assist [the Creeks and Americans] that they might live upon their own Land" and defeat the hated British? His answer was in the affirmative. With these points in mind, Tame King reasoned that the Creeks and Georgia had much in common and should embark on the next phase of alliance-building.[24]

In the postwar era, as at wartime, Tame King's leadership gained traction among the Lower Creeks. When he closed his talk with Georgia's officials in 1782, he presented them with "a number of white Beeds as a Token [of] Friendship from . . . Sundry Towns." Most were affiliates of the Chattahoochee province, including Cusseta as well as Hitchiti, Apalachicola, Oconee, and Sauwoogelo. The Lower Creeks tasked the headman with voicing their interests in parleys with Georgia and, by extension, the European empires with whom he was in dialogue. Like Tame King, they wanted peace in Creek country following the American victory. For example, Fat King of Cusseta later told Georgia authorities that "We the red People and the white should live in Peace." Upper Creeks who cast their lot with Tame King are more difficult to identify, however, although Tallassee's "Head Warrior" joined Tame King in Augusta and swore "nothing but Peace and goodness" with state officials. Many stood behind Alexander McGillivray, who opposed Tame King's recurring meetings with Georgia. For the moment, Tame King partnered with Fat King and other Lower Creeks desirous of good relations with the US republic.[25]

It was with these shared concerns in mind that Tame King and Fat King later ceded land to Georgia. In November 1783, they and a handful of Creeks, primarily from the Lower Creek towns, signed the Treaty of Augusta. The treaty relinquished Creek land east of the Oconee River to Georgia in return for that state's obligation to carry on "a Trade." Whether the Creek delegation possessed treaty-making authority has been the subject of debate since 1783. Scholars take their cue from McGillivray; he dispatched a talk to Georgia governor John Houstoun in 1784, arguing that the Oconee Cession lacked national support and stood null and void to Creeks. McGillivray explained that only duly appointed national leaders like himself exercised the authority to cede Creek lands and reinforced that point by affixing to his talk "S. C. N[.]," which stood for "speaker of the Creek Nation." Historians echo McGillivray's nationalist biases by arguing that the signatories constituted a "small number" of Creek headmen who lacked Creek national approval. Compounding that illegitimacy, as some have suggested, is that Georgia threatened the Creek delegates into signing the treaty.[26]

These perspectives are rooted in a framework of nationhood that assumes that the only legitimate Creek headmen were those, like McGillivray, who claimed to speak for a nation in diplomatic situations. These viewpoints marginalize Tame King's own understanding of the treaty negotiations and ignore his nimble ability to build coalitions on a provincial scale, win political support, and lead Creeks through postwar dangers. His role at Augusta was justified because he expected plenty of concessions from Georgia in exchange for the Oconee lands. He discussed these concessions in a subsequent round of talks with Georgia in 1784. Alighting in the state capital, he informed Georgia officials that he had attended the treaty conference seeking presents and other goods as a reward for his alliance with the rebels in the late war. Georgia authorities had long promised him "a Drum & Am.^{n} flag," he said, while the Georgians "a good while ago promised" Tallassee King "a great coat." He complained that state authorities never produced these gifts. Furthermore, he stated that he and "the Fat King" had agreed to the treaty because it stipulated that Georgia sell ample trade goods to the Creeks. This had long been a foreign policy objective of the headmen, although it never materialized. Tame King signed the Augusta treaty for all these reasons, but Georgia ignored its treaty obligations and reneged on old promises.[27]

Lastly, Tame King reminded Georgia that Creeks normally approved treaties after careful deliberation among all Creek headmen. When he put his mark to the Treaty of Augusta, he did so for his own town and the Lower Creek towns that had authorized his diplomacy with Georgia as well as the French and Spanish. He signed the Augusta document in that capacity. Alongside other signers, he "Could only give up their own right and the Rights of the people of the towns they represented." The "land was not his," he said of the Oconee Cession, and he refused to speak for "a Man of Any town who has not ceded his right to that ground." These revelations capture a headman still invested in riverine governance, which promoted cooperation and discussion among three rivers. Just as Mortar knew that treaties needed kin approval, so Tame King argued that the Augusta treaty was a temporary agreement pending approval from other

Creeks. To that end, he advised state authorities to sponsor an assembly with the Creeks and to distribute "a few presents" to the attendees. If, after rigorous discussion, the "gift of that ground should be confirmed by all the Towns in the nation," then settlers would be permitted to live on the ceded lands. Tame King acknowledged that a land cession treaty required far more consent than his own, but he also realized that the damage was irreversible. Georgia settlers continued to settle on the Oconee and illicitly "mark land" as far west as the Ocmulgee. He could not "tell where they would stop" on these westward journeys.[28]

Land-hungry Georgians ignored Tame King's proposal to convene with the remaining Creek leadership and thus secure Creek support for the Oconee Cession. While failing to sway the state, Tame King hewed to the cooperative ethos of eighteenth-century Upper Creek leadership. Like others before him, he wished to construct partnerships and strike agreements with those sharing his political outlook. This style of leadership created unity during moments of disunity. Consequently, Tame King pinned his hopes on a Creek–Georgian meeting intended to give Creek towns the option to ratify or reject the Oconee Cession, thereby achieving consensus among Creeks and minimizing Creek–Georgian discord. McGillivray chafed at the idea, dismissing Tame King as a co-opted headman whose leadership was both misguided and dangerous. Seen from Tame King's political worldview, however, the evidence indicates that the Tallassee leader attended the Augusta negotiations as the head of a coalition that tried to secure goods and promote peace with Georgia—nothing more, nothing less.[29]

Tame King and his Lower Creek partners sensed the changes afoot in the revolutionary Native South. In September 1783, shortly before they ceded land to Georgia, US and British ambassadors signed the Treaty of Paris. According to this agreement, Britain recognized the independence of the United States and ceded to the new country all territory east of the Mississippi, south of the Great Lakes, and north of the thirty-first parallel, or what is today Florida's northern border. Without indigenous consultation, however, the treaty authorized the transfer of much land controlled by indigenous people, including the Creek Indians. Georgia paid no mind to the Creeks' absence in Paris and promptly demanded land from Creeks who convened in Augusta just two months later. Although the resulting Treaty of Augusta favored Georgia far more than the Creeks, Tame King and his coalition affiliates tried to fashion the best possible settlement with Georgia. Plus, Tame King oversaw the treaty process within a political framework that remained Creek. In his negotiations with Georgia as well as European powers, Tame King rejected nationhood and embraced a tight-knit partnership consisting of peoples drawn from the Chattahoochee. His world remained a nucleus of provincial collaboration.³⁰

"Good child"

Having accumulated years of experience as a coalition-builder, Tame King earned a new title in the mid-1780s. He became known as the "good child" for leading diplomatic initiatives that originated with his network of allies, specifically Tallassee King, who still advised the young man after the Augusta treaty. Taking direction from this relative, Tame King launched a final round of negotiations with Georgia and pressured state authorities to pay for the Oconee Cession with trade provisions. This was a fair resolution, he believed, because the Augusta treaty bound the state to offer compensation for the Oconee lands. To execute this agenda, he reactivated the Tallassee–Okfuskee–Cusseta partnership that lay dormant. Yet during his meetings with Georgia, Creek warriors raided the Oconee settlements to reclaim Creek land and reverse the Augusta treaty. Creek raids and counterattacks by Georgia militias culminated in the Oconee War. Against this backdrop of aggression, Tame King made a last-ditch attempt at international peace.³¹

In September 1784, Tame King met with Governor John Houstoun in Augusta. There he transmitted a "big Talk" from Tallassee King, who stayed home. Assembling with the governor and executive council, Tame King explained that Tallassee King desired one last audience with "his friends . . . before [his] breath [was] taken." Cognizant of his mortality, the ailing Tallassee King reflected on his relationship with Georgia since the late War for Independence and argued that the alliance between the Creeks and former rebels must guide Creek–Georgian relations through the present war. Speaking for Tallassee King, Tame King invoked the late George Galphin, whose "good talk" the mico "never means to throw away." He lauded Galphin as one of few rebel traders who made an honest attempt to supply Creeks with wares before dying in 1780. In that vein, he informed Governor Houstoun that the Creeks "expect to receive Something" in return for the Oconee Cession. He urged Houstoun to fulfill the state's treaty obligations, since "the white people have Surrunded their Land" by settling on the Oconee and even invading unceded lands. At minimum, Tame King informed the governor on Tallassee King's behalf, "The upper & lower Towns [deserved] to have a full supply" of goods when "the Stores in augusta gets full."³²

Although the "big Talk" failed to wrest payment from Governor Houstoun, Tame King revealed an additional motivation for going to the state capital in 1784. While concerned with reparations, he was equally uneasy about the political backlash against him. As the face of the Creek–Georgian alliance, he had incurred criticism for his role in the Augusta treaty and resulting cession. He explained to the governor that Creeks had "accused him" of fabricating information regarding the extent of that cession. In particular, the migrants settling beyond the Oconee contradicted his assurances that the treaty he signed had established the Oconee as the Creek–Georgian boundary. To set the record straight, he traveled to Augusta with Creek "witnesses" so that they might "hear" from Governor Houstoun himself. The governor did Tame King that favor in the presence of the delegates by expressing "Concern to hear that some of our people have marked the Trees beyond the line agreed upon" in the treaty. Additionally, Houstoun promised to "prevent" settlers from crossing the Oconee and to "make [them] pay . . . for" Creek lands they presently and illegally occupied beyond that river. The governor confirmed the Oconee boundary and pledged to hold settlers to it, thereby restoring some confidence in the bruised Tame King.[33]

The headman capitalized on this minor victory by inviting Governor Houstoun to participate in a nascent diplomatic agenda meant to bring peace across the Native South. Its authors were none other than "the three Creeks of Oakfustees Tallassies & Cussataws," meaning the Okfuskees, Tallassees, and Cussetas. The coalition of three rivers lived! According to Tame King, these towns had been communicating with the Choctaws and Chickasaws to enact the agenda. These Native populations had agreed with the Creeks to "One Talk," binding everyone in a mutual alliance premised on good relations and lucrative trade with Georgia. By disclosing these plans to Houstoun, Tame King offered the governor buy-in, extending to him the opportunity to forge alliances with the South's most powerful indigenous peoples and to generate revenue for the state via trade. The benefits cut both ways, enabling the Indians to gain access to American goods and limiting the Indian–white violence sweeping the region, including ongoing raids between Creeks and Georgians along the Oconee. This plan visualized unity among white and Native peoples.[34]

The multiethnic alliance involved Fat King of Cusseta as well as Tame King, who introduced his colleague to Governor Houstoun, remarking that "the fat King [and] the Chickasaws are one fire." Southern Indians who were "one fire" (*totekitcau humgoce*) shared a common ancestor, forged a mutual compact in the distant past, and delegated a broker from each polity to represent the other in diplomatic contexts. In Augusta, Fat King served as broker for the Chickasaws and their Choctaw allies, neither of whom attended the proceedings. In that capacity, the Cusseta headman put Governor Houstoun in contact with the Chickasaws and Choctaws by recommending that the governor open trade with these friendly groups. Then Fat King displayed "a string of white beads as an emblem of the path from those nations down to the white people" in Georgia and handed the diplomatic gift to the governor. Houstoun thereupon accepted what he called "the Tokens of Peace." Acknowledging the Chickasaws' and Choctaws' need for goods, the governor expressed a "Wish [that] the [trade] Path from this Place ... to the Mississippi [River will] always" remain open. Excited by new customers and allies far to the west, Houstoun assured Fat King that "the Chickesaws [and] Choctaws ... will see more Goods in their Towns, than ever they did before."[35]

While Houstoun's pledge to shower his new allies with goods was predictably bombastic, it spoke to the diplomatic acuity of the Creek delegation. Creek leaders brought different strengths to the table as they tag-teamed negotiations in the Georgia capital. Tame King showed his commitment to shared governance in Creek country. By cultivating ties around the Creek provinces, he improved relations between Creeks and state officials in Augusta, as the Oconee War showed no end in sight. Meanwhile, Fat King further strengthened Creek–Georgian dialogue by leveraging his town's ancient connection with Chickasaw country and easing relations between Georgia authorities and Native peoples along the Mississippi. On hand at the 1784 conference, finally, were Okfuskee leaders, who invited Georgia agent Daniel McMurphy to attend a future "Talk in the Okefuskies" to continue discussion about the ceded lands. Just as Governor Houstoun hosted his Creek allies in Augusta, so the Okfuskees planned to host Georgian representatives in their town.[36]

The Creek–Georgian meeting at Okfuskee materialized nearly two years later, in summer 1786, when Tame King and other Creek headmen gathered with McMurphy. It was at this gathering that town leaders, warriors, and other Creeks named Tame King the "good child," which honored his years of diplomatic service with Georgian officials. In the Creek language, "good" (*herē*) is akin to the adjectives "friendly" and "peaceable" (*herkē*) or the nouns "peace" and "goodness" (*herkv*). A good person in Creek culture upheld peace and exhibited warmth. Tame King evinced these rare traits in a region scarred by violence. Furthermore, the honorific recognized his kin tie to Tallassee King. As one who carried talks of peace from his elder paternal relative, Tame King was a "child" (*hopuewv*) of Tallassee King, with whom he shared a tight bond.

Tame King had come into his own as a diplomat by the mid-1780s, but neither he nor the Creeks who attended the Okfuskee meeting ignored his attachment to Tallassee King. Guided by this kinsperson, Tame King led negotiations with the new American republic as well as European empires in the region.[37]

Stepping into the role of "good child," Tame King thanked the Creeks in Okfuskee, saying, "My freinds and brothers, you Stile me Such & you call me so and I ame a going to Speake to you as such." In that capacity, he addressed Agent McMurphy and expressed "hope" that the Oconee War "will not grow . . . Larger." Rather, "I hope that we will agree that our children will grow up in friendship" and exchange abundant goods along a trade "path [that] will not be Dark[e]ned" by more bloodshed. Tame King repeated the common refrain of peace and trade with mixed success. On one hand, the conversations with McMurphy laid the basis for a subsequent treaty that Tame King, Fat King, and hundreds of other Creeks signed with Georgia commissioners on Shoulderbone Creek, a branch of the Oconee River. During that treaty convention, the state followed through on past promises to the Creeks by supplying the delegation with clothing, food, dye, razors, handkerchiefs, and rum. On the other hand, the treaty negotiations were beset by coercion and outright kidnapping. The commissioners held five of the Creek delegates hostage as compensation for settlers killed in the Oconee War, while armed guards "surrounded [the remaining delegates] and made them all prisoners." According to a later report, Tame King "thundered out a furious Talk and frightened the Georgians from their purpose of keeping them." Both sides parted ways on ice-cold terms, except for the five hostages who remained in Georgia's custody.[38]

While Tame King had been misled by Georgia before, Shoulderbone Creek permanently ruptured the Creek–Georgian alliance that he had been constructing since the 1770s. One historian aptly writes that Shoulderbone Creek was "an exercise in intimidation" by Georgia authorities. Yet the gambit backfired, for Tame King allied with the national government in later years. In 1790 he attended treaty negotiations with Secretary of War Henry Knox in the US capital of New York City and put his signature to the resulting treaty. The Treaty of New York confirmed the original Oconee Cession, thereby rendering null and void Georgia settlements beyond the Oconee. This constituted the first treaty between a Native population and the federal government under the new US Constitution. Tame King thus circumvented Georgia by negotiating directly with the US government. As well, he used military force against the state to curb settler expansion. Throwing diplomacy out the window, he and other Creek warriors

Tame King of Tallassee/Halfway House, 1790

Tame King was a leading advocate for peace and trade with colonial powers. He pursued alliances with the American rebels in Georgia as well as the Spanish and French, who entered the War for Independence on the rebels' side. After the Treaty of Paris recognized an independent United States, Tame King doubled down on diplomacy with Georgia. Supported by an influential patron, he exercised a mandate to speak for three Creek provinces during this tumultuous era. By 1790, when this sketch was completed by John Trumbull, he had renounced Georgia and forged a relationship with federal officials. He dons the traditional Creek turban and displays his connection with the United States by wearing a gorget, small peace medal, and a waistcoat. He was a masterful diplomat who wanted nothing more than to preserve his riverine world. Public domain; courtesy of New York Public Library.

attacked and killed Georgians who defied the New York treaty and continued to settle west of the Oconee heartland in the 1790s. No longer the "good child," Tame King made war on his former allies.[39]

There was nothing inevitable about his decision to substitute war for diplomacy, however, since Tame King fought hard to mold relations with Georgia after the Oconee Cession as well as before it. With guidance from an influential relative, he relied on the trusted Fat King and won new adherents from Okfuskee as he sought friendly relations with Georgia. His leadership pushed the envelope, as he attempted not only to stabilize Creek–Georgian relations but also build a trade path that ran from Augusta clear across Creek country to the Chickasaw and Choctaw towns on the Mississippi. Influenced by Tallassee King, he envisioned a grand alliance between Native groups and the United States. The Creeks recognized these ambitions by calling him "good child," signaling a peaceful alternative to the violence that gripped the region. Although eventually swept up in that violence, he had long served the Creeks as an astute diplomat.[40]

Tame King achieved political recognition at a time when a new colonial power claimed Native-controlled lands west of the Atlantic Seaboard and deemed the Native peoples there an impediment to national progress. Georgia's dogged pursuit of the Oconee lands and beyond typified the first generation of American colonialism. In response, Tame King treated with Georgian representatives and opened talks with European powers to protect the waters that flowed through Creek country and sustained its towns and clans. As a riverine leader, he nurtured relationships with the Upper Creeks and gained followers among the Lower Creeks via a strategic partnership with the Cussetas, especially Fat King, who offered Tame King political access. Still, Tame King was subject to the imperatives of on-the-ground actors who shaped Creek governance in the revolutionary era. Tallassee King was one such actor, advising the young Tame King in a fruitful kin relationship. Together, the two relatives pursued multilateral diplomacy with numerous powers in the region. As leader of three rivers, Tame King moved from one embassy to the next in search of goods, allies, and peace. That strategy remained in place as the Creeks braced for more war at the end of the century.

Chapter 4

"The three rivers have talked, and wished for peace"

American and Chickasaw Threats

Beginning in the 1790s, Creeks on the Coosa, Tallapoosa, and Chattahoochee Rivers experienced a one-two punch of warfare. The Oconee War evolved into a larger conflict pitting Creeks, Cherokees, and other Native peoples against American settlers. This international conflagration sprang from the founding and growth of southern states and territories whose existence threatened southern Indian autonomy. Tame King was on the front lines of this battle for indigenous livelihood. As the Creeks slid deeper into war with settlers, tensions between Upper Creeks and Chickasaws boiled over into armed conflict. Officials from the Southwest Territory, which became the state of Tennessee, welcomed the Creek-Chickasaw War as an opportunity to expand into Muscle Shoals on the Tennessee River and other fertile lands. They especially encouraged Chickasaw attacks on the Upper Creeks, whose communities had impeded territorial expansion. The fever pitch of war with two enemies overwhelmed the Creek world.[1]

To check violence with the US South and Chickasaw country, Creek headmen in the National Council summoned riverine power. They were drawn from the Abeika, Tallapoosa, and Lower Creek towns, and together they ratified a policy designed to cultivate peace with their enemies. As Cusseta leaders explained to US major Henry Gaither, who was stationed on the southern frontier, "The three rivers have talked, and wished for peace." Another federal official, well versed in Creek political norms, called the headmen's agreement a "resolution." These shards of evidence capture a rare glimpse into Creek political thought late in the century and indicate that headmen named this peace policy the Three Rivers Resolution. They identified Creek country not as a nation but as a layer

83

cake of provinces, which enveloped clans, towns, and other local spaces. When regional emergencies threatened those provinces, headmen made a bid for unity. They "talked" and engaged in rigorous discussion before consenting to the multi-provincial resolution. Governance by partnership and collaboration still swayed the leadership. The Three Rivers Resolution played double duty too, as it spurred Upper Creek leaders to sue for peace with the Chickasaws. Equipped with a novel policy, Creek headmen looked to temper the violence.[2]

The Three Rivers Resolution culminated decades of riverine leadership. By convening as the three rivers, Creek headmen drew inspiration from a triad of Creek provinces. They crafted the policy in early 1793, mere weeks after Alexander McGillivray passed away, which suggests the swift repudiation of national rulership and the ongoing embrace of riverine power. The weight of history rested on the shoulders of the policymakers. They walked in the shoes of a prestigious lineage of Upper and Lower Creek leaders who had popularized multi-provincial collaboration since mid-century. These political ancestors ranged from Okfuskee Captain and Mortar in the colonial era to Tame King and Fat King more recently. It was with the past in mind, then, that Creek headmen codified the Three Rivers Resolution and encouraged the Creeks to work together to ease tensions with settlers and Chickasaws alike.[3]

Policy woven from Creek provinces, however, necessarily rested on the influence of local Creeks. These Creeks included headmen's relatives and other persons about whom little is known from the available records but who nonetheless guarded kin interests. They determined whether the Three Rivers Resolution would succeed or fail in Creek country; indeed, it failed for years. Many Creeks put their needs before the policy, worsening international tensions and clashing with a leadership intent on pacifying the region. Challenges to Creek policy stemmed from a train of clan customs. Creeks redeployed practices honed in the colonial period to quiet the ghosts of the slain and replenish the power of clan lineages. Creek headmen seeking conflict resolution with American settlers and Chickasaw warriors butted heads with Creeks who coolly ignored or outright defied the Three Rivers Resolution through retaliation and other attempts to protect kin. More defiant and autonomous than in previous decades, local peoples addressed threats from the east and west on their own terms.[4]

Creek country experienced unprecedented emergency in the 1790s. The United States was more populous and more committed to territorial expansion than the British Empire. The ultimate objective of US expansion in the Native South was the conquest and expulsion of its first inhabitants. Kathleen

DuVal asserts in *Independence Lost* that the United States "advanced its own independence through exclusivist citizenship and military might." Meanwhile, the Chickasaws were deadlier and fiercer enemies than the Choctaws or Cherokees. Chickasaw headmen and warriors exerted additional military power by virtue of commercial alliances with white southerners. War with Chickasaws and settlers alike posed the direst threat to Creek country up to that point. There was a silver lining, however for these conflicts produced moments of stunning creativity as Creeks sculpted diplomacy and conducted warfare as they saw fit. Creek headmen and the communities in which they lived followed the established rhythms of provincial politics.[5]

"The Upper Creeks and Cussetahs" Devise a "resolution"

Demographic imbalance set the stage for the Three Rivers Resolution. The American South nearly tripled in population, from 614,000 in 1760 to 1,686,000 in 1790. While Creek country grew in this time span, there were fewer than fifteen thousand Creeks, a mere 1 percent of the 1790 total population. The 55,900 other southern Indians made up 3 percent of the region's total population in the same year. Accounting for the remaining 96 percent of the region's inhabitants were more than one million settlers of European descent, including Americans, and five hundred thousand people of African descent, both enslaved and free. Georgia alone contained 52,886 whites, 29,264 slaves, and nearly 400 free Black people. Similarly, 67,000 whites and 13,800 Blacks lived in the Southwest Territory by 1790. The staggering numerical disparity between Native and non-Native peoples captured major regional changes, including the acceleration of chattel slavery and the proliferation of white settlements dedicated to commercial agriculture and the expropriation of Native land. As white Americans populated frontier settlements in larger numbers, they undercut Creek independence by traveling on roads and rivers, hunting game, ambushing hunting encampments, and killing individuals in Creek country.[6]

Across the region, immigrants moved in multiple directions and invaded multiple indigenous landholdings. White homesteaders established farms and plantations in a vast semicircle that began at the Oconee, stretched to the Cumberland and Tennessee, and ended as far west as the Mississippi. These rivers were vital arteries of economic activity for immigrant farmers, enslavers, merchants, and other whites seeking money and goods from local, regional, and transatlantic markets. In particular, Georgian and territorial settlers used rivers to travel short and long distances and to sell commodities, including Black slaves, foodstuffs, livestock, and other vendible items. Moreover, the allure of cheap land for cotton cultivation on the Mississippi caused many settlers to travel through Creek country without Creek permission, crossing rivers like the Chattahoochee to access the Mississippi delta. Political and ideological agendas motivated American settlers as much as commercial and financial considerations. In western Virginia and North Carolina, debt-ridden farmers cast off the yoke of coastal elites and established independent governments in Kentucky, Cumberland, and Franklin. Cumberland and Franklin accepted federal jurisdiction in 1790 as the Southwest Territory and forerunner of Tennessee, while Kentucky achieved statehood two years later. The circulation of settlers, slaves, goods, animals, and ideas profoundly transformed the region and threatened the autonomy of Native peoples in it.[7]

Frontier settlement kindled armed clashes between the newcomers and southern Indians. Upper and Lower Creek warriors defended Creek lands from American incursion by burning illicit settlements, killing settlers, and taking captives, especially women and children. Popular targets of Creek raiding were settlements on the Oconee, Tennessee, and Cumberland Rivers. On occasion, Lower Creeks teamed up with Seminoles and attacked settler communities along the Altamaha and St. Marys Rivers in Georgia, Seminole country, and the Spanish Floridas. Creek war parties, as Joshua Haynes has argued, constituted "border patrols" to enforce Creek territorial and political integrity. Moreover, war parties consisting of Upper Creeks and Chickamauga Cherokees regularly attacked the Muscle Shoals intruders.[8]

Frequent conflict between settlers and Indians belied the US policy of "expansion with honor" devised by President George Washington's secretary of war, Henry Knox. Knox championed peace with the southern Indians and pleaded with southern state officials and settlers to do the same. The Washington administration's peace policy bore little fruit, and many in Creek country blamed states like Georgia for the failure of the Knoxonian plan. Coweta warrior John Galphin, son of the Coweta woman Metawney and the late deerskin trader George Galphin, told Georgia governor Edward Telfair in 1793, "[Y]ou well know the reason of discontent [between Creeks and Georgians] has ever been the limits and border of our Country." According to Galphin's message, Creek warriors justly defended Creek country from trespassers.[9]

Cooler heads tried to rein in the warriors. As war between Indians and settlers raged, Upper and Lower Creek headmen formed a bloc dedicated to peace with the United States. It featured Mad Dog of Tuckabatchee, White Lieutenant of Okfuskee, and Bird Tail King of Cusseta. These and other Creek leaders argued that Creek raiding on American settlements was irresponsible. They recognized that settlers who lived in rural communities misinterpreted small-scale raids as a general declaration of war and responded with undue force by killing innocents. They were aware, too, that property theft committed by both settlers and Creeks led to confusion that triggered disproportionate force used by state militias against Creeks. In this supercharged atmosphere, the slightest misunderstanding claimed lives. It was for these reasons that Creek leaders issued apologies to Americans after war parties raided white settlements. They addressed their communiqués to federal agents, such as James Seagrove and Timothy Barnard, who worked on behalf of Secretary Knox and President Washington. Creek headmen reasoned that federal officials who desired peace on the southern frontier could be trusted more than state officials who tended to leverage Creek raiding by calling for the seizure of Creek lands. Creek headmen weighed these delicate geopolitical considerations as they charted peace with the United States.[10]

Warriors had other plans, however. Incensed by Georgia's occupation of Creek lands west of the Oconee, Tame King led a war party of fellow Tallapoosas against settlers there. By April 1793, the warriors had killed two. To deter a military response by Georgia, Upper Creek headmen counseled patience in a message to Agent Seagrove. The message was composed by Alexander Cornells, a Tuckabatchee headman who served as an interpreter for the United States. Cornells explained that most Creeks favored peace with settlers and that Tame King and his men were "mad people . . . running crazy." As Tame King repulsed the Oconee settlements, warriors from the Lower Creek town of Chehaw attacked Agent Seagrove's trade stores on the St. Marys, setting "fire to the buildings" and killing several men, including Seagrove's own brother. Like Cornells, Lower Creek headmen expressed frustration at unruly warriors and avowed that most Creeks were America's "friends."[11]

As Creek leaders attempted to repair the damage, they began to shift diplomatic tactics. Dispatching peace talks after warriors had destroyed property and killed settlers appeared reactive and weak. Instead, leaders took the reins and actively devised a peace policy meant to curb raiding and persuade federal officials that the Creeks were indeed good neighbors. The headmen who enacted that policy got started as early as summer 1792, months before the St. Marys and Oconee raids, when White Lieutenant addressed a talk to Agent Seagrove promising that Creeks "stand by" the "great Talk that our beloved men had with your

Beloved men of new York" in 1790. He added, "[T]his is the mouth of the greatest part of the headmen" in Creek country. He urged Seagrove "to Keep your people in peace and we shall do the Same." White Lieutenant's peace message reflected and reinforced conversations among headmen that resulted in a grand meeting with Deputy Agent Timothy Barnard. Cusseta hosted the meeting on March 22, 1793. The attending Upper and Lower Creek headmen appointed Mad Dog as their speaker. He was a strong choice for this position because he had accrued years of diplomatic experience and because his town had played a notable role in regional diplomacy since the colonial era. Although having sided with the British in the late War for Independence, he was prepared to advance relations with the young United States. At Cusseta, he communicated the headmen's determination to eliminate frontier discord, assuring Seagrove in a message penned by Deputy Barnard that Creek country desired peace with settlers.[12]

Two weeks later, Mad Dog addressed Agent Seagrove in a second message written by Barnard. The headman explained from Tuckabatchee that he, White Lieutenant, and other Upper Creek leaders supported all peace talks with the Americans. Since war hindered face-to-face communication, Mad Dog stated that "when you see my talk, it is all the same as if you [had] seen me." He dispatched this talk to Seagrove with two beaded belts intended to establish good relations with the recipients. Woven into the first belt were stripes symbolizing "General Washington," "Mr. Seagrove," and the "brothers of the United States." American men were half the equation, however, for Mad Dog sent a second belt meant "for Mr. Seagrove and his lady." By addressing the belt to husband and wife, Mad Dog invited American women to participate in diplomacy between American and Creek authorities. He made the reasonable assumption that male leaders in the United States were as dependent on relatives' input as were headmen like himself. While "lady" Seagrove's role in these negotiations is uncertain, Mad Dog sought an ironclad peace settlement with multiple US allies.[13]

These peace gestures were part of a coordinated effort among Creek headmen to frame the Three Rivers Resolution. Just as Mad Dog managed negotiations with Agent Seagrove from the Upper Creek towns, Cusseta headmen announced the policy to the United States in April 1793. On the thirteenth, Bird Tail King and the mico of Cusseta sent a talk to Major Henry Gaither, a federal officer stationed along the Creek–Georgian border. In it, they declared, "The three rivers have talked, and wished for peace," adding that Creeks wanted "to have things settled to the satisfaction of both" Creeks and Americans. According to the Cussetas, the Creeks had decided as a body of coordinated provinces

Bird Tail King of Cusseta, 1790

Bird Tail King of Cusseta coauthored the Three Rivers Resolution and worked tirelessly to advance peace with the United States in the 1790s. His town also played a leading role in the negotiations that ended the Creek-Chickasaw War late in the decade. This sketch was done by John Trumbull in New York City in 1790. It illustrates a headman proud of his Creek heritage and adept in the field of diplomacy. Bird Tail King is shown with the traditional accoutrements of Creek men, including a turban, beaded hair, and a pierced earlobe. Yet he exhibits his ties with American officials via a gorget, peace medal, and waistcoat of American manufacture. His name might refer to the white avian feathers that symbolized peace in southern Indian diplomacy. Public domain; courtesy of New York Public Library.

to conduct peaceful relations with the republic. Creek nationhood had little purchase for Creek headmen seeking stability with an expansionist colonial power without sacrificing inherited political customs that had marked Creek governance since mid-century. The leadership remained wedded to the provinces, where leaders cooperated across towns, coauthored messages to the United States, and reached agreements intended to benefit the Creek body politic. As Barnard explained to Gaither, the "resolution [was one] that the Upper Creeks and Cussetahs have fell into." Creek policy was the product not of a nation but of the Abeikas, Tallapoosas, and Lower Creeks.[14]

Confronting interminable war between settlers and warriors, Creek leaders achieved a remarkable degree of unity in the early 1790s. Scrapping nationhood, they invested in the constituent parts of Creek country by producing the Three Rivers Resolution. Its framers accomplished distinct but complementary tasks to bring the peace policy to fruition. While White Lieutenant, Mad Dog, and other Upper Creek headmen contacted US authorities, Bird Tail King and other Cusseta headmen acted as the press corps for Creek affairs. Residents of a peace town, the Cussetas were eloquent communicators, skilled diplomats, and forceful defenders of the three rivers. Plus, they were nearer to US backcountry settlements than many other Creek polities, making them essential to the mechanics of peace. Altogether, the leadership from Cusseta, the Abeikas, and the Tallapoosas devised a policy that augured good relations with their white neighbors.

"The Loss of thaer Relations Kild by the Georgians"

The Three Rivers Resolution faced resistance from the get-go. By devising policy that carved out political space for all Creeks, headmen fell prey to warriors and other local persons who undertook courses of action that obstructed peace with the United States. Creek–US relations demanded that all Creeks look the other way following settler violence and abandon clan-centered traditions that had empowered them since 1750. Yet few Creeks accepted the derogation of clan power necessary to achieve friendliness with the Americans. Instead they adhered to kinship customs that shattered Creek diplomacy, destabilized negotiations with federal officials, and renewed war with settlers. Arrayed against headmen calling for peace with the republic, then, were Creeks who protected local interests and tightened their grip on the reins of power.[15]

One source of political tension was the death of Agent Seagrove's brother, Robert, following the Lower Creek raid on the St. Marys in early 1793. By mid-May, Mad Dog and White Lieutenant had joined the Cusseta leadership to talk strategy. They met with a Lower Creek headman named John Kinnard in his town of Hitchiti. Kinnard assumed importance in this matter likely because his town shared political and kinship connections with the killers' town of Chehaw. Following discussion among the headmen, Kinnard sent a message to Seagrove explaining away the Chehaws' ill behavior and averring that only "some" Chehaws had participated in the St. Marys raid. Most, he alleged, were "your friends." He said the real blame fell on Tame King and other warriors from five Creek towns that were "always against the frontiers." These warriors doggedly refused the headmen's diplomatic pleas. "I have talked [with these warriors] until I am tired, likewise the [Cussetas], and the rest of our head-men," Kinnard complained, "but to no purpose." Since the unrestrained warriors jeopardized the remaining Creek towns, he proposed that Seagrove "send your people up, and give [the holdouts] one drubbing, and burn their towns." Frontier peace required the military defeat of the "mad" warriors and their communities.[16]

Seagrove agreed with Creek headmen's proposal of military force. To that end, he wrote Secretary Knox that the five defiant towns deserved "chastisement," adding, "I see no alternative" but to deliver a "severe blow" to those communities. No US soldiers materialized in Creek country, however, probably because Seagrove's recommendation contradicted the Washington administration's peace policy in the Native South. Discarding full-scale invasion, Seagrove insisted on a less drastic measure—that Creek headmen punish the ringleaders of the St. Marys raid. The headmen complied with that request on June 8, when twenty-four Upper Creek headmen and eight Lower Creek headmen met in Tuckabatchee. There they resolved to kill "six of the ringleaders." The Tuckabatchee headman, David Cornells, carried the verdict to Cusseta and reported to its headmen that the ringleaders must be executed "by order" of the Tuckabatchee council. Men were subsequently "appointed and sent of[f] by the cussetaw to do the business of killing" the culprits.[17]

But none was killed, which strongly suggests that the men selected to mete out punishment remained mindful of clans. These men had no business killing other Creeks, for clans exercised sole jurisdiction over wayward relatives. Each clan alone tried, punished, and in rare cases executed its own members; kin barred non-kin from participation in these decisions. Consequently, these traditions rendered null and void the execution order issued by the Creek headmen and supported by Seagrove. There may have been another reason that caused the directive to go unenforced. When Creeks of one clan killed those of another, the domestic custom of blood revenge permitted the offended clan to kill an equal number from the offending clan. The killers themselves or anyone from their clan were fair targets for retribution. Had they killed the ringleaders, then, the would-be executioners would have jeopardized their relatives' safety as well as their own. Through inaction they prevented the likelihood of civil strife and additional fatalities in Creek country. Creek headmen and Seagrove soon dropped the issue.[18]

The men who abstained from putting the St. Marys raiders to death protected not only Creek lives but also clans' decision-making in Creek political and juridical affairs. While the execution order has been deemed a "shocking attempt at nationalist coercion," the execution squad never killed its targets and may have let them escape. Neutering the headmen's directive, the warriors reminded headmen that governance still rested on clans as well as towns late in the century. This political episode demonstrates overall the abject failure of coercive nationhood in the last decade of the eighteenth century. Historian Joshua Piker sheds light on the relationship between coercion and kinship among Creeks. Decades earlier, in 1752, Coweta leaders seeking to preserve ties with the British Empire had a Creek leader named Acorn Whistler and his nephew executed. Piker reminds us that although the chief strategist behind the executions positioned himself as a nationalist, Creek nationhood was "more aspirational than actual." In 1793 Creek nationhood was even more aspirational because, unlike the 1752 executions, Creek headmen could not persuade anyone to kill the St. Marys ringleaders. Clearly, the voices of Creek localism had grown louder by the end of the century.[19]

Months later, clans remained in the spotlight following an attack in Creek country. On the morning of September 21, Georgia militiamen "plundered and burnt" a talofa named Little Okfuskee. Founded by Okfuskee townspeople earlier in the century, the village lay on the Chattahoochee River east of the mother town and north of the Lower Creek towns. The aggressors torched ten houses, killed six men, and captured several women and children to punish Little Okfuskee for recent horse thefts in the Georgia backcountry. The destruction was so thorough that Little Okfuskee soon became known as Burnt Village. Unfortunately, as Seagrove reported to Knox, the villagers were "among the most friendly of the Creeks, and no way concerned in stealing horses." Several of White Lieutenant's relatives perished in the attack, and one of the captive women was his "own relation" and "wife to a head-man of [Okfuskee]." Although bound by custom to retaliate against Georgia, White Lieutenant may have assumed that a counter-raid would jeopardize the captives' safety. He supported calls for peace by Cusseta headmen and advised Upper Creek leaders to cool warriors' passions. He expected Seagrove to participate in these conciliatory measures and specifically "to have the prisoners women & Children ready to come up" from Georgia. Additionally, Mad Dog and other Upper Creek headmen were "fully determined to do every thing they could to Settle apeace [sic] with the White people."[20]

While Creek leaders turned to Seagrove, Creek warriors denounced Georgia. On October 4, following a meeting among Lower Creek leaders, the Coweta warrior John Galphin sent a message to Georgia governor Edward Telfair. He exclaimed, "We view with astonishment the steps taken by your people when sending Peace Talks in our Nation continually: We were at a Meeting in [Okfuskee] to [hear] a Talk that you sent up" when Georgia militiamen came "into one of our out-towns [Little Okfuskee] and carried off eight women and children, besides killing the old men in the Town, burnt our provision & houses, [and] took off all the property you could find." Galphin accused Governor Telfair of deliberately sending talks of peace "to deceive us" and demanded that he promptly return "our Women and Children" so that both sides may "live in peace and friendship." Lacking confidence in Telfair and Seagrove, however, Galphin prepared for war. He revealed as much in a letter to William Panton, cofounder of the merchant house Panton, Leslie & Company (PLC), based in Spanish Pensacola. If after "twenty days" state and federal officials failed to repatriate "our Women & Children," Galphin informed Panton, he and other warriors would attack Georgian settlements. He requested from the PLC head "Arms or ammunition" so that he and his men might ready themselves for war. Meantime, "We have fixed out strong guards in all the roads [because we] cannot sit still and see our Women and Children carried off and our Towns and Provisions laid in flames."[21]

Yet other Creek warriors were one step ahead of Galphin. Just days before Galphin addressed his letter to Panton, Pensacola commandant Enrique White reported to the governor of Spanish Louisiana and West Florida, the Barón de Carondelet, that war between Creeks and Georgians had already begun. Nor did warriors wait for Panton to supply them, for they traveled to Pensacola throughout October "to ask for munitions." The commandant granted requests for ammunition after the 'government schooner" bearing trade goods arrived in Pensacola's harbor that month. Many warriors were Lower Creeks trying to defend their towns from additional raids by militias. A nugget of evidence indicates, too, that some of those Lower Creeks were grief-stricken individuals whose relatives had perished in the September attack on Little Okfuskee. The "young people [warriors] Regraetts mutch the Loss of thaer Relations Kild by the Georgians," a translator named James Durouzeaux reported to White in mid-October, and they opposed headmen "Very Decieroes of a peace," especially "The White Lieutt^n. of the Ockfuskays and the Mad Dog of the Tuckabatches." This report strongly suggests that the principle of retaliation compelled warriors to exact violence on Georgia. In these ways, then, clans adopted offensive and defensive measures to combat American invaders.[22]

As some relatives quieted the crying blood of the slain Little Okfuskees, others moved to repatriate the Little Okfuskee captives. As Creek headmen and Seagrove dragged their feet in negotiations with Georgia, Creek warriors redeployed the precontact tradition of captive-taking to settle the hostage crisis. During the 1793–94 hunting season, warriors possibly from Upper Creek towns raided the Cumberland settlements near present-day Nashville, Tennessee, and captured "three white women," including one named Alice Thompson. These white American captives were pawns in the warriors' attempt to pressure Creek headmen and the agent to secure the Little Okfuskees' release. If retaliation addressed the problem of ghosts, captive-taking dealt with the living. By summer 1794, a new Georgia governor named George Mathews had released three of the captives in exchange for the three Cumberland women. Whether the remaining hostages remained in Georgia's custody or later returned home is unclear. Still, the Creek captors forced Georgia's hand by speeding up the slow engine of diplomacy.[23]

From mid-1793 to mid-1794, local actors rebuffed the Three Rivers Resolution. This diplomatic policy ran afoul of clans and the lineage members within them. The resistance against both Upper and Lower Creek headmen striving for peace with the United States unfolded within a clan-driven framework. Creeks refused headmen's execution order because it demanded the submission of clans to headmen as well as to Agent Seagrove. More practically, Creeks refused to risk their safety and that of their clans by fulfilling the headmen's wishes. Clanship additionally spurred the renewal of fighting between Creeks and Americans as warriors launched attacks and ransomed kin. In these ways, defiant Creeks amplified both domestic and international tensions.

"Peace with all Nations and people"

While the Three Rivers Resolution failed to build lasting peace between Creeks and Americans, the Upper Creek headmen who coauthored it wished to suppress hostilities with the Chickasaws as well as the Americans. Unlike the Lower Creeks, the Abeikas and Tallapoosas were engulfed in moments of conflict with two equally dangerous and formidable adversaries. The Chickasaws and United States constituted a dual threat to the Upper Creeks in the last decade of the eighteenth century, which explains why several Upper Creek headmen pursued peace concurrently with Chickasaw emissaries and American officials. In particular, Mad Dog of Tuckabatchee and other Upper Creek leaders participated in this two-pronged diplomatic initiative. They believed that the Three Rivers Resolution might relax violence with warriors and settlers alike.[24]

Clustered in small towns on the upper Tombigbee River in present-day northern Mississippi, the Chickasaws were known for their military prowess and diplomatic acumen in the eighteenth century. By 1790 they, like the Creeks, faced down the barrel of a swelling population of non-Native immigrants in the region. Whereas Chickasaw country totaled thirty-one hundred inhabitants, the white and Black population of the nearby Tennessee, Cumberland, and Ohio watersheds exceeded eighty thousand. To preserve Chickasaw autonomy against the US onslaught, Piomingo of Long Town and other Chickasaw headmen forged an alliance with the governor of the Southwest Territory and the future state of Tennessee, William Blount. Piomingo secured gifts of guns and ammunition from Blount in exchange for protecting Cumberland and other US settlements from Upper Creek raids. The Upper Creeks responded to the Chickasaw–Blount tie by purchasing weaponry of their own from PLC merchants. The arms race exacerbated ongoing competition between Upper Creek and Chickasaw hunters for scarcer herds of white-tailed deer. Mad Dog observed that "our deer and game is almost gone," thereby impeding hunters' longtime ability to trade deerskins and other animal products for manufactured goods. These regional shifts created the conditions for the Creek-Chickasaw War.[25]

In December 1792, Upper Creeks moved to cut off the Chickasaws from Governor Blount. On December 10, Upper Creek headmen dispatched a war talk to the Chickasaws "announcing that they were determined to go and kill all the Whites [allied with Piomingo] . . . just as they have also resolved to destroy the ammunition that . . . Piamingo has stored." Chickasaw warriors answered the taunt by assailing a party of four Creeks near the Cumberland in January 1793. They killed two from the Abeika town of Woccoccoie ("Wackakay") and captured the other two. After Upper Creeks learned the news, they killed a prominent war leader known as the Warrior of Piomingo. A furious Piomingo blamed his warrior's demise on the Spanish who had permitted the PLC to sell weapons and ammunition to the Upper Creeks. In a message to the Barón de Carondelet, he exclaimed, "[W]e are going to take revenge" on the Upper Creeks who "receive ammunition from you and [who] kill all the white [American] traders in the [Chickasaw] nation and pillage anything they can lay their hands on." By late February, a Chickasaw war party had retaliated by killing "three or four" Creeks.[26]

Among the slain were two relatives of Mad Dog. The Tuckabatchee leader expressed his grief in a message to William Panton, saying "[I]t is hard for a red man who loses both his brother and nephew to not take revenge; no person can either blame or prevent me." Both his communiqué to Panton and a report by Spanish commissary Juan de la Villebeuvre indicate that Mad Dog and his relatives acted accordingly. By April 1793, they had captured and burned the nephew of a Chickasaw headman named Wolf's Friend. The torture and execution of war captives by fire was a common practice in eighteenth-century southern Indian warfare. After tying the captive to a wooden rod, grief-stricken women and children taunted and beat him as flames consumed his body. Traveling through Creek country in the mid-1770s, at the tail end of the Creek-Choctaw War, the naturalist William Bartram learned from British traders there that Creeks were known to burn war captives "to ashes." Clans practiced this ritual both to expiate relatives' grief and to capture the enemy's spiritual powers. Mad Dog and his kin honored these traditions at the outset of the Creek-Chickasaw War.[27]

Mad Dog's retaliatory act paved the way for a peace initiative with his indigenous enemies. The burning of the Chickasaw captive restored balance to the headman's clan, so there was no need to remain in a state of war with Chickasaw country. Consequently, Mad Dog partnered with hundreds of other Upper Creeks in May "to propose peace to the Chickasaws." This diplomatic maneuver piggybacked on his conversations with US officialdom, including President Washington and Agent Seagrove. This meant that Mad Dog and like-minded Creeks had chartered the Three Rivers Resolution to reach peace with Chickasaw warriors as much as the United States. The initial round of Creek–Chickasaw negotiations was observed by Benjamin Fooy, a Dutchman serving as Spain's agent to the Chickasaws. Fooy arrived in Chickasaw country on May 20, when he "found two Creeks, who have been sent by the chiefs of a party of 800 men who came by surprise to the Chickasaws to propose peace." Wolf's Friend was present. Although his nephew had been tortured to death by Mad Dog's clan, he "accepted the talks" from the envoys. In return, he presented his guests with "some beads to assure the Creeks that [the Chickasaws] ask nothing better than to live at peace with them."²⁸

Yet to have any teeth, the Creek–Chickasaw accord needed the support of Piomingo. He was an esteemed headman whose decision to make peace with the Upper Creeks would carry weight among the Chickasaws. To open a line of communication with him, Mad Dog contacted the Choctaws, who remained neutral. In a message to Franchimastabé, a Choctaw headman of the West Yazoo village, Mad Dog requested that Choctaw leaders mediate between Piomingo and the Tuckabatchee leader. On May 22, Franchimastabé convened an assembly in West Yazoo, where "all the [Choctaw] chiefs" agreed to broker peace between the two high-profile men. Just days later, on June 1, Piomingo hosted a conference with Choctaw leaders from his house in Long Town in Chickasaw country. During the proceedings, a Choctaw leader held a "belt of Wampum" that Mad Dog had dispatched to the Choctaws to present to Piomingo. A Chickasaw leader named Mucklasso Mingo accepted the belt on Piomingo's behalf and thought "well of our making peace with the Creeks." He then handed the object to Piomingo, who said, "I have now taken the peace string of Wampum [from] the Creeks [as delivered] by our brothers the Chactaws." According to a Spanish report, the Long Town meeting resulted in "Peace" between the Upper Creeks and Chickasaws. Mad Dog's diplomacy with Piomingo and Wolf's Friend bore fruit.²⁹

Throughout spring and summer 1793, Mad Dog busied himself in negotiations with Native and non-Native peoples. He was the common denominator in a flurry of Creek diplomacy meant to unite the three rivers around peace with the Chickasaws and Americans. No evidence better captures the linkage between Creek–Chickasaw and Creek–US diplomacy than a talk addressed to the Chickasaws via the Choctaws by Mad Dog and his Abeika colleague, White Lieutenant. The two men were fellow co authors of the Three Rivers Resolution and respected diplomats in international affairs. The political duo composed the talk from Tuckabatchee on January 19, 1794. They confessed that "our Land hath been in much confusion and trouble for some years past" and that the Creeks had committed much "mischief to our friends and neighbours both white and Red." Yet the Creeks had turned a new page, for "The Eyes of our whole nation we think is now open and it is detirmined by the Chiefs of our Land that we Establish afirm [sic] and lasting Peace with all Nations and people." This remarkable language indicates that headmen around Creek country shared the belief that peace with the Chickasaws reinforced that with the United States. To that end, the speakers invited the Chickasaws to attend a peace conference in Tuckabatchee scheduled for this "Coming Spring." Evidence indicates that the Choctaws carried the peace talk to the Chickasaws, for Wolf's Friend later informed a Spanish ally that he "Expect[ed]" to attend the Tuckabatchee meeting.[30]

Like Wolf's Friend, the Upper Creeks expected peace to triumph over war in the approaching months. Mad Dog was principally responsible for creating the conditions for intertribal stability. He had drafted the Choctaws for arbitration, brought Piomingo into the diplomatic fold, and negotiated a Creek–Chickasaw ceasefire. As a riverine leader, however, he accomplished these diplomatic feats by coordinating with other Creek headmen who shared his propensity for good relations with the upper Tombigbee peoples. Both he and White Lieutenant ensured that the Three Rivers Resolution applied to "all Nations and people," not least the Chickasaws.[31]

"My own relations"

After planning to convene with Creek leaders in Tuckabatchee in spring 1794, Wolf's Friend stayed home in his town of Thisatera. He justified his about-face in a talk to his Spanish ally, the governor of Spanish Natchez, Manuel Gayoso de Lemos. To Gayoso he confided his doubts about the Creek–Chickasaw truce, stating, "[I]t seems that the Sun is not likely to [get] just now out of the Cloud." Intertribal peace was too fragile to withstand the antagonism that lingered between the two groups. Subsequent events proved him correct, as the Chickasaws and Upper Creeks plunged into another round of conflict lasting three years. Calls for retaliation led to deaths on both sides and engulfed Upper Creek headmen like Mad Dog in the second phase of the Creek-Chickasaw War. Foreign interference aggravated this conflict because frontier officials like Governor Blount funded Chickasaw attacks on Upper Creeks.[32]

Mere months after Wolf's Friend expressed doubt about peace with the Upper Creeks, the Chickasaws killed another relative of Mad Dog. In response, Mad Dog assembled a war party that included dozens of men and at least one other grieving family member from Tuckabatchee. These men aimed to kill Wolf's Friend. Upon learning the alarming news, the Chickasaw headman dispatched a message to Governor Gayoso, apprising him of Mad Dog's deadly plan. Fresh tensions between the Upper Creeks and Chickasaws reset the diplomatic clock. Despite successful efforts to cultivate ties with Wolf's Friend, Piomingo, and other Chickasaws, Mad Dog remained caught in the same web of clanship that shaped warriors' decisions to raid American settlements in the wake of the Three Rivers Resolution. An obedient relative, he heeded the call for retributive justice.³³

Upper Creek headmen filled in for Mad Dog by attempting to stop the Creek–Chickasaw accord from crumbling in summer 1794. As Mad Dog's war party was en route to Chickasaw country, two Tuckabatchee headmen, known only as Spandahayo and Neuhayo, sent "Express News" to Wolf's Friend, warning the Chickasaws of Mad Dog's violent intentions. The two Tuckabatchee men advised the Chickasaws "to be on there Gard" and "to kill Anny of the Creek they Should Meet With" in Chickasaw country. Spandahayo and Neuhayo sought to preserve peace with the Chickasaws at all costs, going so far as to alert Chickasaw warriors of Mad Dog's whereabouts. This news spared Wolf's Friend and possibly other Chickasaws from the Tuckabatchee war party, for no records indicate that Mad Dog and his men killed any Chickasaws in mid-1794. By funneling information to the enemy, moreover, Spandahayo and Neuhayo endangered themselves. Had the Chickasaws slayed even one warrior from his party, Mad Dog possessed the obligation to attack either the Chickasaws or the Tuckabatchee emissaries who had compromised the party's safety. The conflict in Mad Dog's town exposed cracks in the Upper Creek headmen's formerly united agenda to make peace with their indigenous neighbors.³⁴

Tipping the scales toward the reignition of war was the meddlesome war hawk Governor Blount. He sought congressional support for war against Creek country, especially Upper Creek towns, whose warriors had long raided the Southwest Territory's settlements along the Tennessee and Cumberland watersheds. In December 1794 he wrote Brigadier General James Robertson, who lived in the Cumberland settlements, that "the present Session of Congress will order an Army" in spring or summer 1795 "to humble if not destroy the Creek Nation." The destruction of Creek country, in Blount's estimation, promised to "give Peace to the Southwestern Frontiers." Although no federal army invaded Creek country in 1795, Blount stoked the flame of war as part of his bid for Tennessee statehood. In fact, some Chickasaws endorsed Blount's militant stance and desired "open war" with the Creeks. By late January 1795, the Chickasaws had "Killd five Creeks" on the Tennessee River and presented "the Scalps" to General Robertson as proof of the Chickasaw–American alliance. The second round of the Creek-Chickasaw War had begun.³⁵

Chickasaw assaults on the Creeks persisted into February, when PLC trader Benjamin James wrote Spanish commissary Villebeuvre that three Chickasaw "partys" had departed for the contested "Hunting Grounds" of the Chickasaws and Upper Creeks. One Chickasaw party "[has] returned," James reported on the February 12, and its warriors had "killed nine, [and] took six prisoners." The Chickasaw vanquishers "let one Boy make his Escape to carry [the] News" to Creek country to taunt headmen there. A few days later, Agent Fooy informed Governor Gayoso that "four or five" Chickasaw war parties went out "to kill some parties of Creeks," perhaps near the Tennessee. The multipronged Chickasaw offensive shocked the Upper Creeks. Hard hit was the Abeika town of Aubecooche, located on a branch of the upper Coosa River. The Aubecooche headman Dog Warrior expressed confusion in a talk to William Panton, saying, "I thought I had peace all around [but] the Chickasaws have fell on us." He confided to the merchant, "I don't know what to do now, I am setting inactive [as] the ennemy [is] killing up my people in the woods."[36]

Amid the death in Abeika country, clans weighed the decision to exact retaliation. Dog Warrior lost "three of my own relations," which caused some of his relatives to assemble a war party destined for the Chickasaws. According to a PLC trader named Joseph Stiggins, however, Dog Warrior and other Aubecooche leaders "stopped" them in February 1795. By contrast, violence prevailed in nearby Coosa. The Coosas shared kin ties with some of the Upper Creeks slain by the Chickasaws in the opening months of 1795. Unlike their Aubecooche neighbors, the Coosas responded with shocking horror by slaying three Chickasaw women married to Coosa men in the town. The Chickasaw victims had "thought themselves Safe under their [Coosa husbands'] protection," but they were sorely mistaken. The logic of retaliation spared neither women nor men from harm. As the Creek-Chickasaw War intensified, the Coosa assailants deemed the Chickasaw women convenient targets for execution and, possibly, a fifth column.[37]

The Coosas' lethal action stemmed from a broader Upper Creek offensive meant to quiet crying blood and to wage war from a position of strength. Mad Dog and White Lieutenant, former champions of intertribal peace, positioned themselves at the center of this military campaign. To secure the requisite weapons and ammunition, they contacted Spanish officials perhaps under the assumption that Spain would enjoy challenging Blount's influence by arming Upper Creek warriors against his Chickasaw allies. Or perhaps the headmen decided that American officials could not be trusted to supply Upper Creeks since the Chickasaws appeared to be the republic's favored indigenous ally. Whatever their motives, they identified Spain as trustworthy. On February 19, Mad Dog convened with Commandant Enrique White in Spanish Pensacola at the helm of eighty Tuckabatchees and fifty-seven other Tallapoosas and Abeikas. The headman presented Commandant White with a "belt of seven strings of white Wampum with five purple rhumbs [lines?]." The wampum belt represented Spanish authorities, including White and King Carlos III, as well as the Upper Creek polities of Tuckabatchee and Okfuskee. Mad Dog explained that the belt symbolized "perpetual friendship" between Spaniards and the Creeks who alighted in the port city. After days of visiting and negotiation, the commandant supplied Mad Dog's delegation with "ten guns, 150 pounds of powder, [and] 300 pounds of ball." A blacksmith also repaired the guns that many delegates carried to the city.[38]

Despite these gains, however, the Upper Creeks were routed by the Chickasaws. Around October 1795, Mad Dog led a war party into a disastrous skirmish with Chickasaw warriors, who killed thirty-six of his men. The Chickasaws' decisive victory was the consequence of superior military expertise and fruitful relations with Governor Blount and other officials who had disbursed guns, ammunition, and other goods to the Chickasaws throughout the decade. Records indicate that the Chickasaws received far more goods from the Americans than Mad Dog did from Spanish officials like White. Well-supplied Chickasaw warriors easily outmaneuvered Mad Dog on and off the battlefield. Moreover, they imperiled his military standing among Upper Creeks. Mad Dog proved unable to command men, ensure success in battle, and return home with minimal casualties. These shortcomings probably explain why no records identify him as a war leader for the remainder of the Creek-Chickasaw War.[39]

War continued through mid-1797, nearly two years after Mad Dog suffered irrecoverable loss to his martial reputation. Once an advocate of peace, Mad Dog succumbed to clan obligations that undermined his diplomacy and motivated him to assault the Chickasaws. Coupled with retribution, intervention by American officialdom altered the calculus of war. By presenting his Chickasaw allies with military goods, Governor Blount contributed to the renewal of Creek–Chickasaw hostilities and increased Upper Creek casualties to boot. The expanding US republic thus shaped the terms on which southern Indians interacted and produced crises for indigenous leaders like Mad Dog and White Lieutenant. Furthermore, the rhythms of localism apparent in the Creek-Chickasaw War were more strident than in previous decades. There was nothing particularly new about ghosts crying out for blood and relatives snagging headmen in clan dictates. But the context within which these trends played out, along with the growing influence of local actors in Creek country, demonstrates that Creek leaders could barely hold on to power.[40]

The "warers women and Children will live in Peace"

The combatants soon laid down their weapons. As Benjamin Hawkins, the new US agent for the southern Indians, remarked in October 1797, "[T]here was now a prospect of a happy accommodation of all past differences" between the Upper Creeks and Chickasaws. The peace settlement took shape from months of effort by the agent himself, southern Indians beyond Creek country, and the Lower Creeks. The Cussetas were particularly effective mediators. They had coauthored the Three Rivers Resolution, belonged to a peace town, and remained allies of the Chickasaws, with whom they shared "one fire." A Cusseta headman named Tussekiah Mico led his town's negotiations with the Chickasaws in what may have been Chickasaw country. There, he instructed his Chickasaw hosts "to behave well and mind their hunting" should they encounter Upper Creeks during the upcoming winter hunts. The Chickasaws later responded by sending a peace talk with "some beads and tobacco" to their former adversaries, namely the Abeikas and Tallapoosas. At that point, the Cusseta headman met with "the Chiefs of the Abbecohatchee [Abeikas] and Tallapoosahatchee [Tallapoosas]" and advised them "to mind their hunting and think of nothing but peace" with the Chickasaws.[41]

All parties complied with Tussekiah Mico's advisement, and by winter calm filled the air. No documents confirm intertribal clashes during the hunting season of 1797–98. Moreover, the Upper Creeks were so jolted by war that few wished to reignite hostilities with a consistently superior indigenous enemy. Outgunned and outmatched, Mad Dog desired peace and shepherded the intertribal settlement in the following months. A disgraced war leader, he reassumed the position of diplomat by inviting Chickasaw headmen to his town in summer 1798 to affirm peace. During the parley, Mad Dog warned his guests of the ill consequences of aligning too closely with the Americans and encouraged them to accept the newfangled peace, which promised to bolster southern Indian lands against Georgia and the new state of Tennessee. The "Land was But Small that We Live on," he reminded the Chickasaws, and that was enough for him to take his former adversaries "fast by the hand." Mad Dog drew a connection between intertribal peace and southern Indian sovereignty; each strengthened the other. To keep white southerners at bay, indigenous southerners had to work together.[42]

Just as the Creek-Chickasaw War had been dictated by clan activity, so the war's conclusion rested on the shoulders of kin exhausted by years of violence. Mad Dog captured Upper Creek sentiment when he expressed "hope [to the Chickasaws that] Ouer warers [warriors,] women and Children will live in Peace." By invoking on-the-ground Creeks, he revealed that his legitimacy continued to emanate from women, children, and other relatives craving peace with the Chickasaws. His relatives had previously approved his raids against that group to defend and strengthen the clan. When he neglected to protect his warriors in battle, however, kin barred him from the military sphere and tasked him with intertribal peace-making instead. Mad Dog had become more useful to his relatives as a diplomat than as a killer. Thus Upper Creek clans supervised high-ranking men like him during the war and subsequent peace talks.[43]

In closing, the Creek–Chickasaw peace contrasted sharply with ongoing warfare between Creeks and Americans in the late 1790s. An exhaustive study of Creek–Georgian border raids indicates that Creek warriors frequently "raided surveyors" who marked Creek lands and "extorted non-Indian" migrants who traveled through Creek country and settled in it without permission. Young Creek men killed these intruders on occasion. If Creek–US relations were plagued by violence, then Creek–Chickasaw relations were defined by peace. This disjuncture illuminates an intricate political calculation that the Creeks made late in the century. The ferocity of American-backed Chickasaw warriors and the rapid expansion of the United States prompted the Creeks to identify the Americans as the common enemy shared by all southern Indians. War with the Chickasaws no longer served a useful purpose and constituted a mere distraction from settler invasion. Creeks at the ground level made this decision and acted accordingly. Just as Creek assaults on American migrants "reflected popular opinion in Creek country," according to one historian, so "[warriors,] women and Children" approved friendship with the Chickasaws. They identified the real enemy as the century closed.[44]

The Creeks fought a two-front war in the 1790s. The growth of Georgia and the creation of the Southwest Territory ignited Creek conflict with various peoples from the Oconee, Tennessee, Cumberland, and Tombigbee watersheds. In response, Creek headmen attempted to reduce violence by framing the Three Rivers Resolution. Led by Mad Dog, White Lieutenant, and Cussetas like Bird Tail King, political leaders from three core provinces negotiated vigorously with American authorities, Chickasaw diplomats, Choctaw intermediaries, and Spanish imperials. Local peoples subverted that project, however, especially headmen's kin and those motivated by kin interests. They called for retaliation, killed enemies, and took captives. Clanship dictated the cadences of war and peace and etched its mark on an unstable region. Mad Dog exemplified headmen's inability to control local situations. Whether leading war parties or peace talks, he was sensitive to relatives' needs. As the nineteenth century dawned, local actors guided the Creek leadership more vocally and with greater impact than in previous decades. While three of the Creek "rivers" were as strong as ever, the fourth and final one was poised for a grand entrance.[45]

Part III

Four Rivers: Alabama Adumbration, 1798–1815

Chapter 5

"No more Land . . . to White people"

The Quest for Intertribal Union

At the turn of the nineteenth century, an Upper Creek headman named Singer emerged as an instrumental figure in Creek governance. He lived in the Alabama town of Hickory Ground, shortly north of the confluence of the Alabama, Coosa, and Tallapoosa Rivers, and served on the National Council. Like other Upper Creeks, he championed intertribal union as the best method to defend southern Indian lands from the American republic. That method reached its zenith in 1803, when he hosted southern Indian leaders in his town. Among other things, they discussed indigenous southerners' common problems, including recent land cessions to federal officials. The Hickory Ground gathering resulted in an intertribal agreement that codified resistance to American desires for indigenous land. Southern Indian leaders vowed to relinquish "no more Land . . . to White people" and to discuss strategy with one another before meeting US authorities at the treaty table. The intertribal compact to which Singer belonged was a portent of sorts. While it cultivated strength among the southern Indians, its swift collapse foreshadowed a civil war in Creek country.[1]

The southern Indians launched pan-Indian movements as early as the seventeenth century and adapted them in the next to slow the piecemeal absorption of land by the British Empire and United States. More immediately, the pan-Indian coalition on display at Hickory Ground originated from Tame King's diplomacy with southern Indians during the late War for Independence and Mad Dog's newfangled outlook that the southern Indians must end intertribal tensions to stop US expansion. The Native leaders who assembled in Singer's town therefore worked in a preexisting leadership structure designed to coordinate strategy and circulate information across tribal lines. The road to Hickory

Ground was neither straightforward nor preordained, however, for the Upper Creeks worked diligently to foster the conditions that enabled the 1803 compact. Five years earlier, in 1798, Singer, Mad Dog, and other Upper Creek headmen began to communicate with neighboring Indians in earnest. They did so in messages recorded by American and Spanish officials, encoded in wampum belts, and spoken in public square grounds. As skilled provincial coalition-builders in Creek country, they were prepared for a robust era of intertribal politicking.[2]

The main cause of southern Indian land loss at the turn of the century was trade debt. The creditors who pestered southern Indians to discharge the debt were US agent Benjamin Hawkins and John Forbes, who reorganized the Pensacola-based Panton, Leslie & Company as John Forbes & Company (JFC). Debts to the JFC and United States compromised the southern Indians' financial solvency and continued access to wares. Compounding the problem were diminishing herds of white-tailed deer, which prompted hunters to buy goods on credit absent deerskins and other ready sources of currency. Hunters' inability to pay their debts angered traders and merchants, themselves bound up in transatlantic credit networks. In some cases, the United States and JFC accepted land cessions for debt payment; in other cases, the JFC joined Agent Hawkins in a multinational scheme by which Hawkins secured land from indigenous leaders in return for promises to extinguish their debts to company merchants. The United States then sold parcels of the ceded lands to farmers, plantation owners, and other settlers to finance westward expansion and apply some of the profit to JFC coffers. The southern Indians denounced these facets of colonialism at Hickory Ground in 1803. In doing so, they attempted to hold the line against foreign creditors.[3]

Crucial to this strategy were the Alabamas. Some Alabamas relocated west to the Mississippi River and Red River valleys at the beginning of the nineteenth century. According to one historian, the Alabama outmigration constituted a diaspora "with the goal of preserving and re-creating" the Alabama world free of American intrusion. Unlike these diasporic peoples, Singer and his kin were "stayers." They partnered with other Upper Creeks to solve the ills plaguing all southern Indians. As a stayer, Singer poured his energies into an intertribal program designed to protect southern Indian land from American officials and settlers. He walked in the shoes of another Alabama, the late Alexander McGillivray, who had formed what one historian calls the Southern Confederacy before his death in 1793. That intertribal body was far more militant toward the United States than that led by Singer. Still, both men defended southern

Indian land from settler encroachment and simultaneously raised the profile of Alabamas in Creek politics. By the new century, Singer had staked a claim to equal political status in Creek governance, helping to bring the Alabama stayers into the Creek fold.[4]

In the early nineteenth century, southern Indian coordination rested on local actors, whose political influence in Creek country gathered strength. Singer recognized the political and cultural impact of women and specifically his sister, who acted as an important broker in the cross-Indian ties emanating from his town. Meanwhile, warriors and other young men changed the tenor of Creek politics. When Hawkins pressured Singer and other Creeks into a land cession that violated the non-cession policy, Creek warriors assassinated the Alabama leader. It was at this point that a new phase in Creek history and that of the Native South dawned. By killing a high-profile headman, the assailants legitimized political violence and established the conditions for a civil war that ended in American conquest. During this rapidly changing era, the promise of intertribal unity in the Native South succumbed to Americans' unrelenting pressure for land and sharper political discord in Creek country.[5]

"To Remaene in Peac[e] with Red And White"

The principal architects of the southern Indian coalition in the late eighteenth and early nineteenth centuries were Singer and Mad Dog. They possessed the diplomatic savvy to align southern Indian interests in the pursuit of land preservation. They initiated this project when they contacted the Seminoles, whose attacks on US backcountry settlements had destabilized the gulf coastal plain. The headmen reasoned that Seminole aggression would increase American appetites for southern Indian lands and that the preservation of those lands would demand peace between the United States and the region's Native peoples. Mad Dog captured this outlook in a talk to the Seminoles, advising them "to Remaene in Peac[e] with Red And White [people] So Long As the Sun Rises." To safeguard the territorial domain of the southern Indians, then, both he and Singer encouraged the Seminoles to conduct friendly relations with the republic.[6]

The Seminoles were descendants of Lower Creeks who had migrated to present-day northern Florida earlier in the century to dodge British settler intrusion. Like their forbears, they built towns, farmed land, and hunted game. When American settlers overran Seminole country in the generation after the War for Independence, they found an ally in the Maryland-born adventurer, merchant, and loyalist William Augustus Bowles. Like them, he opposed

US intrusion into the region. He was a thorn in the side of American officials like Hawkins, who complained that Bowles enticed Seminole warriors to raid the backcountry. Seminole warriors needed no direction on whom to raid, of course, but Bowles was a convenient scapegoat for Americans seeking their country's orderly ascent. Creek headmen were equally alarmed by Bowles's relationship with the Seminoles. Mad Dog attempted to convince Seminole leaders to restrain their warriors and cooperate with Creek leaders like himself to bring peace to the region.[7]

Mad Dog made progress on an evening in late May 1798, when he convened with Hawkins and leaders from Seminole and Creek countries. He opened talks in Tuckabatchee by holding a wampum belt depicting "two white ends, two rows of blue wampums on each edge, and two rows of white wampums thro' the middle." He interpreted the belt for Hawkins, saying that the two middle rows of white beads signified "the path of perpetual peace, leading from one white end to the other." Further, the two white ends represented "the beloved man [Hawkins] . . . and . . . the Creeks and Seminoles" all joined in union. The ritual belt visualized the Seminoles' and Creeks' promise to live in peace with the Americans and to rely on Hawkins to mediate future disputes between whites and Indians. "It is with a view to join the hands of the people of the United States and the people of my land that I offer this belt" to the agent, who accepted it. Likewise, Mad Dog expressed hope that the United States, Creeks, and Seminoles "may never again be separated or at enmity."[8]

Although he regarded the Seminoles as an autonomous population, Mad Dog referred to these Creek offshoots as "our people" to maximize Creek–Seminole togetherness. He revealed this complex attitude in April 1799 by advising "the Seminoles . . . not [to] do any [mischief] but take [his] Talk and behave [themselves] like a good people." His injunction aimed to calm Seminoles at a time when a team of surveyors led by the United States was demarcating the boundary between the southern United States and Spanish Floridas. Fearing that each colonial power would carve up their lands, Seminole warriors harassed the boundary-marking expedition. Mad Dog grasped Seminoles' anger, saying "it is [necessary] to be On [our] Gard Aganst intruders." Yet he encouraged them to resist the newcomers with pan-Indian diplomacy. He guaranteed that no southern Indian "Nation Shall Part With Any of [its] Land with Out the head Men of the fower [four] Nations As Present" at treaty councils. All southern Indians had to therefore "set Down in Peace" and invest in leaders like himself who pledged to negotiate fair agreements with colonial powers. Making a final bid for unity, he exclaimed, "we Are All Red People." Mad Dog assured the Seminoles that intertribalism would preserve southern Indian lands.⁹

He met with mixed success in Seminole country. Among his allies there was Methlogee, "a second Chief of the Mackasookey Indians." The Miccosukee headman expressed support for Mad Dog during a conversation with former agent James Seagrove in June 1799. He approved "the advice of [the] old and principal Chiefs" of Creek country, he told Seagrove, and "restrained" Seminole warriors from killing "those people who were running the line" through Seminole country. This peaceful stance was "the voice generally" of a unified Creek–Seminole body and "the other three great Nations[,] namely the Chickesaws[,] Chocktaws[,] and Cherokees." Aping Mad Dog's words, Methlogee informed the ex-agent that these "four Nations are all now United and were determined to support each other" in interactions with the United States. Other Seminoles objected to Creek interventionism, however. They included a headman named Okaiegigie, who lived on the lower Flint River. Although "we have always sat Still & lisined to Our friends" in Creek country, he railed against the "Line . . . drawn through [Seminole country] which we Cant see the use of or what Cause or reason [there] is for it." The Seminoles "never Can agree to" that act of colonialism, he railed, and the headmen of Creek country "[know] it." Thus many Seminoles conducted their affairs apart from Creek country, thwarting Mad Dog's aim to unify Creek and Seminole interests.¹⁰

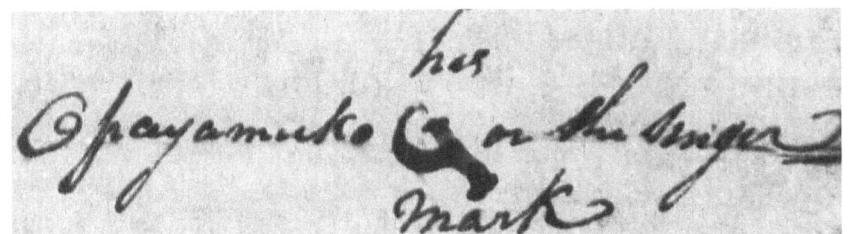

"Opayamuko or the [S]inger, his mark" in 1803
Singer of Hickory Ground cut an instrumental figure at the turn of the nineteenth century. He possessed the acumen and charisma to lead the Creeks through an era of land loss and crippling debt. During his tenure, he partnered with Upper Creek colleagues to advance a grand project of southern Indian union meant to preserve indigenous lands from John Forbes & Company and the US republic. His crowning achievement was to help charter the non-cession agreement of 1803 from his hometown. His subsequent assassination sent the Creek world into turmoil. Detail from Singer to Governor Folch, 8/21/1803, Hickory Ground (?), in Papers of Panton, Leslie and Company, University of West Florida, Pensacola. Courtesy of UWF Archives and West Florida History Center, University of West Florida Library.

Determined to rein in the Seminoles, the Creeks launched a "pacific mission" to Seminole country in 1800. Although Mad Dog's foregoing communication with the Seminoles laid the groundwork for it, Singer led the way. Identified by Hawkins as "Mucclassee Hopoie of Ocheubofau [Hickory Ground]," Singer had been active in intertribal affairs since at least 1797. In that year he served as an "ambassador" for the Upper Creeks and Chickasaws by ferrying talks of peace between both groups. This diplomatic service suggests that he counted indigenous allies beyond Creek country, and it explains why he occupied a prestigious role as go-between for two groups. The title "Mucclassee Hopoie" also hints at Singer's allies in the nearby Tallapoosa town of Muccolossus or in an indigenous polity far from Creek country (or both). Singer exercised spiritual power that further enhanced his intertribal diplomacy. His name implies that he was a crier or singer who communed with the spirit world, while records identify him by the war title Hopoie Micco, meaning "far-off king." A warrior of this stature possessed the power of clairvoyance and knowledge of faraway lands suitable for long-distance communication and alliance-building. Equipped with a rare skill set, Singer leaned into his mandate to bring peace between the Seminoles and the United States.[11]

Headmen from all four Creek provinces participated in the peace mission with Singer and Mad Dog. In addition to Lower Creek headmen, Okfuskee leaders named Fushatchee Micco and Cussetuh Tuskeinchau represented the Abeikas. They inherited the mantle of peace from White Lieutenant, who had died in 1799, one year earlier. Despite this coordinated effort, Seminoles remained defiant of Creek leaders, intransigent to US interests, and supportive of Bowles, who seized property belonging to the former Panton, Leslie & Company at St. Marks. Seminoles eluded restraint. Creek leaders tried again in 1802, when Mad Dog addressed the Seminoles in a stern talk on behalf of the four rivers: "the Aubocoes, the two Upper [Tallapoosas and Alabamas] and the Lower rivers," or "the whole Creek nation." "You must no longer persist in the conduct you have hitherto pursued; you must drop it; stop where you are, and adopt another course of conduct." Unless the Seminoles abandoned Bowles's and other talks that had "misled" them, Mad Dog warned, "it will be to your injury." To ensure that Mad Dog's talk reached its intended recipients, Singer appointed two allies to escort a courier safely to Seminole country. They were Hopoie Yauholo of Tuskegee (Alabama) and Yaufkee Emautlau of Autossee (Tallapoosa). Both men were "accustomed to [diplomatic] business," according to Singer, who deemed them imperative to the embassy.[12]

Creek efforts to cultivate a durable relationship with the Seminoles fell flat. Creek headmen undercut the Seminole agenda instead by ceding land to the United States. Under extraordinary pressure to abolish Creek debts, Singer and Mad Dog convened with Agent Hawkins and other federal commissioners at Fort Wilkinson, Georgia, in summer 1802. The headmen put their mark to a treaty on June 16 after lengthy discussion. In return for funding the debt to the trading store at Fort Wilkinson and securing annuity monies, they relinquished Seminole lands near the St. Marys River and Creek lands along the western bank of the Oconee. The specter of trade dependence compromised ties between Creeks and Seminoles and anticipated more treaties of land cession in the future. As well, the Treaty of Fort Wilkinson undermined the intertribal diplomacy championed by Singer and Mad Dog. The problem of debt inserted a wedge between Creeks and Seminoles, forcing the headmen to cave to US colonial interests.[13]

By the early 1800s, Creek leaders were juggling the competing demands of southern Indian unity and Creeks' financial solvency. Bound in ever-tightening webs of debt, the Creeks sold land to the United States to allay economic hardship and demonstrate good faith to US officials. Yet, although trade debt posed an obstacle to intertribal cooperation, Mad Dog and Singer were hardly failures. They tried to protect southern Indian lands by forming and directing a coalition that spanned all Creek provinces and held out the possibility of Seminole cooperation. The coalition participants aimed to mute Seminole violence against settlers and, more broadly, create peace between "Red And White" peoples.[14]

"We must [be] at Peace [and] Asist each Other"

The Creek attempt to court allies in Seminole country was one dimension of a broader Creek agenda to forge alliances with all southern Indians, especially the Cherokees, Choctaws, and Chickasaws. No longer adversaries, these three groups shared the Creek belief that southern Indians must work together to bar intruders and outlaw cessions. Intertribal conflict had been futile; intertribal cooperation promised results. To that end, Mad Dog and Singer communicated with these southern Indians in messages and meetings that encouraged recipients to be "at Peace [and] Asist each Other." The exchanges facilitated by this political duo spawned mutual arrangements that resolved disputes and created moments of unity among the involved parties. In short, Mad Dog and Singer looked to generate centrifugal waves of intertribal alliance that would blunt the centripetal waves of finance eroding the southern Indian domain.[15]

Mad Dog took the lead in Creek country to erect the pillars of southern Indian peace. Just as he contacted the Seminoles in 1798, so in the same year he met with Cherokees, Chickasaws, and Choctaws in an undisclosed location. He summarized the meeting in a subsequent talk recorded by a federal agent named Richard Thomas. According to Mad Dog, the participants "all met And Agree[d] to Burey All" desire to harm the United States. Showcasing agreement, they pledged to stop warriors from stealing settlers' horses, cattle, and other property on "the frontears" and to "Set matters to Right" should marauders return home with pilfered items. Furthermore, the Indians agreed to designate guards to police tribal boundaries separating them from the United States. Mad Dog explained that "the Chacktaws will Pay Due Attencon from Tom Bigbie to Natchez and the Chickasaws will Gard [the] frontere [with Tennessee settlers] and the Cherokees will [do what they can] on ther Part as far as [the] Appalache [River]." Drawing a correlation between rivers and autonomy, Mad Dog sought to hold the line of American expansion at the Tombigbee, Tennessee, and Apalachee. The "fower Nations," he concluded, should be of "On[e] mind."[16]

Enforcing riverine borders between southern Indians and American settlers was meant to give hunters better access to game and other resources with which to service debts. Talks from Mad Dog and Singer illustrate the importance of the traditional winter hunts to financing debt at the turn of the nineteenth century. Both talks derive from the period shortly before Panton, Leslie & Company reorganized as John Forbes & Company. In a talk to Forbes, who joined Panton, Leslie in the 1790s, Mad Dog pleaded for an extension on behalf of Creek debtors. The Tuckabatchee headman informed the merchant that "there is many little people going about picking up the Skins," adding that Creeks "shall use [the upcoming] winter to make good hunts and pay off our debts" to the merchant house. Likewise, Singer alerted William Panton to his plans to hunt in "the Woods . . . with all my people" during the approaching winter. He pledged to "visit you [in the spring] with all the skins I can collect" to pay for goods he had purchased on credit for himself and kin. Hunting improved economic and social relationships with foreign entities, as well as supplied the wherewithal to procure wares.[17]

Because American settlers restricted access to southern Indian hunting grounds, however, hunters trod new lands in search of game. The establishment and growth of Tennessee forced Upper Creeks to hunt on nearby Choctaw lands. In April 1802, a Choctaw headman named Mingo Homastubbee addressed this issue in a talk to the Upper Creeks. He had "heard of a new settlement formed by your people on the Choctaw land," along the Black Warrior River in present-day western Alabama. He raised "no objection to your people hunting on our land" unmolested by settlers, and he considered "your warriors as ours." But "I do not wish to see you settle on it"; nor would "I . . . permit even my own warriors to settle out in the hunting grounds" on the Black Warrior. Herds of deer needed time to repopulate following the winter hunts, Mingo Homastubbee reasoned, so the founding of an Upper Creek settlement in this area threatened herds on which both societies depended. Thus "the land on Black warrior [must] be preserved for hunting." To "preserve a good understanding between our Nations," he forwarded the talk to two headmen conversant in intertribal negotiations: Singer, who "I hope will join me to prevent this settlement," and Mad Dog, who might "lend his aid to check this settlement."[18]

Some "papers" kept by Singer at his home in Hickory Ground indicate that he and Mad Dog responded favorably to Mingo Homastubbee. Among those files was a speech that the Choctaw headman delivered in Choctaw country months later, in October 1802. He explained in the speech that he had been "appointed & Authorised" by the Choctaws to carry on talks with the Creeks. In this capacity, he had been "into that [C]reek] nation" and "received and Acknowledged as such by their head Chiefs," meaning Singer and Mad Dog, among others. The Creek "Chiefs" agreed with the Choctaws that Mingo Homastubbee should ease Creek–Choctaw tensions arising from the territorial dispute on the Black Warrior. His speech and other evidence further suggest that the Creeks endorsed his leadership because he, like them, promoted southern Indian politicking on the broadest scale. For instance, Mingo Homastubbee "sincerely wish[ed] to preserve peace with [every] nation" and to issue "friendly talks to . . . our red Brothers" across the region. His intertribal outlook clearly aligned with that of Singer and Mad Dog.[19]

If Mingo Homastubbee served as the Creeks' point person in Choctaw country, Singer was fast becoming the southern Indians' contact in Creek country. He was the recipient of at least one of Mingo Homastubbee's talks. He was an important voice for the Chickasaws during the negotiations that ended the Creek-Chickasaw War. He was one of few Creek leaders who oversaw relations with the Seminoles. And he was an ally of Doublehead, a prominent Cherokee headman concerned about the hemorrhaging of Cherokee land. Yet he owed his intertribal reputation to Mad Dog, whose diplomatic initiatives paved the way for the Alabama headman. There was no Singer without Mad Dog. Furthermore, Mad Dog cemented Singer's prominence in international relations by naming him the speaker for the Upper Creek towns in the National Council in 1802. Mad Dog was so advanced "in age [and unable to] do as I used to do" that he decided to retire from the daily bustle of Creek politics. Henceforth Singer represented Upper Creek interests in talks and councils with the southern Indians.[20]

Mad Dog also "transfered the seat" of all subsequent Council meetings in Upper Creek country from Tuckabatchee to Hickory Ground. He recognized the ways in which his successor's town would aid the southern Indians. Records indicate that Hickory Ground, like the Lower Creek town of Cusseta, was "a white or peace town" that encouraged alliance-building between Creeks and outsiders. As a result, this Alabama polity was ripe for southern Indian exchange in the early nineteenth century. Hickory Ground was also a convenient meeting place for southern Indians wishing to join hands with one another and close ranks against foreign creditors. As Mingo Homastubbee put it, Singer lived "on the frontier of his [the Creek] nation," meaning the western edge of Creek country, nearer Choctaw country than the remaining Creek towns. Hickory Ground had become a beacon for southern Indian peace and unity, lending Singer additional clout with which to build intertribal connections.[21]

Singer made Hickory Ground the site of a grand council in spring 1803. A who's who of southern Indian headmen joined him there, including Mad Dog, an up-and-coming Tuckabatchee named Big Warrior, Mingo Homastubbee of the Choctaws, and Doublehead of the Cherokees. Investing in southern Indian union, these headmen gathered with Singer under the belief that no indigenous population should part with any more land to the United States. Opposing them were Benjamin Hawkins and John Forbes, who attended the council. Both officials wished to secure the Indians' approval for a land cession that would advance the joint interests of the United States and the JFC. Deep in Alabama country, the southern Indians' fate hung in the balance.[22]

"The four mothers"

Guiding indigenous leaders in Hickory Ground were local peoples equally anxious to preserve land. They set the council's tone, informed its discussions, and participated in its achievements. They ensured that this was a meeting of what Singer called "the four mothers." By coining this phrase, he equated diplomacy among the southern Indians with the localist contours of southern Indian leadership. He articulated the long-held Creek practice of headmen's relatives and other local actors shaping high-profile diplomacy. Constituted as "the four mothers," the Creeks/Seminoles, Cherokees, Choctaws, and Chickasaws in Hickory Ground drew strength from communities. Moreover, by invoking mothers and women more generally, he mounted a gendered defense of southern Indian lands. As farmers, Singer understood, women would need to be central to discussions about land. Whether his acknowledgement of women was an oblique comment on matrilineal or bilateral kinship reckoning is uncertain; perhaps it was a little bit of both. More likely, he underscored women's ongoing inclusion in public affairs in the early nineteenth century. They and other ground-level peoples formed the bulwark of pan-Indian politics.[23]

Among them was Singer's sister. A rare glimpse of her life appears in the journal of Estevan Folch. A representative of the Spanish crown, he trekked with Forbes from Pensacola to Hickory Ground in May. On the evening of May 15, Folch and his companion approached Hickory Ground from the "top of a little mountain" and observed "smoak" billowing from the square ground fire. The men soon made their way into town and, according to Folch, "went strait to the Singer's sister's house." There she presented the travelers with "a dish of thin drink" made with lye. This was the popular Creek dish known as *sófki*. Made from ground corn, water, and ash, sófki demonstrated women's culinary skills and their centrality to rituals of greeting and hospitality. Southern Indian women had welcomed foreigners into their communities since the colonial era, a practice that Singer's sister continued in the early 1800s. By serving food to Folch and Forbes, she built trust between the Native and non-Native attendees at the upcoming council. Moreover, her culinary service was a political act because it gently reminded her guests that subsequent discussions about land must take her and her kin into consideration.[24]

Southern Indian emissaries began to arrive in her town in late May. Creek headmen welcomed them to the square ground, where they staged rituals meant to build intertribal ties. Folch wrote on May 21 that Creeks received Mingo Homastubbee and other Choctaw "deputies . . . with much ceremony at the square." Four days later, Cherokee, Choctaw, and Chickasaw leaders who had recently completed their journeys delivered formal "addresses" to one another in the square. Doublehead's speech was "singularly dignified and impressive," according to Folch, although its contents are unknown. Later that evening, southern Indian leaders convened nearby in a conical structure known as the hot house. There they performed a dance that resembled, as Folch put it, the "actions and steps as the forest bear when he is taught." These intertribal acts culminated with Mad Dog's lecturing "the young warriors" on the southern Indians' shared history and traditions. The retired headman imparted his wisdom by interpreting "the different belts of wampum [brought by] the several embassies" to Hickory Ground and closed his speech by encouraging the warriors to "preserve the records after his death." The momentous conference at Hickory Ground needed to be memorialized for southern Indian posterity, involving as it did people of all ages, genders, and ranks.[25]

It commenced on Thursday, May 26. Folch and Forbes as well as Hawkins, who had arrived the previous weekend, sat quietly in the square ground as Creek headmen heard several talks from the Native delegates, including Doublehead. During another "long harangue," Doublehead spoke "in favour of unanimity" among the Indians. His colleagues later endorsed his call for unity by appointing what Folch called "a king," who would advocate for the southern Indians. The person who filled this position was Singer's trusted Choctaw ally Mingo Homastubbee. Folch noted that the Choctaw man sat on a "white deerskin" in the square ground as a ritual tea known as the black drink cooled nearby. Two men soon entered the square. One of them "spoke with considerable force of gesture respecting the ceremony that was to be performed . . . and the virtues necessary to be possessed by a king." Then each one "put into the Chactaw's hand a white wing" to conclude the "ceremony." Afterward, the assembled Indians shook hands with Mingo Homastubbee and celebrated with black drink.[26]

The ceremony recorded by Folch appears to be a nineteenth-century update of the institution of the Fanni Mingo. Meaning "squirrel king," a Fanni Mingo was a man of high status adopted by a group of people, whom he represented among his own. He was a fictive kinsman and cultural broker. His adopters' interests and those of his natal group were one. This practice originated as early as the seventeenth century when the Choctaws and Chickasaws adopted proponents of peace from both groups to end bouts of conflict between them. The Creeks relied on similar intermediaries in the eighteenth century to facilitate trade and mediate conflict between Creek country and the British Empire. Although Singer and other Creeks may have tasked Mingo Homastubbee with representing the Creeks in Choctaw councils, the political context at Hickory Ground strongly suggests that southern Indian headmen charged Mingo Homastubbee with advancing a vaster agenda designed to burnish intertribal ties and defend indigenous southerners' domain from agents of colonialism. These headmen were drawing on past lessons to meet present challenges. Furthermore, the appointment of a Fanni Mingo required elaborate ceremonialism that cleansed the adoptee and symbolized peace between him and his adopters. Thus Mingo Homastubbee sat on a white deerskin, received two white wings, and enjoyed the sacred black drink. In Hickory Ground, the past and present converged.[27]

The selection of a Fanni Mingo dashed the hopes of the notorious adventurer William Augustus Bowles. He had arrived in Hickory Ground with the Seminole delegation expecting to "be made king of the four nations." Yet both the Native and non-Native attendees opposed his ambitions. They considered him a regional disturbance who impeded calm negotiation between duly appointed authorities. The southern Indians' "voice was for Singer," who called Bowles "a black speck in the sky." Clearly, the headmen in Hickory Ground voted against Bowles when they chose Mingo Homastubbee as "king" of the southern Indians. Even members of the Seminole embassy sided with their colleagues. That much is suggested by the appearance of Methlogee, Mad Dog's ally, at the council. Bowles was soon cuffed in irons and placed in a canoe downriver, where according to Folch, a "crowd of men, women, and children immediately pushed it off." Bound for Morro Castle in Havana, Cuba, Bowles later died there under Spanish custody. His demise stemmed as much from that "crowd" of local actors as from high-profile diplomacy. Hickory Ground pulsed with intertribal unity in spring 1803.[28]

Southern Indian leaders reached the zenith of pan-Indianism in the days following Bowles's expulsion. On May 30, Forbes assembled in the square with indigenous leaders and implored them to pay their debts to the JFC. He was most concerned about the Creeks and Seminoles, who were in arrears for $113,512. That figure constituted more than half of the $204,000 owed by all southern Indians to the JFC. Like others in his day, he lumped Creeks and Seminoles into one group, prompting his request that they fund their joint debt by selling land along the Apalachicola River near JFC headquarters in Pensacola. This was mainly Seminole land that Forbes had long espied. His demands left the Creeks and Seminoles in disbelief. Singer later examined the JFC account book with Upper Creek colleagues Big Warrior and Alexander Cornells to assess the transactions with which Forbes calculated the Creek–Seminole debt. Hours of discussion failed to break the logjam between the Indians and Forbes. Keenly following the exchange was Hawkins, who advised Singer to accept Forbes's claim and consider parting with the Apalachicola tract. Yet the headmen remained "disagreable," Folch noted in his journal.[29]

Singer delivered a formal reply to Forbes the next morning. "It is a very large thing [the debt] you have put to us," he exclaimed; "[h]owever, we think we have got it to bear." He assured Forbes that Creeks and Seminoles intended to settle up with the merchant house. He exempted land as a medium of payment, however, and instead proposed that Creeks raise money from the property of deceased "white and red" traders who had long supplied the Creeks. Big Warrior agreed to handle the sale of pigs, cattle, and other items from the estate of the late traders. Natural resources possessed financial value too, as Singer broached the idea that Creeks sell "cedar . . . and other woods" from their landholdings. The Creeks were "poor people," after all, with little else to vend. Likewise, Singer opposed a cession of the Apalachicola lands without consulting the rightful owners. On this issue he deferred to a Seminole headman named Semothle, who pledged to "look into" the matter after returning home. Native southerners promised everything but land to Forbes.[30]

These conversations sparked a bold moratorium on land sales. Shortly before the gathering disbanded, in early June the Cherokee headman Doublehead addressed the Euro-American officials and declared, "Here we have met. We have become the four nations as one people, and we [have] resolved to sell no more lands but with the consent of the whole [southern Indian] confederacy." According to Doublehead, the southern Indians collectively decided to pull land from the negotiating table. White interlopers must accept that choice, he implied, and recognize that indigenous people alone decided whether, when, and on what terms to part with land. Although Folch believed that the Cherokee delegation had "induced" the others to "thwart" Forbes, he was mistaken. Doublehead was merely a spokesperson for southern Indian leaders who for weeks had discussed the common interests that led to the non-cession pact. The appointment of a Fanni Mingo, the arrest of William Bowles, and the participation of local actors in conference activities spurred on pan-Indian union. The southern Indians were a formidable bloc in Hickory Ground.[31]

Singer expressed as much in a talk to the governor of Spanish West Florida, Vicente Folch, more than two months later. He called Doublehead's announcement a "resolution" that bound the southern Indians to decline Euro-Americans' requests for land except for cases when the "whole confederacy" consented. Singer explained that "in [the] presence of your Son [Estevan Folch] & Mr Forbes [w]e . . . concluded to give[?] no more Land away to White people." That decision had stopped Forbes in his tracks, denying him the Apalachicola lands. Further, the southern Indians had decided to bar indigenous lands from all "White people," especially the United States and its indomitable agent Benjamin Hawkins. Singer grasped the danger posed by Hawkins, who tirelessly leveraged southern Indians' financial weakness in negotiation after negotiation and tracked southern Indians' dealings with JFC merchants like Forbes. Singer expressed confidence to Governor Folch that the southern Indian "resolution" would frustrate Hawkins as well as other whites desirous of indigenous lands.³²

The Hickory Ground council was an exciting, if rare, moment of intertribalism in the Native South. Southern Indian leaders united across tribal lines, coauthored a policy that slowed land cessions, and mapped out a bright future for indigenous people in the early nineteenth century. The council also fulfilled years of intertribal diplomacy involving Singer, Mad Dog, Methlogee, Mingo Homastubbee, Doublehead, and other political heavyweights. By convening in Creek country, these leaders were subject to the ongoing forces of localism that had shaped Creek politics since the mid-eighteenth century. While women conducted rituals of hospitality, a diverse crowd of Indians exiled Bowles. Singer captured these on-the-ground moments when he likened the southern Indians to "the four mothers" and acknowledged that women and other local Creeks aided the effort of intertribal union.³³

"The most influential man in the nation"

Shortly after the Hickory Ground council, Singer met with an unceremonious death and faded from the pages of Creek history. His fall from grace was as unexpected as precipitous. Few Creek leaders more adamantly defended the southern Indian domain from foreign intrusion, and few Creek leaders possessed as much recognition in Creek country as he did. "The Singer[,] it appears, is now the most influential man in the [Creek] nation," remarked JFC official William Simpson in 1804, one year after the Hickory Ground council. Little escaped the headman's notice or mark. Yet the perennial issue of trade debt compromised his leadership by forcing him to accept treaties of land cession as the only means of erasing debts to commercial entities. The recent Fort Wilkinson treaty had taught him that land sales provided an easy fix to Indians' economic woes and relieved pressure from Euro-American authorities who harassed Native southerners with requests for land. With limited options, Singer abandoned the Hickory Ground compact and regrettably paid with his life.³⁴

The waning years of his leadership are illuminated by a conversation between him and Euro-American officials in November 1804. He convened then with Hawkins and Simpson at the US agency on the Flint River. The three men discussed a recent "grant" made by the Seminoles and Lower Creeks to the JFC. The grant in question was the Apalachicola tract for which John Forbes had badgered southern Indian leaders earlier in Hickory Ground. In return, the JFC excused a portion ($66,534) of the Creek–Seminole debt. The Forbes Purchase, as it became known, outraged Singer, who cast doubt on its validity by alleging that "the men who have granted it had not the power, & that it will not hold good." Those men had violated the Hickory Ground resolution, circumventing its provision that southern Indian headmen consult one another before ceding land to the whites. Singer, observed Simpson, felt "neglected & mortified at not having been consulted" about the land grant. The headman stated that the merchant house "ought to have" known better than to seek land from very few headmen in one "corner" of the Native South. Rather, numerous leaders were bound to agree to land grants. Singer thus "expresse[d] his disapprobation" for the JFC's divide-and-conquer tactic.[35]

Yet in the same breath he queried Simpson and Hawkins about whether the "Oakmulgee lands" might "pay" the remaining debt owed by the Creeks and Seminoles. The lands in question resided in the fork between the Oconee and Ocmulgee Rivers in present-day eastern Georgia. By dangling the fertile Ocmulgee lands to both parties, Singer looked to erase the outstanding debt with John Forbes & Company and to satisfy Agent Hawkins, with whom he had been discussing the Ocmulgee cession for several months. The idea was that the United States would purchase the land in question from Creek leaders and fund the Creek–Seminole debt through land sales to westward-moving settlers. A canny negotiator, Singer knew that the cession promised to fulfill the interests of two foreign powers and improve the Creeks' and Seminoles' financial standing to boot. The transcript bearing his conversation with Hawkins and Simpson also suggests that he had no choice but to accept the elaborate scheme and secure the best outcome for the indebted parties. To escape the vice of debt, Singer and other Creeks signed the Treaty of the Creek Agency with Hawkins on November 3, 1804. A delighted Simpson mused that the JFC will "reap" all kinds of "advantages" from the agent's "friendship & knowledge of Indian affairs."[36]

Whether Lower Creek leaders approved the Ocmulgee cession is uncertain, but that land belonged to them. Lower Creeks had hunted game in the Ocmulgee Valley since the colonial period. More recently, they had clashed with Georgia settlers for control of the area. In 1794 Georgia militiamen "Cross'd the Oakmulgee" onto Lower Creek lands to pursue two Cusseta men presumed to have killed a settler and stolen two horses. After militia officer John Clark and his party encountered the suspects, the soldiers opened fire, killing and scalping one and wounding the other. Other examples of Lower Creek–settler violence abound. Furthermore, the Lower Creeks cherished the Ocmulgee lands for their sacred import. Adjacent to the river were the Ocmulgee Old Fields, where Creeks' ancestors "sat down (as they term it) or established themselves, after their [historic] emigration from the west," wrote William Bartram in the 1770s. By the nineteenth century, the Lower Creeks objected to federal and state attempts to survey the Creek–Georgian border in the Ocmulgee and vicinity. Agent Hawkins grumbled in his journal that the "disposition of the Indians who claim the lands [made] it impracticable to" complete the task.[37]

Lower Creek headmen participated in renewed negotiations over the Ocmulgee lands in November 1805. Joined by an Upper Creek representative, the headmen met in Washington with President Thomas Jefferson, Hawkins, and other federal authorities. No evidence suggests that Singer attended the convention. His name is absent from the resulting treaty, and no conference minutes place him in the US capitol. Instead, a small body of headmen led by William McIntosh of Coweta put their mark to the Treaty of Washington. Soon ratified by the Senate, it confirmed the transfer of the Ocmulgee from Creek country to the United States. Additionally, the treaty permitted US engineers to construct a horse path known as the Federal Road through Creek country, thereby hastening the movement of citizens, slaves, and goods between the Atlantic Coast and Mississippi Territory (founded 1798). In return, McIntosh and the other signers received exclusive rights to own and operate ferries, stands, taverns, and other commercial enterprises along the route.[38]

The Hickory Ground resolution was but a dead letter in 1805. Saddled with trade debt, Creek and Seminole headmen reduced the southern Indian domain by granting land piecemeal to "White people," including US treaty authorities and the JFC. The 1804 Forbes Purchase and the 1805 Treaty of Washington exemplified the most recent transfers of land from southern Indian to Euro-American control. The southern Indians had been troubled by debt and signed treaties of land cession to foreign entities since the previous century, but the non-cession agreement reached at Hickory Ground had been designed to reverse the damage. Southern Indians vowed to cede no land to anyone unless they agreed to do so following rigorous intertribal consultation. Before long, however, the Hickory Ground council receded from view. The headmen who consented to the Forbes Purchase and the Treaty of Washington ignored fellow southern Indians. Nor did Singer draft southern Indians beyond Creek country as he negotiated with Hawkins and Simpson regarding the Ocmulgee cession. Falling prey to Euro-American requests for land, headmen accepted guarantees of debt reduction and financial reward in return. Southern Indian land cessions after 1803 illuminated how debt, trade, and finance cleaved the southern Indians into competing interest groups and weakened their commitment to intertribal unity. These economic forces overwhelmed headmen like Singer.[39]

He was assassinated, according to Hawkins, "during the winter" of 1805–6. The agent reported to Georgia governor John Milledge that the assassins were "two men of Cussetuh." Although Singer had remained in Creek country during the Washington treaty convention, the Cusseta assassins apparently blamed him for the post-treaty fallout. The Treaty of the Creek Agency was the genesis of the Treaty of Washington, after all, and Singer's role in the former enabled the latter. Moreover, Singer was the linchpin around which Creek politics in the early nineteenth century revolved. As the "most influential man" in Creek country, he bore responsibility for leading Creeks in the proper direction. When he faltered by parting with lands outside his political jurisdiction, they marked him for death. Undermining Creek confidence in Singer was the perception that he had been co-opted by Hawkins. This view was held by the Cussetas' ally Tame King, an outspoken critic of Singer. He may have even had a hand in Singer's downfall by encouraging the Lower Creeks to resist headmen like Singer, whose relationship with Hawkins smacked of corruption.[40]

The assassination of Singer was a watershed in Creek history. Since the eighteenth century, warriors and other on-the-ground individuals had criticized leaders and temporarily removed them from power to amend the direction of Creek country. The "two men of Cussetuh" had committed an unprecedented political act in Creek country, however, when they killed a high-profile and popular headman. In doing so, they legitimized violence as a political tool and sowed the seeds for the civil war soon to erupt in Creek country. Furthermore, the Cusseta men and other possible co-conspirators belonged to a growing movement of "young people" that Hawkins called "improvident and ungovernable." By drawing a correlation between poverty and intransigence, Hawkins captured the horrific impact of colonialism on Creek country. Their "hunting [was] nearly done[,] their [trade] expenses [were] accumulating on them and the land speculators [were] eager to misrepresent" them. As dubious persons swarmed Creek lands, drained Creek resources, and demanded Creek cessions, they jeopardized Creeks' ability to secure food, procure skins, and maintain autonomy. The Creek leadership offered no direction, Creeks believed, as "the old Chiefs" like Singer had become listless and ineffectual.[41]

Singer's violent undoing demonstrates the limits of southern Indian union in the early nineteenth century. He and other regional indigenous leaders never devised a method of debt payment that could simultaneously guard land and satisfy the interests of John Forbes & Company and its unflagging patron, Benjamin Hawkins. Euro-American officials held the winning hand. By leveraging the Indians' debt problem, they made incessant requests for indigenous land, placed indigenous leaders in untenable positions, and contributed to the shattering of the inter-indigenous unity achieved at Hickory Ground. Yet while the gradual transfer of land from southern Indians to Euro-Americans was bound up in debt, ground-level actors shaped the region's territorial reconfiguration as much as high-profile authorities. The Cussetas who took Singer's life sent a bloody rebuke to Creek leaders who participated in cessions of land and who appeared irresponsive to local needs.

From the late eighteenth century to the early nineteenth, the Creeks sought an intertribal salve for trade debt and land erosion. Led by Mad Dog of Tuckabatchee and Singer of Hickory Ground, they constructed alliances with fellow indigenous leaders who shared Creek fears about the financial grip of Pensacola-based merchants and US authorities. Mad Dog and his Alabama partner excelled in the craft of intertribal diplomacy, using talks, wampum belts, councils, and other forms of communication to advance togetherness among the Indians. These leaders were in tune with the political mood of Creek country and cultivated support among local persons, ranging from sisters and children to warriors and other men. Thus Creeks at the top and on the ground agreed that intertribal collaboration was the best way to retain indigenous land and the autonomy that flowed from it. Because power still rested on local input, however, Creek leaders who appeared to pander to Euro-Americans faced sharp criticism and even newfound violence from below. These developments proved fatal to Singer. He represented in microcosm the promise and peril of Creek political leadership in the new century.

Chapter 6

"The four rivers ... is for us to Live upon"

The Creek War and the Paradox of Riverine Leadership

Following Singer's assassination, two Upper Creek headmen competed to fill his vacancy. One was Tame King, resident of the Tallassee village of Halfway House. An inveterate enemy of the United States, he opposed settler incursions, construction of the Federal Road, and Benjamin Hawkins's grip on the Creek government. More than anything or anyone, however, he despised council headmen who failed to undo these changes and who appeared to be complicit with the US agent. He was a Creek patriot to the bone. His rival was Big Warrior of Tuckabatchee. Once an ally of Singer, Big Warrior absorbed the diplomatic stance of his predecessor and called for peace with other Indians as well as the Americans. Although he agreed with Tame King that US expansion jeopardized the Creeks, he opposed Tame King's hard-line position, believing that it promised not security but invasion. As a result, Big Warrior cooperated with American authorities and sought alliances with other indigenous leaders under the belief that regionwide diplomacy best served Creek independence. These two headmen drew the political battle lines in Upper Creek country, facing off in the ensuing Creek War of 1813–14.[1]

A subset of the War of 1812, the Creek War was an epic struggle between the National Council and the Redstick Creeks. Named after the red implements carried into battle by medicine men, the Redsticks championed Creek traditions in the face of American expansion. Like Tame King, who served as a Redstick leader, they abhorred settler intrusion, treaties of land cession, and other acts of US colonialism that weakened the Creek domain. Furthermore, they looked to dismantle the federal government's "plan of civilization." Former secretary of war Henry Knox had designed this policy in the 1790s to remake the southern

Indians in white Americans' image and thereby bring peace to the southern frontier. Hawkins embraced this program with zeal. He encouraged Creek men to abandon hunting and take up farming. By plowing fields of wheat and tending herds of cattle, he reasoned, Creek men would earn a steady income that avoided the vicissitudes of the deerskin trade. Likewise, he directed Creek women to move from the cornfield to the household, so that they would perform domestic work like their white counterparts. The Redsticks decried these changes and the headmen, especially Big Warrior, who seemed to condone them. Anticolonial heroes, the Redsticks sought to restore Creek country to its former glory.[2]

Despite the enmity between the Redsticks and aligned Creeks, each side participated in the shared field of riverine politics. Headmen gained adherents, boosted morale, deployed warriors, and outmaneuvered enemies by constructing partnerships with like-minded people. Who claimed power, on what basis, for what purpose, and with which allies were questions that animated each side. The riverine mode of governance remained intact, creating overlap between the war's oppositional duo: Big Warrior and Tame King. These headmen shared more in common than they or their contemporaries recognized. Just as Tame King advocated for Creek independence, so the Tuckabatchee headman defended Creek country, stating "the four rivers we have in our Country . . . is for us to Live upon. [I]t is our whole dependence." Cherishing Creek freedom, both leaders demonstrate that the Creek War originated from and unfolded on familiar political terrain.[3]

By invoking "the four rivers," moreover, Big Warrior commented on the warriors, women, and other local Creeks beyond positions of formal leadership. They held an equal stake in the direction of the civil war. They needed to know that choosing a side was worth the danger to themselves, to kin, and to town. Women and men made bold, calculated risks that guided Big Warrior and his Redstick nemeses A paradox soon emerged, however, for governance that involved input from above and below proved fatal in a time of civil strife. As Redstick and council headmen rallied their bases, they formed competing partnerships within and across the provinces, hardening political boundaries in Creek country. If riverine leaders had sought peace and unity in the past, they began to work at cross-purposes during the war.[4]

Ultimately, the Creek War resulted in the US conquest of Creek country. Southern military forces used the war as a pretext for invasion, crushed the Redsticks, and approved a land grab that expanded cotton cultivation and Black chattel slavery in the Deep South. Still, Creeks defied US colonialism and held to a localist ethos in the postconquest era. Redstick survivors fled to the Florida panhandle and peninsula, where they resisted US territorial expansion in league with the Seminoles into the 1850s. Nor was Creek removal to Indian Territory inevitable. Headmen forced another round of treaties with the United States in the 1820s and early 1830s, while Creek rebels launched a war against Americans in 1836. Some even dodged expulsion altogether and later created the Poarch Band of Creek Indians in the state of Alabama, where they remain today. Creeks did not go down without a fight.[5]

"Our families, our Children"

Before the Creek War, Big Warrior and Tame King sought to protect Creek country from the perils of US colonialism. The Tuckabatchee headman applied his experiences from the famed Hickory Ground meeting to rally Creeks behind another project of southern Indian union. He made his town the seat of intertribal alliance-building and, like Singer, argued that a diplomatic agenda represented the surest measure to bolster southern Indians' independence. More focused on the Creeks, Tame King threw out diplomacy and countered US expansion by building up Creek military reserves. He united warriors under his able leadership and prepared them for war against the encroaching Americans. Despite differences on the surface, then, both headmen shared the common pursuit of Creek unity and power. Whether or not they knew it, they agreed that Creek country was off-limits to whites.[6]

Big Warrior launched his plan as early as 1809, when Americans illegally navigated Creek rivers in ever larger numbers. He was alarmed by these foreigners who traversed the Coosa River to establish a route between Tennessee and areas south of Creek country, including Mobile Bay. He was equally alarmed by Cherokees from Little Turkey's Town on the upper Coosa who were granting Americans free navigation. In May, Big Warrior fired off a stern message to Path Killer, a resident of that town, scolding him for the Cherokees' decision to open "our Country" to American intruders, who threatened to "disturb our young people." Path Killer seemed to think that "us Creek people [want to be] mix'd with the white families," but "we do not Like it." These unwanted travelers belonged nowhere near Creek rivers and lands. To guard indigenous spaces against the United States, Big Warrior proposed that the Cherokees and Creeks unite with the Choctaws and Chickasaws to re-create the kind of intertribal unity achieved in Hickory Ground a mere six years earlier. Referring to the "four nations," Big Warrior instructed Path Killer to resist Americans' subsequent requests for passage through Creek country. "[W]e all should be of one mind, and one sentiment," he said, "and not to do, any thing contrary To that Talk."⁷

Big Warrior advanced this outlook in the following months. In April 1810, Hawkins reported to Secretary of War William Eustis that Big Warrior, "his associates," and "some . . . Chiefs of the Upper Creeks" made "an other attempt . . . to unite the four nations under the Muscogee" leadership. Anxious to turn away US intruders, leaders from Tuckabatchee and other Upper Creek towns rallied behind Big Warrior. Furthermore, this headman shifted the center of the southern Indian alliance from Hickory Ground to the Tuckabatchee "square" to manage intertribal relations. Taking inspiration from Singer, he designated his natal town as the site from which southern Indians would cultivate unity and weaken Americans' "claim on our lands." In case Americans misconstrued his intentions, Big Warrior assured Hawkins that no members of the anticipated intertribal alliance would harm settlers, for he wanted "nothing but peace and friendship with all Nations." "We [in this] part . . . of the Creek nation," meaning the Upper Creeks, "have all a good heart and [are] true friends" to Natives and whites alike.⁸

Big Warrior worried about protecting relatives as much as land from the tentacles of US expansion. The southern Indians must preserve their domain, as he told Path Killer, "for our families [and] our Children." Intertribal union was futile without the security of clans and especially children, who ensured clans' survival from generation to generation. He upheld a future of indigenous landownership based on the early nineteenth-century needs of youth and their elders. Although Big Warrior's own clan is unconfirmed in the documentary record, Hawkins once observed that political leadership in Tuckabatchee passed through the "Eagle family," which suggests that the headman was an Eagle kinsman. Awash in a world of kin ties, he worked with fellow southern Indian leaders to guard land, rivers, and other resources for his relatives, for those of his Creek colleagues, and for those of his indigenous allies. Intertribal networking gave Big Warrior the means to defend the Native South from escalating US intrusion.⁹

Tame King similarly opposed the US reach into Creek country. In May 1811 he dispatched a message to President James Madison laying out his political strategy. As "speaker for our warriors," he decried the construction of the Federal Road authorized by the 1805 Treaty of Washington. This post path opened Creek country to a torrent of unwanted newcomers, not merely mail carriers, who illicitly traveled through, took resources from, and settled on Creek lands. Tame King and other Creeks feared that this engineering project would restrict Creek mobility. As the Federal Road neared completion, Tame King declared firmly to Madison, "[Y]ou ask for a path and I say no." "[M]y chiefs and warriors . . . tell [me] I must not allow it and must say no." Like his Tuckabatchee rival, this soon-to-be Redstick leader broadcast his affinity for clans. He warned the president, "I have a large family of people in the [Creek] Country and cannot govern all so as to preserve a good understanding" between Creeks and America. Tame King was prepared to sic these relatives on the United States unless Madison took appropriate action by banning travelers through Creek country and even tearing up the Federal Road.[10]

Tame King framed his talk in the familial nomenclature of Creek politics. A Creek headman like him derived legitimacy from kin or, as he put it, "a large family of people in the [Creek] Country." These family members included "chiefs and warriors," who looked to him for honest leadership as relations with the United States soured. He acknowledged their concerns and reported them to Madison. Tame King may have layered additional meaning onto his talk to the president. His bold invocation of "a large family of people" reflected and reinforced an interclan support network that spanned multiple provinces and could be summoned at the outset of the Redstick movement. Tame King's strategy fit into a preexisting nexus of Upper Creek leadership that called for discussion with numerous constituents, including relatives. As civil war approached, he prepared to deploy this "large family of people" to roll back American expansion.[11]

The eruption of the Creek War two years later destroyed Big Warrior's and Tame King's shared pursuit to retain Creek autonomy in the Native South. Pressure from Hawkins and action by Big Warrior lit the fuse that ignited civil war. In early 1813, Hawkins demanded that the National Council punish the ringleaders of Creek war parties who had recently killed American settlers. Big Warrior responded to Hawkins by exacting coercive power against Creeks. He appointed a posse of experienced warriors to execute the ringleaders, eleven of whom lay dead by late April. While clans exercised sole jurisdiction in the punishment of wayward kin, Big Warrior undermined that tradition and drew the ire of the incipient Redstick movement. He used the council to overwhelm local actors with deadly force. By this point, as Kevin Kokomoor argues, "Creek state violence" was "as common as it was welcomed." Thus the success of the execution squad in 1813 reflected an increasingly entrenched atmosphere of political violence following Singer's death early in the century.[12]

Yet the council-backed violence does not mean that Creek headmen had come to embrace coercive nationhood to appease federal authorities and thereby suppress local interests. Big Warrior and his ilk believed instead that coercive rule had become a last-ditch option in Creek–US affairs. His decision to approve the executions resulted from Hawkins's uncompromising position and from a need to defend his riverine world. As Big Warrior pointedly explained to the agent, "You have told us, that if we did not punish all of [the ringleaders], that we should lose our land to Chattahoochee, and to Coosa waters." The blame lay with Hawkins, whose imperialist ambitions on behalf of the United States threatened Creek country from the Chattahoochee on the east to the Coosa on the west. Since the four rivers lay in danger, the "chiefs thought best to save their land" by putting the ringleaders to death. As a result, Big Warrior remained in the agent's good graces and headed off invasion by federal and state entities itching to expropriate Creek land. He served not a nation but a constituent group of provinces whose families needed protection from the US republic.[13]

A report from Assistant Agent Nimrod Doyell also indicates that the 1813 council executions involved the relatives of at least two of the men slated for death. He wrote to his superior that before the executions, the council "chiefs sent two parties after" two Okfuskee ringleaders, whose "uncles went with the [council] warriors and pointed them out." Kinship custom dictated that clans and specifically uncles punish kin for past transgressions; thus the uncles who aided the executioners assumed some control in the death of their young nephews. Although Creek intraclan deaths rarely surface in the historical record, the logic that relatives took care of their own remained in place. This line of reasoning suggests that Big Warrior and the execution squad needed clans' stamp of approval to enact an otherwise unpopular decision. Local actors and the customs that had animated them for decades continued to shape council headmen in the fateful year of 1813.[14]

Still, the damage was done. The Abeikas, Tallapoosas, and Alabamas descended into civil war as young men joined the Redstick movement and opposed established leaders throughout spring and summer 1813. The Redsticks expelled, assaulted, and killed headmen who condoned, if not accepted, the council's authority and, by extension, Hawkins's influence over the Creeks. In Okfuskee, for example, Redsticks "killed five Chiefs" deemed co-conspirators with the council. Northwest of Okfuskee, Redsticks in Aubecooche killed three headmen and injured a fourth. In Tallapoosa country, Autossee Redsticks had "driven off their Chiefs" by June. The Redsticks also attacked headmen's property that smacked of the US civilization plan. After the Okfuskees killed their headmen, they "destroyed almost all the cattle in town." The Alabama towns descended in violence too. Once a center of peace and unity under Singer's leadership, the Alabama province became a Redstick spiritual hub for the duration of the war.[15]

The Creek War was the perfect storm of US colonial aggression and political instability unleashed by Singer's assassination less than a decade earlier. Following Singer's death, Big Warrior and Tame King attempted to head off the very civil strife that later consumed them. Each tailored his prewar leadership to the protection of families and the sustenance they drew from Creek lands, rivers, and other resources. While one flexed his muscles in the intertribal arena, the other gained support among warriors. They moved from bitter rivals to irreconcilable enemies when Big Warrior relented to Hawkins's forceful interventionism. Redsticks in the Upper Creek towns denounced the council executions, which symbolized compromised leadership in the National Council.

"Chatteeck, chu, fau, lee" and the Paradox of Leadership

The enmity between Big Warrior and Tame King evinced the growing liability of riverine governance as civil unrest erupted. Since the mid-eighteenth century, headmen had identified common threats to Creek country and formed partnerships within and across the provinces to neutralize those threats. Tensions between headmen and local actors dogged unity with regularity and frustrated agendas to forge alliances, secure goods, and pursue other routes to autonomy. Yet political unease rarely caused internal violence and never produced civil war. By 1813, however, a large group of Abeikas, Tallapoosas, and Alabamas had banded together as Redsticks, arguing that the treasonous behavior of Big Warrior and other council members merited death. To build the Redstick movement, Tame King and other Redstick leaders fashioned partnerships that purposefully deepened civil strife and erased the organizational effect of riverine leadership. Based in "Chatteeck, chu, fau, lee," or Halfway House, he energized the Redstick base by attracting Lower Creeks to a movement composed largely of Tallapoosas, Abeikas, and Alabamas. Vowing to fight to the death, Tame King refused the entreaties of Big Warrior, who sought the reabsorption of the Redsticks into the Creek mainstream.[16]

Halfway House offered the Redsticks secure access points from which to cultivate solidarity in and launch attacks from Upper Creek country. As Tallassee's lone talofa, this polity was known as Middle Town, a transitional space between the Lower Creeks to the southeast and the Upper Creeks to the northwest.

It may have become the capital of the Tallapoosa province over time because Tame King hosted the National Council in Halfway House at least twice (in 1810). Additionally, the name of this community symbolized fellowship, alliance, and power. A "big house" (*cukofv rakko*) was a council house where headmen met for discussion. Verbs with the root *cuko-* point to the act of visiting someone, as during a political gathering. Likewise, *cuko rakko* was a ceremonial ground. Underscoring the spiritual dimension of town square grounds, this term speaks to the spiritual importance of Halfway House in a movement dependent on otherworldly forces. Tame King himself combined human and other-than-human agency during the Creek War when at one point he bragged about the "magic powers he possessed." Halfway House thus encapsulated the political, cultural, and religious contours of the Redstick insurgency.[17]

From this base Tame King reanimated the Halfway House–Cusseta tie first forged during the American War for Independence. Since Cusseta was a white town, he needed to convince its townspeople to endorse the Redsticks without abandoning the town's banner of peace. In late spring 1813, he addressed a message to "Cussetah Micco" about prophets in Alabama country who had recently killed members of the council's execution squad, including a Tuckabatchee headman named Tustunnuggee Hopoie. The victims, Tame King explained, had accidentally stepped into a prophet's magical circle and "immediately seized with madness [had] died." Supernatural power rather than human agents had caused these deaths. He set the record straight about the Redsticks and invited a polity long allied with his own to join them.[18]

Tame King's reception among the Cussetas is detailed in a report to Hawkins from Tuckabatchee headman and translator Alexander Cornells. Representing the National Council, Cornells met with the Cussetas in June 1813 to gauge their loyalty to the Redsticks and especially to "Hoboheilthle Micco," or Tame King. According to him, the townspeople "seemed willing to apologize for" the prophets' "conduct." Further, he learned that Tame King had courted other towns in the province, writing to Hawkins that the Halfway House leader had "directed" Cusseta Mico to recruit supporters from "all" the Lower Creek towns downriver from Cusseta. Cornells confirmed that the Cusseta headman had indeed forwarded Tame King's talk to unidentified Chattahoochee towns. Thus Tame King remained a trusted figure among the Cussetas, who in turn trusted his read on the Redsticks' motives and powers. The line of communication between Tame King and Cusseta Mico spread the Redstick message far and wide among the Lower Creeks.[19]

Cusseta Mico endorsed the Redstick insurgency not only by allying with Tame King but also by withholding military assistance from Big Warrior and other council leaders in Tuckabatchee. When a Cusseta war leader named Tuskeenohau prepared to travel to Tuckabatchee to defend it from a Redstick siege, Cusseta Mico objected, refusing to "help the [council] chiefs" isolated there. Incensed, Tuskeenohau "reprimanded [Cusseta] Micco for his pusillanimous conduct" and overrode the mico's objection by leading his warriors to the endangered town. Timid conduct aside, Cusseta Mico affirmed his political connection to Tame King and, in the process, aided the Redstick militants by letting the council fend for itself. Other Lower Creeks, including members of Yuchi, backed the Redsticks too. Whether this town was among those where Cusseta Mico disseminated Tame King's overtures is unknown. Still, Cusseta and Yuchi shared kin ties dating to the middle of the eighteenth century, which suggests a possible collaboration between Cusseta Mico and the Yuchis. In short, the Cussetas did the heavy lifting for Tame King and his Redstick allies in Lower Creek country.[20]

Yet Tame King encountered resistance on the Chattahoochee. People in Cusseta and neighboring Coweta allied with Big Warrior and other council leaders. This meant that few Creek towns aligned exclusively with the Redsticks or the council; an either/or scenario of allegiance elides the messy political realities of civil war. The war leader Tuskeenohau is a case in point. His denunciation of Cusseta's mico opened a political wedge in town and presented Big Warrior with an opportunity to compete for Cusseta allies. Since Cusseta was one of the most populous towns in Creek country, Big Warrior desperately needed its warriors to defend the council from the Redsticks. He also sought allies from the esteemed town of Coweta, where the council had occasionally gathered before the war. To that end, he teamed up with Tuskeenohau and a Coweta headman named Atchau Haujo. These men served as his emissaries and in one case carried a message from the council to Tame King. They met their contact in Halfway House shortly before or on July 5 and implored the Redstick leader "to have [his] war sticks and projects thrown aside."[21]

Tame King predictably stayed the course. According to the Cusseta and Coweta emissaries who met with him, "the old man rejected" the peace overtures and "declared his determination to persevere until he destroyed all who [had] aided and assisted" Big Warrior in the council-led executions. The defiant headman referred to those Creeks who had participated in or condoned the executions "as people of the United States." In his rejoinder to the emissaries,

Tame King also shared the Redsticks' determination to march "to Ogeechee" and push "the white people' back to the "sea coast." This may have referred to a treaty signed nearly a century earlier, in 1739, codifying the original boundary between Creeks and Georgians. Since then, westward-moving Georgians and other whites had eroded the Creeks' domain. Tame King hoped "to crush" these Americans as well as the National Council.[22]

The Tame King–Big Warrior rift highlighted the dangers of political coordination during the Creek War. If Tame King leaned on Halfway House's relationship with Cusseta, Big Warrior countered by drafting members of Cusseta and Coweta. Yet the reliance on cross-provincial leadership drove a deeper wedge between Creeks, subverting the purpose of riverine power. In the past headmen ranging from Okfuskee Captain to Mad Dog had led political aggregates whose goal was peace and stability in the Creek world. Although these headmen fell prey to divisions that forced them to make last-minute alterations to their leadership, Creek politics had always been fractious and dependent on local currents from below. Riverine rulers expected and engaged with that tension. Seldom had this form of governance proved fatal, but the newfound culture of political violence reshaped politics, turning rivals into enemies, annoyances into altercations, and instability into incivility. Tame King and Big Warrior captured this tectonic shift in Creek country.

Tame King was the more effective leader of the pair, for he and other Redsticks outmaneuvered Big Warrior, who struggled to gain followers beyond Tuckabatchee, Coweta, and Cusseta by mid-1813. Alexander Cornells apprised Hawkins in late June that seven towns "nearest [Tuckabatchee] refused to oppose the prophets" and support Big Warrior. Hawkins recognized as much when he grumbled to Georgia governor David B. Mitchell that despite goading the council "to attack and destroy the prophets without delay," the headmen "seem not equal in their present state of alarm and confusion to such an enterprise." Although Big Warrior preferred words to bullets, few Creeks seemed interested in cooperating with him to eliminate the Redstick threat (with or without violence). Bereft of allies, Big Warrior lay helpless. The Redsticks moved to action on July 22, when as many as 320 of them besieged Tuckabatchee. The town had been palisaded in anticipation of the siege, which lasted one week. Of the hundreds of women, children, and men who huddled together in town, none died and "one woman [was] wounded, her arm broke." Thirteen Redsticks perished. In the aftermath, Big Warrior fled to Coweta, where he remained in the following months.[23]

Throughout late spring and summer 1813, the Redsticks gained momentum and marginalized Big Warrior, unable to cultivate more than a handful of allies beyond his town. By contrast, Tame King enlarged the Redstick base. He contacted allies in Cusseta and made new ones elsewhere on the Chattahoochee by touting the spiritual prowess of the Alabama prophets. From the Alabama towns on the west to the Lower Creek towns on the east, Tame King summoned partnerships far beyond his perch at Halfway House/Middle Town. The cross-provincial partnerships that he and other Redstick leaders pieced together fueled the Creek War, however, and heightened intratribal violence. Big Warrior, too, worsened this fatal development for his role in the springtime executions and by forging his own coalition meant to weaken the Redsticks. Ultimately, Redstick and council headmen in Upper Creek country repurposed riverine leadership as they encouraged people to unite against rather than with one another.

"The women hid the canoes": Undermining the Redsticks

As the Redsticks and the National Council maneuvered for political advantage, women did not sit idly by. According to Kathryn E. Holland Braund, one of few historians who has studied women's participation in the Creek War, they exercised "great power to shape opinion and influence events." While most contributed to the Redstick movement, some cast their lot with the National Council. They believed that the Redsticks' militant stance inched Creek country closer to war with the United States. Calculating that the insurgents posed a greater danger to Creek country than the council leadership, they devised ways to thwart the Redsticks. These women obstructed the Redsticks' mobility, gathered information about their strength and tactics, and sent news about their objectives to Big Warrior and Agent Hawkins. In short, they made critical decisions that affected the political and military dimensions of the war.[24]

The women who aligned with the National Council acted as unofficial diplomats. In that capacity, they sought to ensure the well-being of their relatives and towns, protect the land on which they grew crops and tended livestock, and empower council headmen to make informed decisions about the war. They were more than prepared to meet these challenges. Since sustained contact with colonial powers in the late seventeenth century, Creek women had attended European–Indian and intertribal councils, gaining experience in foreign affairs and learning how headmen conducted high-profile diplomacy. They had also prepared food for male emissaries and forged workable relationships with European and, later, American newcomers by marrying traders and other outsiders. Comfortable in multiple worlds and anxious to protect Creek livelihood, Upper Creek women mounted an appreciable, if limited, opposition to the Redsticks.[25]

Some tried to restrict the Redsticks' ability to move freely at the outset of the war. Around April 1813, the council's execution squad was hot on the trail of Redstick warriors who had recently attacked American settlements on the Ohio River. Squad members soon caught word that among those Redsticks, "one of the murderers, and his brother" were holed up in the Tallapoosa town of Hoithlewaulee. After arriving in town, the executioners killed one of the brothers. Assistant Agent Doyell learned from the mico of Hoithlewaulee that the surviving brother "got his gun and set out the morning after, to kill white people" in response. But women intervened. Doyell wrote, "The women hid the canoes" and obstructed the Redstick man's getaway. By hiding a major vehicle of waterborne transportation in early nineteenth-century Upper Creek country, the Hoithlewaulee women both limited the Redsticks' mobility and attempted to arrest Redstick warriors.[26]

The Redsticks soon captured Hoithlewaulee and set up encampments in and around the town. The camps sat astride the Tallapoosa River, supplying Redsticks with freshwater and a natural defense against US and council enemies. Redsticks there suffered from privation, however, as war disrupted the spring planting season, produced food shortages, and led Hawkins to stop the flow of trade goods to the Redsticks. As the Hoithlewaulee camps deteriorated, some Redsticks began to question their commitment to the movement. One such person was an unnamed woman who left the camps for the council, where she furnished intelligence to Big Warrior. On the evening of August 4, 1813, the headman apprised Hawkins of "a red woman of Ho,ith,le,wau,lee" who had come "strait from that Town" to inform on Redstick military strength. According to her report, Redstick leader and prophet Peter McQueen had secured "Ammunition" from Spanish Pensacola. Moreover, she told Big Warrior that she had seen the "scalps" of two white men "with her own eyes" before she left town.[27]

Although she failed to share her motivations, she may have resorted to espionage both to weaken the Redsticks at Hoithlewaulee and to preserve peace between the United States and her relatives, including her spouse. She was married to white trader "Hardy [Reed]." Like other intermarried traders, Reed joined his wife's clan upon marriage and incurred the expectation that he furnish his new wife and other affinal kin with affordable and abundant trade goods. Journal entries from Hawkins show that Reed had supplied Upper Creek towns like

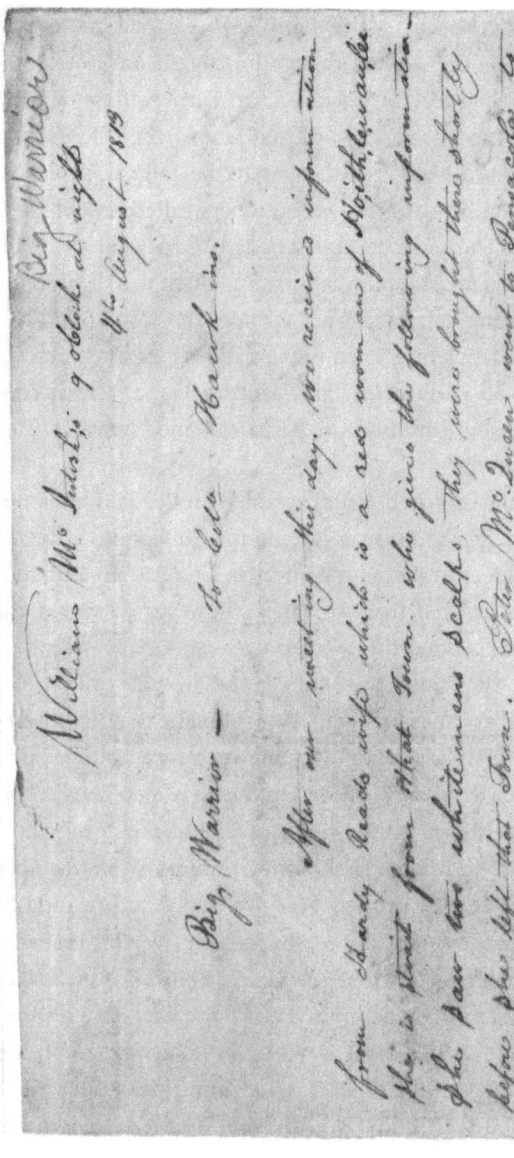

Report from "a red woman of Ho,ith,le,wau,lee," 1813

This "red woman of Ho,ith,le,wau,lee" so impressed Big Warrior with her knowledge about the Redsticks that he featured her in an address to US agent Benjamin Hawkins at the height of the Creek War. A woman like her coordinated efforts to limit civil strife, protect loved ones, and guard land from white Americans. Courtesy of Georgia Archives, File II Subjects, Folder: Indians—Creeks—Big Warrior, 1813.

Hoithlewaulee with goods since at least 1797. Bound by marriage to Reed, the Hoithlewaulee woman sought to maintain access to US wares by ensuring her husband's safety. Moreover, her actions suggest that she loved her husband and wanted to protect him from the Redsticks, who targeted Indian countrymen like him for execution. They considered him an interloper whose vendible goods symbolized Creek dependence on US colonialism.[28]

If evidence hints at the purpose of the Hoithlewaulee woman's report, other evidence reveals the method by which women collected information about the Redsticks. Creek women in Tallapoosa country engineered networks of communication to gather, examine, and swap knowledge about the militants. The wartime communication nodes activated by these women are illuminated by a dispatch that Hawkins received from a Creek man named Hoithleponiyau in August 1813. Hoithleponiyau explained to the agent that the Redsticks had marked for death all who had "assisted the Chiefs" in implementing the council's executions earlier that spring. He revealed that "My wife," who lived in Muccolossus, ' informed me" of those Redstick "plans." By sharing this vital information with her husband, the Muccolossus woman enabled Hawkins and the council to anticipate Redstick actions. She was also living proof that some Creeks favored a peaceful relationship with the United States.[29]

As peacekeepers, women along the Tallapoosa River produced and controlled networks of knowledge meant to counter the Redsticks. Historian Alejandra Dubcovsky has argued that southern Indians in the colonial era prized accurate information so as to shape regional developments. During the Creek War, similarly, Hoithleponiyau's wife stayed one step ahead of the Redsticks, managing the content and transmission of news about them. She probably understood that reliable information saved lives too. Since Hoithleponiyau's report to Hawkins implied a connection between the two men, she may have worried that the Redsticks would try to kill her husband for his complicity with the enemy. To spare him and possibly others from the Redsticks' wrath, she funneled news along the communication corridor that was the Tallapoosa valley.[30]

Further, the Muccolossus woman acted in concert with other like-minded women, for her report indicates that she positioned herself as a middleperson between her husband and a woman from the Alabama towns. She received the information reported to her husband "from a near female relative" of an elderly Alabama headman and Redstick prophet named Molton, who lived just downriver from Muccolossus. The Alabama woman may have been Molton's sister or niece. Although her agenda is difficult to confirm, she and her Tallapoosa counterparts must have opposed the Redstick movement and feared that the escalation of civil strife would cause the United States to grow increasingly nervous about the Redstick militants. For these reasons, she coordinated with the woman from Muccolossus in a fluid chain of communication.[31]

In league with Alabama women, then, Tallapoosa women undercut the Redstick movement to uphold peace with the Americans. They obtained and traded information about the Redsticks from the Alabamas, whose ties to the Tallapoosas had been strengthened by the late Singer and his recent partnership with Mad Dog and Big Warrior. In this way, Alabama and Tallapoosa women leveraged those preexisting ties in the attempt to cultivate peace in Upper Creek country. Yet evidence that suggests let alone confirms the involvement of Abeika women in these exchanges is scarce. The Abeika towns were beset by violence throughout spring and summer 1813, which may have diminished opportunities for Abeika women to collaborate with the more distant Tallapoosas and Alabamas. Hawkins reported in September, for example, that the Redsticks had recently killed "two distinguished Chiefs of Wewocau," bringing a fresh round of violence to Abeika country. Based on the extant documentation, Tallapoosa women engineered and led a rich communication nexus with support from Alabama women.[32]

Upper Creek women along the Tallapoosa corridor deftly navigated the vicissitudes of civil war. As diplomats in all but name, they tried to protect their communities from Redstick warriors as well as the specter of US soldiers. To ensure the livelihood of Creek country, they hindered Redstick mobility and collected intelligence about the opposition's leaders, supplies, and plans. Agent Hawkins, Big Warrior, and other council leaders were dependent on the bold actions of these women. While some hid vehicles, others shared knowledge directly with Big Warrior. Still others reported to husbands, who in turn put that information in the hands of the US agent. By charting a path of peace with the United States, Upper Creek women left an indelible mark on the Creek War.

"Conquered towns": US Invasion

Meanwhile, the Redsticks upped the ante. Sixty of them arrived in Spanish Pensacola in July 1813 to meet with Governor González Manrique. Led by the prophet Peter McQueen, they attempted to enlist Spanish support for the Redstick movement. The governor declined but did supply ammunition to his guests. On July 27, on their way home, the Redsticks made camp at Burnt

Corn Creek in Mississippi Territory. Suddenly, in the afternoon, 180 militiamen from the nearby Tensaw district opened fire on the encampment. The Tensaw assailants included white Americans and métis Creeks, who traced descent from European and Creek parentage. Many of these métis had migrated from Alabama towns to the Tensaw in the late eighteenth century and developed an economy inspired by the US civilization plan. Like their white neighbors, they practiced commercial agriculture and owned Black slaves. The Redsticks harbored a strong animus toward the Tensaw métis, deeming them cultural traitors, no better than headmen like Big Warrior. The Redsticks expressed no reservations about fighting the métis as well as whites at Burnt Corn Creek. Equipped with fresh ammunition, they inflicted a stunning victory, killing about one hundred white and métis militiamen. Only six Redsticks perished.[33]

According to Robert G. Thrower, historic preservation officer for the Poarch Band of Creek Indians in Alabama, Burnt Corn Creek was the "beginning of sorrows for the Creek Nation." This battle set off a chain reaction that ended in the Redsticks' defeat and the US conquest of the Upper Creeks. Emboldened by their victory, the Redsticks prepared to launch an assault on the Tensaw in August 1813. The Tensaw inhabitants responded by fleeing their homes and banding together in hastily erected stockades. Wealthy and retired trader Samuel Mims hosted one such stockade on his plantation. Known as Fort Mims, it sheltered roughly 440 settlers, soldiers, and métis Creeks. On August 30, the prophet Paddy Walsh and tactician William Weatherford besieged the fort with 726 Redsticks. By the afternoon, the Redsticks had killed 247 people. The Redsticks sustained the loss of three hundred men, however, making their victory a pyrrhic one.[34]

The Redstick attack on Fort Mims reverberated across the United States as the Fort Mims Massacre. Newspapers and other print media exaggerated the death toll, claiming that the Redsticks had slain as many as four hundred people. The propaganda slogan "Remember Fort Mims" became Americans' rallying cry. It blamed all Creeks, hostile or friendly to the United States, for the slaughter at Fort Mims and charged them with conspiracy to kill whites indiscriminately on the southern frontier. Few Creeks had participated in the August massacre, however, and those who did trained their sights primarily on métis Creeks and secondarily on white Americans. Still, southern planters, politicians, and military officers exploited Fort Mims to drum up support for the US invasion of Creek country. They reasoned that the invasion and assured conquest of Creek country would pave the way for a slave-based economy across the Deep South. The Creeks thus impeded white southerners' dreams of wealth and power. By fall, Georgia, Tennessee, and Mississippi Territory had organized three armies to spearhead the invasion. Tennessee planter and lawyer Andrew Jackson commanded his state's division as major general.[35]

Big Warrior responded to this frightening news by doubling down on peace with the United States. Although many Creeks had disavowed him in prior months, he garnered supporters from at least nine towns, including the Abeika towns of Okchai and Wewocau and the Lower Creek towns of Coweta and Cusseta. Headmen from these polities reminded Hawkins that at least some Creeks opposed the Redsticks. They argued that peaceable Creeks should not be punished for the Redsticks' actions and that US invasion would cause the destruction of innocent towns and the deaths of innocent people. One member of Big Warrior's peace coalition who adopted this outlook was Hoboheilthle Haujo of Fish Ponds, an Abeika town about thirty miles upstream from the deserted council headquarters in Tuckabatchee. After explaining in a message to the Redsticks that most of his "towns people . . . are determined not to kill red or white people," he forwarded it to Hawkins to demonstrate Creeks' peaceful intentions.[36]

Despite these measures, the United States invaded Upper Creek country with chilling ferocity. Composed of trained infantry, militiamen, and volunteers, the three US armies destroyed nearly twenty towns and talofas in the Redstick heartland from November 3, 1813, to March 23, 1814. During the same time frame and in the same area, US forces demolished hundreds of domiciles. In one day alone, on November 29, 1813, the invaders razed two hundred homes in the Tallapoosa town of Autossee and another two hundred in an "adjoining" town that harbored refugees. Nor were the nearby Alabamas spared. In late December, for example, soldiers destroyed two hundred houses in Holy Ground (Ecunchate), a Redstick base. Another twelve towns and talofas were abandoned from August 1813 to July 1814. A manifestation of ethnic cleansing, the destruction of Upper Creek country laid bare American colonial policy that called for the erasure of indigenous populations from the region. While the Redsticks had committed one massacre at Fort Mims, American military bodies waged a "total war" against the Upper Creeks, inflicting repeated massacres and gunning down hundreds.[37]

US soldiers won their first victory at the Abeika town of Tullushatchee on the upper Coosa. There, on November 3, 1813, soldiers under the command of General John Coffee killed every single Redstick in town. Days later the

Hillabees, in the midst of negotiations with General Jackson, were inexplicably mowed down in the Hillabee Massacre. The Creek War culminated at Tohopeka, anglicized as Horseshoe Bend, on March 27, 1814. This was a makeshift fortification and settlement located strategically on a wide bend in the upper Tallapoosa. One thousand Redsticks made a last stand from this riverine bastion. General Jackson attacked with fifteen hundred Americans and hundreds of Native auxiliaries, including five hundred Cherokees and one hundred Lower Creeks. His men overpowered the Redsticks. Eight hundred Redstick men, or less than one-tenth of the total Creek population, had lost their lives by the afternoon. Following the Battle of Tohopeka, American forces obliterated an additional twenty-one towns and talofas in cleanup operations between April 11 and May 3. By July, some eighty-two hundred refugees from what Hawkins called the "conquered towns" had flooded his agency on the Flint River with requests for rations. Upper Creek country lay in ruins.[38]

In August, General Jackson rubbed salt on the wounds by imposing a punitive treaty on the survivors At Fort Jackson, named in his honor, he met with Creek headmen near the junction of the Alabama, Coosa, and Tallapoosa Rivers. On August 9, Big Warrior and thirty-two other headmen signed the Treaty of Fort Jackson. An instrument of American conquest, it excused US actions by shifting blame onto the Redsticks. According to the treaty preamble, the "unprovoked, inhuman, and sanguinary war, waged by the hostile Creeks against the United States, hath been repelled . . . successfully [by] the said States." US forces had acted "in conformity with principles of national justice and honorable warfare." This sentiment trafficked in imperial fantasy, however, for American warfare had been anything but honorable and had claimed innocent Creeks who merely desired peace. If one side had been "inhuman" and "sanguinary," it was the Americans, not the Redsticks. Jackson paid little regard to these details. He tied the "conquest" of the Redsticks to American territorial and economic expansion. In the largest Native American land cession in US history, article 1 authorized the seizure of 21,086,793 acres from the Creeks. This land included two-thirds of the Creek domain, much of which belonged to Jackson's Lower Creek allies, and carved out modern-day Central Alabama, South Georgia, and North Florida.[39]

Unlike prior treaties between the Creeks and the United States, Fort Jackson was a treaty of conquest. The leadup to it illuminates the imperialist tactics of federal authorities. In June, for example, Tame King was held under guard at Fort Jackson, where he sustained unknown injuries. The esteemed riverine leader died on June 12 and was buried just north of the fort. Three days before the signing, moreover, Hawkins failed to announce the exact "line of conquest" to Big Warrior and the other treaty participants, suggesting that they approved a far larger cession than intended. Big Warrior had long feared this possibility. During the late war, Jackson had aggressively pressed for a cession, but Big Warrior declined until the leadership could discuss the matter "in our own minds" without the prying influence of federal authorities. Records indicate as well that the treaty negotiations had violated Creek protocol. Big Warrior complained to Hawkins that the "whole nation did not meet together to hear the treaty"; therefore headmen had never reached a consensus about whether to approve or reject Fort Jackson. Nor did the American commander host the conference in a town square ground, where leaders normally debated matters before the community. Instead, Jackson had forced Creek leaders to meet him "in the woods" away from community reach. All in all, Big Warrior recognized Fort Jackson for what it was: a land grab.[40]

Big Warrior's denunciation of this controversial treaty brings our story full circle. Like Singer, Tame King, Mortar, Okfuskee Captain, and others before him, he remained committed to protecting the provinces and the towns and clans bound by them. During one postwar conversation with Hawkins, he lamented the destruction of the Redsticks' "towns and many of their relations." Community and kin still animated this riverine leader and what remained of the Creek government. Yet he lived in a very different world than his predecessors. Never had Creeks experienced the sort of division occasioned by the Creek War, never had they suffered the kind of destruction caused by American invasion, and never had they faced so bleak and unknown a future in the Native South. The devastation visited upon the Abeikas, Tallapoosas, and Alabamas pushed the entire region in a new, more ominous direction.[41]

Big Warrior lived long enough to witness the Native South's transformation following US conquest. Fort Jackson unleashed social, economic, and political changes that expanded Anglo-American freedom, curtailed southern Indian autonomy, and entrenched Black slavery. As settlers invaded lands confiscated by treaty, they brought with them slaves and purchased new ones from the networks spun by the fledgling interstate slave trade. Plantation owners, farmers, and other settlers spread cotton cultivation across the region and deepened white southerners' control over slaves. Enslavement, profit, and white supremacy became the order of the day. The expansion of King Cotton in Georgia and Alabama (founded 1819) soon sparked a chorus of politicians, editors, settlers, and other white southerners to demand the forcible removal of southern Indians to areas west. In short, the treaty to which Big Warrior had been a reluctant party set the stage for the Indian Removal Act of 1830 and ethnic expulsion.[42]

Still, the road to Fort Jackson and beyond was a contested one. After Singer's assassination in the first decade of the nineteenth century, Upper Creek leaders put forward two competing political visions. One called for the excision of American influence in Creek society, and the other promoted careful alignment with the Americans. Tame King of Halfway House and Big Warrior of Tuckabatchee stood on opposing sides, but they cultivated similar rulership styles that advanced Creek unity while staying aware of kin needs. Indeed, the crisis of this era led both headmen to envision larger kinship formations that intertwined their own kin with those of other Creeks and neighboring indigenous populations. They absorbed the bottom-up pressures exerted by women, warriors, and other local peoples. But the Creek War and subsequent US invasion exposed the liability of riverine leadership at a time of immeasurable chaos. By summer 1813, Tame King and Big Warrior pursued moments of unity that unexpectedly sharpened civil discord among Creeks. Women attempted to prevent the downward spiral, but neither they nor aligned leaders found ways to keep peace with the United States after Fort Mims. The Americans ran roughshod over the creative energies of the male leadership and the influences of Creeks on the ground. The possibility of an autonomous "four rivers" yielded to the reality of American empire.[43]

Conclusion

From Water to Sand

Rivers of Power has traced Creek Indian leadership in the long eighteenth century. It has argued that Creek rivers furnished the conceptual basis on which Creeks engineered power, practiced politics, and asserted autonomy. The riverine system of governance lent flexibility to leaders and preserved influence among local actors, including headmen's relatives, who kept them in check. The impact of the Creek political system was enormous. It generated situations that stymied nation-building and a national leadership structure; propelled cross-town connections within and across provinces designed to curb war, seek trade, and defend land; and ensured that women, children, warriors, and other local Creeks shaped the thoughts, language, and actions of the male leadership. The ingenuity of Creek politics rested on its flexibility. Headmen ranging from Okfuskee Captain and Tame King to Singer and Big Warrior authored coalitions that bent to the Creeks' immediate needs and circumstances. Political adaptability eclipsed political rigidity time and again. While clans and towns remain essential categories of political analysis, it is important to recognize that they belonged (and belong) to larger political formations that point up alternatives to indigenous nationhood. The province or subregional unit is a useful path forward.

When Big Warrior talked about "the four rivers" in his 1809 talk to Path Killer, he explained Creek political culture to his recipient then and scholars today. Each of the four Creek rivers housed a unique mixture of clans and towns and carried a political identity as Abeika, Tallapoosa, Alabama, or Lower Creek. Big Warrior understood, however, that these units neither existed in isolation nor tackled foreign affairs alone. He witnessed, for instance, the coordination among Singer, Mad Dog, and other Creek leaders at the fateful Hickory Ground council. Creek political coordination had its roots in the previous century.

After 1750, Okfuskee Captain represented the Abeikas and Tallapoosas in the resolution of the Creek-Cherokee War and the reduction of tensions with the expanding British Empire. Abeika–Tallapoosa ties strengthened as Mortar and Emistisiguo killed Choctaws and made peace with them on the eve of American independence. The crises unleashed by the birth of the US empire-republic in turn brought Cusseta into the Abeika–Tallapoosa network. Tame King and later Mad Dog massaged relations with that great peace town on the waters of the middle Chattahoochee River. For years headmen from "three rivers" promoted diplomacy with the United States and the Chickasaws. At the turn of the nineteenth century, the Creeks' political brand shifted once again to foster stronger Alabama inclusion. An equal participant of the "four rivers," Alabamas illuminated both the possibility of indigenous independence and the danger of rulership in the face of US expansion.[1]

This book's historical narrative is bound up in the world of rivers that inspired power in Creek country. It takes seriously Creek actions, words, thoughts, perspectives, and ideologies that articulate how Native peoples themselves conceptualized leadership and addressed crisis. The Abeikas and Tallapoosas were the anchor for this ethno-ethnohistorical approach to Creek politics They reeled from the acceleration of settler invasion, the deepening of trade dependence and financial crisis, and the multiplication of land cession treaties after 1750. Their political and territorial autonomy gradually eroded because of these trends. European colonists and American citizens appear only gradually and episodically in this narrative, however, for Abeikas and Tallapoosas expressed more concern about and devoted more energy to other indigenous people. War with the Cherokees, Choctaws, Chickasaws, and finally one another claimed lives, produced grief, and busied leaders. So too did the formation, growth, and breakdown of alliances with these same groups, as well as the Seminoles, over whom leaders such as Mad Dog asserted power. More histories of the early modern Native South must include these intertribal and intratribal coalescences, fractures, and shifts.[2]

Local peoples animate this political history. Beyond the pale of formal leadership, they ranged from women and children to warriors and elders. They shaped the male leadership in innumerable ways and with a creativity that deserves sustained scholarly attention. Acting alone or in common, local Creeks undermined leaders by exacting retaliation, burning captives, and securing booty; defied leaders by ignoring unpopular mandates; assisted leaders by directly and indirectly encouraging peace with enemies, both domestic and foreign; and otherwise policed community interests with kin and other people in mind. The evidence demonstrates, in short, that these Creeks so exercised a check on the leadership that they constituted a kind of leadership in their own right. Whether they spied on the Redsticks for Big Warrior or dragged Mortar into renewed war with the Choctaws, women and men forced leaders to recognize and respond to their agency. Central to this argument is a dialogue with anthropologist Vernon James Knight. He asserts that Creek clanship may have been more capacious than scholars recognize. That assertion, coupled with documentary evidence analyzed in this book, suggests that Creeks practiced bilateral kinship reckoning by the eighteenth century. Clanship was a potent political medium that ensured local actors' relevance in the politics of the Native South. At different times and for different reasons, they protected clan interests by killing some, making peace with others, and signaling agendas to still others. Leaders maintained legitimacy only if they absorbed relatives' needs and wants.[3]

On December 6, 1835, 511 Creeks departed the state of Alabama for a new home in Indian Territory. Congress had established this jurisdiction one year earlier for southern Indians expelled from their homelands in the East. The Creeks who left their home in December 1835 belonged to Cusseta, Tame King's old allied town, and possibly other Lower Creek towns. They reached their destination at Fort Gibson on February 2, 1836. While the journey onboard the steamer *Alpha* and two keel boats proved uneventful, sand marred the travelers' progress on the Arkansas River. Lieutenant Edward Deas, the disbursement agent, complained of a "sand-bar" on January 13, another "Sand-Bar" on January 15, and yet "another Sand-Bar" on January 19. As he grumbled on the January 20, "This River at low water is obstructed by numerous [sand]Bars which are constantly changing." Still another sandbar impeded travel two days later. An Ohio-born businessman named John Hewitt Jones, who traveled with the party, later recalled that near Little Rock, one of the keel boats ran aground "on a sand bar (for [there] are plenty in that river)." Following the disastrous Creek War of 1836, thousands more Creeks arrived in Indian Territory, where water was scarcer than back home. Moving west, they found that rivers of water turned to rivers of sand.[4]

Abbreviations

AHM	*American Historical Magazine.* Digital copies.
ASP/IA	Lowrie, Walter, and Matthew St. Clair Clarke, eds. *American State Papers: Class II, Indian Affairs.* 2 vols. Washington, DC: Gales and Seaton, 1832–34.
Ayer	Edward E. Ayer Manuscript Collection. MSS 797 and 926. Newberry Library, Chicago.
Bartram	Gregory A. Waselkov and Kathryn E. Holland Braund, eds. *William Bartram on the Southeastern Indians.* Lincoln: University of Nebraska Press, 1995.
BMAM	British Museum Additional Manuscripts, no. 21671 Parts 1–4. Library of Congress. Photostats.
CO5	Records of the British Colonial Office. Class 5 Files. Part 1, Westward Expansion, 1700–1783. Edited by Randolph Boehm. University Publications of America, Frederick, MD, 1983. Microfilm.
CRSC I	McDowell, William L. *Colonial Records of South Carolina: Documents Relating to Indian Affairs, May 21, 1750–August 7, 1754.* 1958. Reprint, Columbia: South Carolina Department of Archives and History, 1992.
CRSC II	*Colonial Records of South Carolina: Documents Relating to Indian Affairs, 1754–1765.* 1970. Reprint, Columbia: South Carolina Department of Archives and History, 1992.
CWBH	Foster, Thomas, ed. *The Collected Works of Benjamin Hawkins, 1796–1810.* Tuscaloosa: University of Alabama Press, 2003.
DAR	Davies, K. G., ed. *Documents of the American Revolution, 1770–1783.* 21 vols. Shannon: Irish University Press, 1972–81.

EAID   Vaughan, Alden T., ed. *Early American Indian Documents, 1607–1789.* Vols 11–12, 18. Bethesda: University Publications of America, 1989–2004.
ETHS   Corbitt, D. C., and Roberta Corbitt, eds. "Papers from the Spanish Archives Relating to Tennessee and the Old Southwest, 1783–1800." East Tennessee Historical Society Publications 9–49 (1937–77).
GA/File II Georgia Archives. File II. Reference Services. RG 4-2-46. Original manuscripts and digitized records.
GGL   George Galphin Letters, 1778–80. Edward E. Ayer Manuscript Collection. MS 313. Newberry Library, Chicago.
GHQ   Corbitt, D. C., ed. "Papers Relating to the Georgia-Florida Frontier, 1784–1800." *Georgia Historical Quarterly* nos. 19–25 (1935–41).
IALT   Kappler, Charles J., ed. *Indian Affairs: Laws and Treaties.* Vol. 2. Washington, DC: Government Printing Office, 1904.
LBH   Grant, C. L., *Letters, Journals and Writings of Benjamin Hawkins.* 2 vols. Savannah: Beehive Press, 1980.
OSW/LR   Letters Received by the Office of the Secretary of War Relating to Indian Affairs, 1800–23. National Archives Microfilm Publications, roll 1 (1800–16), folder 1811, microcopy 271. National Archives and Records Service, Washington, DC, 1959.
PPLC   The Indian Trade in the Southeastern Spanish Borderlands: Papers of Panton, Leslie and Company. University of West Florida. Archives Unbound.
Rubenstein David M. Rubenstein Rare Book and Manuscript Library. Duke University, Durham, NC.
SMV   Kinnaird, Lawrence, ed. *Spain in the Mississippi Valley, 1765–1794, Parts I–III.* Vols. 2–4. Washington, DC: Government Printing Office, 1946–49.
SNAD   Southeastern Native American Documents, 1730–1842. Digital Library of Georgia. http://dlg.galileo.usg.edu.
TGP   Thomas Gage Papers, 1754–1807. American Series. Volume 98. November 12–December 13, 1770. William L. Clements Library, University of Michigan, Ann Arbor.

TSRO	Carter, Clarence Edwin, ed. *The Territory South of the River Ohio, 1790–1796*. Vol. 4 of *The Territorial Papers of the United States*. Washington, DC: Government Printing Office, 1936.
WHLP	William Henry Lyttelton Papers, 1755–61. Series I: Correspondence and Documents. William L. Clements Library, University of Michigan, Ann Arbor.

Notes

Acknowledgments

1. Document 1, "Camp at Cedar Creek," 7/7/1759, p. 4 ("I"), enclosed in Edmond Atkin to William Henry Lyttelton, Okfuskee, 11/30/1759, box 13, in WHLP.

Introduction

1. Big Warrior, "Chief and Warrior of the Creek nation," to "Path maker [Path Killer], Chief of the Cherokee," 5/1[?]/1809, Tuckabatchee, in OSW/LR, frame 620 (quotes). Alexander Cornells, who lived in Big Warrior's town, recorded this talk before sending it to Path Killer. Southern Indians referred to written messages as "talks" to underscore both the verbal and sacred dimensions of interpersonal communication. See, for example, Clara Sue Kidwell and Alan Velie, *Native American Studies* (Lincoln: University of Nebraska Press, 2005), 31–35, and Alejandra Dubcovsky, *Informed Power: Communication in the Early American South* (Cambridge, MA: Harvard University Press, 2016), 3–8. On the Eagle clan, see US agent Benjamin Hawkins, "A sketch of the Creek Country in the years 1798 and 1799," in LBH, 1:285–327, here 318.

2. This book is about politics, not rivers, but it echoes early modern indigenous thought by arguing that rivers served as a conceptual device for Creek leaders. Other works bring the South's rivers into focus. Harvey H. Jackson III, *Rivers of History: Life on the Coosa, Tallapoosa, Cahaba, and Alabama* (Tuscaloosa: University of Alabama Press, 1995) is an exhaustive study of the environmental, social, and political history of rivers that shaped the South from the Mississippian era to the formation of the state of Alabama in the nineteenth century. In *Creek Paths and Federal Roads: Indians, Settlers, and Slaves and the Making of the American South* (Chapel Hill: University of North Carolina Press, 2010), especially 5–6, 81–82, and 103–5, Angela Pulley Hudson studies the roads and rivers of Creek country to trace the relationship between territoriality and politics. Specifically, she looks at how Creeks sought to preserve their autonomy by contesting American settlers' use of Creek paths in the early 1800s. On "Indian cores," see Juliana Barr and Edward Countryman, "Introduction: Maps and Spaces, Paths to Connect, Lines to Divide," in *Contested Spaces of Early America*, ed. Juliana Barr and Edward Countryman (Philadelphia: University of Pennsylvania Press, 2014), 1–28, here 24. For "four," see Big Warrior to Path Killer, 5/1[?]/1809, in OSW/LR, frame 620.

3. Adair referred to the Tallapoosa River as the "Okwhuske [Okfuskee]," a reflection of that's town prominence in the eighteenth century. See James Adair, *The History of the American Indians*, ed. Kathryn E. Holland Braund (Tuscaloosa: University of Alabama Press, 2005), 273 (quotes). Prompted by Spanish invasion and a strengthening Indian slave trade, Lower Creeks and other Indians migrated to the Oconee–Ocmulgee watershed beginning in 1690. The principal settlement of the Lower Creeks was at "Ochese Creek," a name the British gave to a branch of the Ocmulgee. By 1716, most Lower Creeks had returned to their former homes along the Chattahoochee. On this temporary migration, see Steven C. Hahn, *The Invention of the Creek Nation, 1670–1763* (Lincoln: University of Nebraska Press, 2004), 50–52, 90–92; Kathryn E. Holland Braund, *Deerskins and Duffels: The Creek Indian Trade with Anglo-America, 1685–1815* (1993; repr., Lincoln: University of Nebraska Press, 2008), 4; and "Observations on the Creek and Cherokee Indians," in Bartram, 139–41.

4. Adair, *History of the American Indians*, 247 ("natives"), 153 ("emblem," "along," "holy"), 154 ("purified," "joyful"), 160–61; Charles Hudson, *The Southeastern Indians* (Knoxville: University of Tennessee Press, 1976), 321–25; Jack B. Martin and Margaret McKane Mauldin, *A Dictionary of Creek/Muskogee* (Lincoln: University of Nebraska Press, 2000), 100 (*posketv/posk-itá*). The Busk's daily format varied by town; see John R. Swanton, *Creek Religion and Medicine* (1928; repr., Lincoln: University of Nebraska Press, 2000), 546–614.

5. "Travels Through North & South Carolina, Georgia, East & West Florida, the Cherokee Country, the Extensive Territories of the Muscogulges, or Creek Confederacy, and the Country of the Chactaws; Containing an Account of the Soil and Natural Productions of Those Regions, Together with Observations on the Manners of the Indians," in Bartram, 42 (first account), 233n17; "Observations," in Bartram, 140 (second account), 268n3. On the importance of lakes, oceans, and other large bodies of water in Creek culture, see Bill Grantham, *Creation Myths and Legends of the Creek Indians* (Gainesville: University Press of Florida, 2002), especially 117, 134–36. On Creek creation stories, see Gregory D. Smithers, *Native Southerners: Indigenous History from Origins to Removal* (Norman: University of Oklahoma Press, 2019), 18–19.

6. Arrows could be fashioned from wetland bushes (*ue-akroswv*). For water-laden terms, see Martin and Mauldin, *Dictionary*, 57, 127–28. On the Tie-Snake, see John R. Swanton, *Myths and Tales of the Southeastern Indians* (Norman: University of Oklahoma Press, 1995), 34–36, and Hudson, *Southeastern Indians*, 130–32. On nineteenth-century missionaries, see Claudio Saunt, *Black, White, and Indian: Race and the Unmaking of an American Family* (Oxford: Oxford University Press, 2005), 18–19, and Gary Zellar, *African Creeks: Estelvste and the Creek Nation* (Norman: University of Oklahoma Press, 2007), 10–40.

7. Document 1, 7/9/1759, Tuckabatchee, p. 12 (quotes), in Edmond Atkin to William Henry Lyttelton, 11/30/1759, box 13, in WHLP; Hudson, *Southeastern Indians*, 313–16.

8. Creek Indian studies is a vast and vibrant subfield of the Native South that involves anthropologists, ethnohistorians, and other researchers. My book cannot engage with all who have published on the Creeks, but my focus on Creek governance allows me to speak to a precise body of scholarship. Regarding the eighteenth century, Joshua Piker argues that headmen built multitown coalitions within a framework of town-based localism, while Steven Hahn similarly traces "acts of confederation" that stimulated nation-building among otherwise local communities. More recently, Joshua Haynes contends

that localized warriors defended a national border from the expansionist United States late in the century, but Kevin Kokomoor goes further by asserting that headmen in the National Council implemented a coercive strain of national leadership to defend land from the United States. James L. Hill, finally, searches for common ground by arguing that Creek diplomacy was a reflection of newfound centralization and persistent localism. See Joshua Piker, *Okfuskee: A Creek Indian Town in Colonial America* (Cambridge, MA: Harvard University Press, 2004), Joshua Piker, *The Four Deaths of Acorn Whistler: Telling Stories in Colonial America* (Cambridge, MA: Harvard University Press, 2013); Joshua Piker, "'White & Clean' and Contested: Creek Towns and Trading Paths in the Aftermath of the Seven Years' War," *Ethnohistory* 50, no. 2 (Spring 2003): 315–47; Hahn, *Invention*, 7 ("acts"); Joshua S Haynes, *Patrolling the Border: Theft and Violence on the Creek-Georgia Frontier, 1770–1796* (Athens: University of Georgia Press, 2018); Kevin Kokomoor, *Of One Mind and of One Government: The Rise and Fall of the Creek Nation in the Early Republic* (Lincoln: University of Nebraska Press and American Philosophical Society, 2018); James L. Hill, *Creek Internationalism in an Age of Revolution, 1763–1818* (Lincoln: University of Nebraska Press, 2022).

These works belong to a larger body of scholarship on Creek history. For analyses of Creek localism, the work of Hahn and Piker should be read alongside Robbie Ethridge, *Creek Country: The Creek Indians and Their World* (Chapel Hill: University of North Carolina Press, 2003). Moreover, Haynes supports the concept of territoriality and incipient nationhood probed in Hudson, *Creek Paths*. Regarding nation-building, Kokomoor should be paired with Claudio Saunt, *A New Order of Things: Property, Power, and the Transformation of the Creek Indians, 1733–1816* (Cambridge: Cambridge University Press, 1999), which first suggested that Creek headmen had devised more coercive forms of leadership by the early nineteenth century, and Evan Nooe, "Common Justice: Vengeance and Retribution in Creek Country," *Ethnohistory* 62, no. 2 (April 2015): 241–61, which examines how the National Council's violation of clan custom sparked the Creek War in 1813. Likewise, Kokomoor explores cooperation between Creek national leaders and federal agents in the 1790s, a pivotal decade in southern history, in "Creeks, Federalists, and the Idea of Coexistence in the Early Republic," *Journal of Southern History* 81, no. 4 (November 2015): 803–42.

Two foundational works on Creek history are David H. Corkran, *The Creek Frontier: 1540–1783* (Norman: University of Oklahoma Press, 1967) and Michael D. Green, *The Politics of Indian Removal: Creek Government and Society in Crisis* (Lincoln: University of Nebraska Press, 1982). Similar to Corkran, Green demonstrated that Creek divisions stemming from local patterns of governance weakened political unity during key historical moments. For other early works on Creek localism, see Hudson, *Southeastern Indians*, especially 202–22; Duane Champagne, *Social Order and Political Change: Constitutional Governments among the Cherokee, the Choctaw, the Chickasaw, and the Creek* (Stanford, CA: Stanford University Press, 1992); and Braund, *Deerskins*.

For other, more recent studies of Creek localism, see Bryan C. Rindfleisch, "The 'Owner of the Town Ground, Who Overrules All When on the Spot': Escotchaby of Coweta and the Politics of Personal Networking in Creek Country, 1740–1780," *Native South* 9 (2016): 54–88, and Steven J. Peach, "The Failure of Political Centralization: Mad Dog, the Creek Indians, and the Politics of Claiming Power in the American Revolutionary Era," *Native South* 11 (2018): 81–116. Bryan C. Rindfleisch, *George Galphin's Intimate Empire: The Creek Indians, Family, and Colonialism in Early America* (Tuscaloosa:

University of Alabama Press, 2019) digs into the Creeks' local world and retrieves those individual relationships that shaped decision-making in the early American South and Atlantic world. A local framework of politics also conditions John T. Juricek's wonderful syntheses on Creek diplomacy in *Colonial Georgia and the Creeks: Anglo-Indian Diplomacy on the Southern Frontier, 1733–1763* (Gainesville: University Press of Florida, 2010) and *Endgame for Empire: British-Creek Relations in Georgia and Vicinity, 1763–1776* (Gainesville: University Press of Florida, 2015).

9. While Upper Creek riverine language is ubiquitous in the records and deserves sustained inquiry, Abeika and Tallapoosa leaders exercised no monopoly on these terms. For one Lower Creek reference to riverine divisions, see Malatchi of Coweta to South Carolina governor James Glen, 5/31/1753, "Thursday A.M.," Proceedings of the Council Concerning Indian Affairs, in CRSC I, 394. For in-text quotes, see Big Warrior to Path Killer, 5/1[?]/1809, in OSW/LR, frame 620 ("four," "rivers"); "Old Tallassee King's Son" to the commissioners of Georgia, 6/18/1777, in EAID, 18:223 ("Three"); document 1, "Camp at Cedar Creek," 7/7/1759, p. 4 ("Abehkas"), enclosed in Edmond Atkin to William Henry Lyttelton, Okfuskee, 11/30/1759, box 13, in WHLP; Red Coat King to Glen, 7/26/1753, in CRSC I, 380 ("Upper").

10. Red Coat King to Glen, 7/26/1753, in CRSC I, 380 ("Upper"); document 1, "Camp at Cedar Creek," 7/7/1759, p. 4 ("Abehkas," "Tallapoosas"), enclosed in Atkin to Lyttelton, 11/30/1759, box 13, in WHLP; Piker, "'White & Clean' and Contested," 318–19; Braund, *Deerskins*, 6–7.

11. I thank Robbie Ethridge for sharing her forthcoming article entitled "The Origins and Coalescence of the Creek (Muscogee) Confederacy: A New Synthesis," in *Studies in Eighteenth-Century Culture* 52 (2023): 113–31, here 116, 123–24. On Okfuskee, see Piker, *Okfuskee*, 7, 10 (quotes). Readers may accuse me of splitting historiographical hairs, but the distinction between town-based and provincial organization is important enough to merit extended analysis. I thank my readers for pressing me on this interpretive issue.

12. Raymond D. Fogelson, "The Ethnohistory of Events and Non-Events," *Ethnohistory* 36, no. 2 (Spring 1989): 133–47, here 134–35. For a volume dedicated to Fogelson's work in Native American anthropology and ethnohistory, see Sergei A. Kan and Pauline Turner Strong, "Introduction," *New Perspectives on Native North America: Cultures, Histories, and Representations*, ed. Sergei A. Kan and Pauline Turner Strong (Lincoln: University of Nebraska Press, 2006): xi–xlii. A former student of Fogelson's at the University of Chicago, Jennifer S. H. Brown applies an ethno-ethnohistorical method in "Fields of Dreams: Revisiting A. I. Hallowell and the Berens River Ojibwe," in Kan and Strong, *New Perspectives*, 17–41, especially 35–38. Based on fieldwork and textual analysis, she contends that dreams are central to how Ojibwes conceptualize and understand their history. Indeed, for Ojibwe people, dreams collapse Western distinctions between past and present. For a Cherokee-centered interpretation of Cherokee politics in the eighteenth century, see Tyler Boulware, *Deconstructing the Cherokee Nation: Town, Region, and Nation among Eighteenth-Century Cherokees* (Gainesville: University Press of Florida, 2011). Smithers, *Native Southerners*, 3–11, roots the South's vibrant history in indigenous perspectives as well.

13. Big Warrior to Path Killer, 5/1[?]/1809, in OSW/LR, frame 620 ("four," "Creek"); Emistisiguo to Charles Stuart, enclosed in John Stuart to Gage, 12/13/1770, TGP ("Abekas," "Tallapousses"); Red Coat King to Glen, 7/26/1753, in CRSC I, 380 ("Upper").

On the need to revise "tribal" studies in the Native South, see Piker, "'White & Clean' and Contested," 319-21, 332-33; Hahn, *Invention*, 5; and Claudio Saunt, "The Native South: An Account of Recent Historiography," *Native South* 1 (2008): 45-60, here 45-49. The best study on the Creek National Council is Kokomoor, *Of One Mind*, especially 18-23, 215-329. On indigenous nationhood and indigenous national identity formation in the eighteenth- and early nineteenth-century South, see Haynes, *Patrolling the Border*, especially 130-34, and Boulware, *Deconstructing the Cherokee Nation*, 2-7, 179-182.

14. On women's influence in Creek and southern Indian history, see Hudson, *Southeastern Indians*, 190-91, 196-202, and Theda Perdue, "Writing the Ethnohistory of Native Women," in *Rethinking American Indian History*, ed. Donald L. Fixico (Albuquerque: University of New Mexico Press, 1997): 73-86, here 81-83; and Bryan C. Rindfleisch, *Brothers of Coweta: Kinship, Empire, and Revolution in the Eighteenth-Century Muscogee World* (Columbia: University of South Carolina Press, 2021), 29-30, 40-41.

15. Although women were not leaders in a formal sense, they were active political agents. This point draws on a rich body of scholarship that traces the ways southern Indian women blunted the impact of European and American colonialism in the eighteenth and nineteenth centuries. For a sampling of this literature, see Jean Chaudhuri and Joyotpaul Chaudhuri, *A Sacred Path: The Way of the Muscogee Creeks* (Los Angeles: UCLA American Indian Studies Center, 2001), 26 ("female," "corn," "rivers"), 186-87; Hudson, *Southeastern Indians*, 190-91, 196-202; Perdue, "Writing the Ethnohistory of Native Women," 73-86, here 81-83; Smithers, *Native Southerners*, 47; and Rindfleisch, *Brothers of Coweta*, 29-30, 40-41. For a useful overview of kinship and gender, see Jay Miller, "Kinship, Family Kindreds, and Community," in *A Companion to American Indian History*, ed. Philip J. Deloria and Neal Salisbury (Malden, MA: Blackwell Publishing, 2002): 139-53, here 139-41, 150. On the related concept of balance among southern Indians, see Hudson, *Southeastern Indians*, 317-18, 336, and Chaudhuri and Chaudhuri, *Sacred Path*, 23-27, 48.

16. One notable exception is an article-length study of Creek-Cherokee ties by Bryan C. Rindfleisch, "Cherokee Kings and Creek Kings: Intra-Indigenous Connections and Interactions in the Eighteenth-Century American South," *Journal of Southern History* 85, no. 4 (November 2019): 769-802, here 771-73, 776-78, 802. On Creek kin in European-Indian relations, see Piker, *Okfuskee*, 115-18, 165-76, and *Four Deaths*, 134-38, 158-59; David Andrew Nichols, *Red Gentlemen and White Savages: Indians, Federalists, and the Search for Order on the American Frontier* (Charlottesville: University of Virginia Press, 2008), 3-16, 44-54, 106-13, 176-89; Natalie R. Inman, *Brothers and Friends: Kinship in Early America* (Athens: University of Georgia Press, 2017), especially 2-9, 15-33; Rindfleisch, "'Owner of the Town Ground,'" 61-63; Peach, "Failure of Political Centralization," 35-86, 92-98; Vernon James Knight, "Puzzles of Creek Social Organization in the Eighteenth and Nineteenth Centuries," *Ethnohistory* 65, no. 3 (July 2018): 378 (quotes); Rindfleisch, *George Galphin's Intimate Empire*, 105-25; Smithers, *Native Southerners*, 78-105; Rindfleisch, *Brothers of Coweta*, 17-19. On kin in other southern Indian populations, see Greg O'Brien, "The Conqueror Meets the Unconquered: Negotiating Cultural Boundaries on the Post-Revolutionary Southern Frontier," *Journal of Southern History* 67, no. 1 (February 2001): 39-72, here 51, 55, 59; Michelle LeMaster, *Brothers Born of One Mother: British-Native American Relations in the Colonial Southeast* (Charlottesville: University of Virginia Press, 2012), 15-50.

For comparable studies of the Native Southwest, readers should consult James Brooks, *Captives and Cousins: Slavery, Kinship, and Community in the Southwest Borderlands* (Chapel Hill: University of North Carolina Press, 2002), 228–34 and passim; and Juliana Barr, *Peace Came in the Form of a Woman: Indians and Spaniards in the Texas Borderlands* (Chapel Hill: University of North Carolina Press, 2007), 27–108.

17. Knight, "Puzzles," 373–89, here 378–79; Haynes, *Patrolling the Border*, 17–21; Ethridge, "Origins and Coalescence," 113 ("coalescent") and passim. Knight interrogates anthropologist John R. Swanton's early twentieth-century publications on which later scholars' understanding of matrilineal clans is based. Knight argues that Swanton's use of "phratries" actually refers to lineage aggregates, which included those related by kinship affiliation and "circumstantial or traditional association" (379). I recognize that my focus on kinship excludes other sodalities that shaped Creek leaders, such as ethnic divisions and trade factions. By isolating kinship as an important political variable, however, I can study precise moments when leaders reacted to on-the-ground situations, contribute to a busy historiography on kinship in the Native South, and improve narrative coherence.

18. On kinship among Lower Creeks, see Rindfleisch, *Brothers of Coweta*, especially 17–19, 129nn9–11. While I agree with Rindfleisch that clans (as well as towns) were the foundation of Creek power, I argue that power stemmed specifically from a headman's lineage, other lineages, and ill-defined interest groups and individuals whose identities are difficult to pinpoint in the records but who nonetheless conditioned leaders. For a related study on kinship among the Cherokees and Chickasaws, see Inman, *Brothers and Friends*.

19. On Galphin, see Rindfleisch, *George Galphin's Intimate Empire*, 11–15, 27–48. Both Robbie Ethridge (Zoom conversation with author, October 11, 2022) and Gregory Waselkov, who read an earlier version of this manuscript, have stoked my thinking about bilateral kinship. Increasingly I find myself unable to reconcile the widespread scholarly use of colonial authors ranging from Galphin to Adair with a selective dismissal of those same authors' ethnographic observations. The criticism that European and US authorities failed to grasp indigenous kinship patterns falls flat when those same authors are consulted about other topics, such as indigenous politics, warfare, trade, and religion.

20. Eric R. Wolf, *Envisioning Power: Ideologies of Dominance and Crisis* (Berkeley: University of California Press, 1999), ix, 5 ("relational," "interdependent"), 1–8, and 69–196. Wolf examines how ideologies of dominance, especially national socialism, spurred violence and war across the globe in the twentieth century. Two of his case studies pinpoint indigenous people in North America, bringing into focus Aztec sacrificial rites and Northwest Coast potlatch ceremonialism. I have explored this conception of power by drawing attention to Mad Dog, a headman of the Tallapoosa town of Tuckabatchee in the eighteenth century, in "Failure of Political Centralization," 83. On power, authority, and legitimacy among other southern Indian leaders, see O'Brien, *Choctaws*, xxiv–xxvii, 1–3, and Dubcovsky, *Informed Power*, 3–8, 128–55.

21. On political contestation in the Native South, see Gene Allen Smith and Sylvia L. Hilton, "Introduction," in *Nexus of Empire: Negotiating Loyalty and Identity in the Revolutionary Borderlands, 1760s–1820s*, ed. Gene Allen Smith and Sylvia L. Hilton (Gainesville: University Press of Florida, 2010): 3–7, here 5 ("remained," "political");

David Andrew Nichols, *Red Gentlemen*, 80 ("set") and *Engines of Diplomacy: Indian Trading Factories and the Negotiation of American Empire* (Chapel Hill: University of North Carolina Press, 2016); Alan Taylor, "Remaking Americans: Louisiana, Upper Canada, and Texas," 208–226, and Pekka Hämäläinen, "The Shapes of Power: Indians, Europeans, and North American Worlds from the Seventeenth to the Nineteenth Century," 31–68 (both in Barr and Countryman, *Contested Spaces*); Kathleen DuVal, *Independence Lost: Lives on the Edge of the American Revolution* (New York: Random House, 2015); David Narrett, *Adventurism and Empire: The Struggle for Mastery in the Louisiana-Florida Borderlands, 1762–1803* (Chapel Hill: University of North Carolina Press, 2015), 3–8; Rindfleisch, *George Galphin's Intimate Empire*, 15 ("negotiated '"); and Daniel S. Dupre, *Alabama's Frontiers and the Rise of the Old South* (Bloomington: Indiana University Press, 2018), 3 ("once").

22. Document 1, "Camp at Cedar Creek," 7/7/1759, p. 4 ("Abehkas"), enclosed in Edmond Atkin to William Henry Lyttelton, Okfuskee, 11/30/1759, box 13, in WHLP; Alan Gallay, *The Indian Slave Trade: The Rise of the British Empire in the American South, 1670–1717* (New Haven, CT: Yale University Press, 2002), 40–69; Paul Kelton, *Epidemics and Enslavement: Biological Catastrophe in the Native Southeast, 1492–1715* (Lincoln: University of Nebraska Press, 2007), xix, 101–59; Robbie Ethridge, "Introduction: Mapping the Mississippian Shatter Zone," in *Mapping the Mississippian Shatter Zone: The Colonial Indian Slave Trade and Regional Instability in the American South*, ed. Robbie Ethridge and Sheri M. Shuck-Hall (Lincoln: University of Nebraska Press, 2009), 1–62, here 2 ("shatter"), 8–15, 42–43n3; Ethridge, *From Chicaza to Chickasaw: The European Invasion and the Transformation of the Mississippian World, 1540–1715* (Chapel Hill: University of North Carolina Press, 2010), 113–14, 246.

23. Gregory A. Waselkov and Marvin T. Smith, "Upper Creek Archaeology," in *Indians of the Greater Southeast: Historical Archaeology and Ethnohistory*, ed. Bonnie G. McEwan (Gainesville: University Press of Florida, 2000): 242–64, here 244, 246, 250–55; Steven J. Oatis, *A Colonial Complex: South Carolina's Frontiers in the Era of the Yamasee War, 1680–1730* (Lincoln: University of Nebraska Press, 2004); William Ramsey, *The Yamasee War: A Study of Culture, Economy, and Conflict in the Colonial South* (Lincoln: University of Nebraska Press, 2008), 34–53; Ethridge, *Chicaza*, passim; George Edward Milne, *Natchez Country: Indians, Colonists, and the Landscapes of Race in French Louisiana* (Athens: University of Georgia Press, 2015), 32–40; Ethridge, "Origins and Coalescence," 123 ("displacements"). The Muscogean language family is divided into Western and Eastern Muscogean. While Chickasaws and Choctaws belong to the western division, the eastern division encompasses Alabama, Koasati, Hitchiti, Mikasuki, and Muscogee proper (or Creek). On language, see Mary R. Haas, "The Classification of the Muskogean Languages," in *Language, Culture, and Personality: Essays in Memory of Edward Sapir*, ed. Leslie Spier, A. Irving Hallowell, and Stanley S. Newman (1941; repr., Salt Lake City: University of Utah Press, 1960): 41–56, here 41–43.

24. Benjamin Hawkins, "A sketch of the Creek Country in the years 1798 and 1799," in LBH, 1:285–327, here 300 ("Aubecuh") and Hawkins to William Eustis, 2/24/1811, in LBH, 2:583. On Okfuskee, see Waselkov and Smith "Upper Creek Archaeology," 255–56; Ethridge, *Chicaza*, 167; Piker, *Okfuskee*, 8; Ethridge, "Origins and Coalescence," 119. For evidence of Okfuskee as Abeika, see document 1, "Camp at Cedar Creek," 7/7/1759, p. 4 ("Abehkas"), enclosed in Edmond Atkin to William Henry Lyttelton,

Okfuskee, 11/30/1759, box 13, and Jerome Courtonne, "List of Headmen of the Creeks, giving information re[:] French and British sympathies," October 1758, box 8—both in WHLP. Courtonne, who conducted the mid-century census, identified ten "abickaw" towns, including "Okchoy," "Okfuskee," "Hilabbee," "Abecootchi," "Breed Camp," "Shalapkcaggee[?]," "Woccukay" (Woccoccoie), "Puckantallahassee," "Little Tallassee," and "Cacoledgee" (Kialijee). Nine towns made up the "Tallapoosee division," including "Mocculussaw[?]" (Muccolossus), "Savanahs," "White Ground," "Coolamee," "Tushatchee" (Fusihatchee?), "Clevawlee[?]" (Hoithlewaulee), "Olassee" (Autossee), "Tuckebatchee," and "Talshee" (Tallassee/Big Tallassee/Great Tallassee). On Creek demography, see Peter H. Wood, "Changing Population of the Colonial South," in *Powhatan's Mantle: Indians in the Colonial Southeast*, 2nd ed., ed. Gregory A. Waselkov, Peter H. Wood, and Tom Hatley (Lincoln: University of Nebraska Press, 2006): 57–132, here 60 (table 1), 81–87.

25. Emanuel Bowen, *A New Map of Georgia, with Part of Carolina, Florida and Louisiana*, 1748, Georgia Archives, Historic Map File, hmf0117. On the "Upper Creeks, Middle Creeks, and Lower Creeks," see John Reed Swanton, *Early History of the Creek Indians and Their Neighbors*, Smithsonian Institution's Bureau of American Ethnology Bulletin 73 (Washington, DC: Government Printing Office, 1922), 216. Swanton wrote that the first is also called "Coosa or Abihka, the second Tallapoosa, and the last Coweta" (216). On European maps of the Americas, see Barr and Countryman, "Introduction," 5–18.

26. On Native historicity, see Fogelson, "Ethnohistory of Events and Non-Events," 134–41; Kidwell and Velie, *Native American Studies*, 7–13; Peter Nabokov, *A Forest of Time: American Indian Ways of History* (Cambridge: Cambridge University Press, 2002), 29–57, 192–217; and Thomas Buckley, "Native Authorship in Northwestern California," in *New Perspectives on Native North America*, ed. Kan and Strong, 211–38, here 211–14.

Chapter 1

1. Document 1, "Camp at the Springs," 7/3/1759, p. 1, and "Camp at Cedar Creek," 7/7/1759, p. 4 (quotes), enclosed in Edmond Atkin to William Henry Lyttelton, Okfuskee, 11/30/1759, box 13, in WHLP. On the southern theater of the Seven Years' War, see John T. Juricek, *Colonial Georgia and the Creeks: Anglo-Indian Diplomacy on the Southern Frontier, 1733–1763* (Gainesville: University Press of Florida, 2010), 242–63; Steven C. Hahn, *The Invention of the Creek Nation, 1670–1763* (Lincoln: University of Nebraska Press, 2004), 245–50.

2. Document 1, "Camp at Cedar Creek," 7/7/1759, p. 4 ("one"), enclosed in Atkin to Lyttelton, 11/30/1759, box 13, in WHLP.

3. On the Creek-Cherokee War, see Hahn, *Invention*, 250–51; Steven J. Oatis, *A Colonial Complex: South Carolina's Frontiers in the Era of the Yamasee War, 1680–1730* (Lincoln: University of Nebraska Press, 2004), 223–63; Joshua Piker, *Okfuskee: A Creek Indian Town in Colonial America* (Cambridge, MA: Harvard University Press, 2004), 45–52; Wayne E. Lee, "Peace Chiefs and Blood Revenge: Patterns of Restraint in Native American Warfare, 1500–1800," *Journal of Military History* 71 (July 2007): 701–41; and William Ramsey, *The Yamasee War: A Study of Culture, Economy, and Conflict in the Colonial South* (Lincoln: University of Nebraska Press, 2008), 148–55.

4. On war and rebellion in the early colonial South, see Peter H. Wood, *Black Majority: Negroes in Colonial South Carolina from 1670 through the Stono Rebellion* (New York: Alfred A. Knopf, 1974); Hahn, *Invention*; Oatis, *Colonial Complex*; and Ramsey, *Yamasee War*. For an abrupt shift in Creek–British relations and especially Okfuskee–British relations at mid-century, see Piker, *Okfuskee*, 42–43, 45–63.

5. On kin shaping male leaders in the colonial era, especially in Indian–European negotiations, see Michelle LeMaster, *Brothers Born of One Mother: British-Native American Relations in the Colonial Southeast* (Charlottesville: University of Virginia Press, 2012), 15–50; and Natalie R. Inman, *Brothers and Friends: Kinship in Early America* (Athens: University of Georgia Press, 2017), 15–34.

6. James Adair, *The History of the American Indians*, ed. Kathryn E. Holland Braund (Tuscaloosa: University of Alabama Press, 2005), 189 ("burned"); Memorandum from George Galphin to William Pinckney, commissioner for Indian affairs of South Carolina, in Galphin to Pinckney, 11/3/1750, Silver Bluff, in CRSC I, 4 ("out"). The British tracked the Creek-Cherokee War with great interest. While traders worried about financial disruptions, authorities like Commissioner Pinckney feared that intertribal conflict might engulf British settlements in violence.

7. William Sludders to Commissioner Pinckney, Okchai, 11/11/1750, in CRSC I, 3 ("Upper," "Lower," "Nothing"); and Affidavit of Timothy Millin, deposed to James Fraser, 7/19/1751, Augusta, in CRSC I, 36 ("Matters," "determined"). On Cherokee geography and history, see Gerald F. Schroedl, "Cherokee Ethnohistory and Archaeology from 1540 to 1838," in *Indians of the Greater Southeast: Historical Archaeology and Ethnohistory*, ed. Bonnie G. McEwan (Gainesville: University Press of Florida, 2000): 204–41, here 204, 205 (figure 8.1), 213–21; and Wayne E. Lee, "Fortify, Fight, or Flee: Tuscarora and Cherokee Defensive Warfare and Military Culture Adaptation," *Journal of Military History* 68 (July 2004): 713–70 here 753–56.

8. Breed Camp was settled by migrant Chickasaws with the consent of Upper Creeks earlier in the century. Affidavit of Timothy Millin, deposed to James Fraser, 7/19/1751, in CRSC I, 35 ("Peace," "out"), 36 ("conclude," "expected"). The Shawnees were identified as "five Savanah Indians who] came in from the Cherokees" (35). For an example of Shawnee diplomacy among the southern Indians, see Henry Stuart to John Stuart, 8/25/1776, "Chote," in EAID, vol. 18, 213–14. Georgia agent Patrick Graham believed that a "Peace" between "Upper Creeks" and "Upper Cherokees" would "soon be ratified" in summer 1751. Since the Abeikas' main enemy was the Lower Cherokees, however, peace remained elusive. See Graham to Glen, 6/15/1751, Augusta, in CRSC I, 81.

9. Lachlan McGillivray to William Pinckney, 12/18/1751, "Upper Creeks," in CRSC I, 216 ("some," "seven"). On The Raven, see "Sciogunster of Keehowe" to South Carolina governor James Glen, n.d., "North Side of Great Saluda River," in CRSC I, 155 ("Upper"). Addressing Glen, The Raven said, "I heard two Men of my Town [Hiwassee] is killed since I left Home. That is 2 Nauchees which he looks upon as his own People" (CRSC I, 155). The Raven's words suggest that kinship ties existed between Hiwassee and Nauchee. See, too, Galphin to Glen, 4/20/1752, Coweta, in CRSC I, 257 ("Man" killed "at the Oakfusskees" and "at the Cossas," "made").

10. John Phillip Reid, *A Law of Blood: The Primitive Law of the Cherokee Nation* (1970; repr., DeKalb: Northern Illinois University Press, 2006), 153–61, 154 ("international"); Adair, *History*, 182–94, 185 ("I"), 186 ("kindred"), 329, 376 ("crying"); Christina

Snyder, *Slavery in Indian Country: The Changing Face of Captivity in Early America* (Cambridge, MA: Harvard University Press, 2010), 80–84; Greg O'Brien, "Quieting the Ghosts: How the Choctaws and Chickasaws Stopped Fighting," in *The Native South: New Histories and Enduring Legacies*, ed. Tim Alan Garrison and Greg O'Brien (Lincoln: University of Nebraska Press, 2017): 47–69, here 48–50.

11. Galphin to Glen, 4/20/1752, Coweta, in CRSC I, 258 ("Oakfusskees," "one"); "Ifa Tuskenia" or "The Captain of the Okfuskee" to Glen, 7/26/1753, Okfuskee, in CRSC I, 381 ("Appearance," "killing").

12. Okfuskee Captain to Glen, 7/26/1753, Okfuskee, in CRSC I, 381 ("whole"), 410 (head count); James Germany to Lachlan McGillivray, 7/15/1753, Okchai, enclosed in McGillivray to Glen, 8/6/1753, Savannah, in CRSC I, 379 ("Head"); Wolf to Lyttelton via "Woolf Warriour of the Fushatches," "pre" 10/28/1757, box 6, in WHLP ("eight"). On the Charles Town delegation, see Proceedings of the Council Concerning Indian Affairs, 5/30/1753–6/4/1753, in CRSC I, 387–408, here 387 ("confirming"). Wolf endorsed Malatchi, a Lower Creek headman from Coweta, who spoke to Glen about forging peace with the Cherokees (388, 397, and 407). On the delegation's makeup: "About 69 . . . of the Upper Creeks [Abeikas and Tallapoosas] had come being all the Head Men of the Upper and Lower Creek Nation excepting the Gun Merchant [of Okfuskee] and Chiggilli [of Coweta]" (387).

13. Red Coat King to Glen, 7/26/1753, Okfuskee, in CRSC I, 380 (quotes). The quote "two Slaves of the Northern French Indians" is also found herein (380). The headman desired that one slave each be sent to the Upper and Lower Creeks. On captive exchange, see Snyder, *Changing Face of Captivity*, 13–45.

14. On the Okfuskee convention, see "Information of George Johnston," n.d., in CRSC II, 10. A careful reading of reports from British traders, such as Johnston, suggests that the Upper Creek meeting at Okfuskee took place around fall 1753. See, too, Lachlan McIntosh to Glen, 11/2/1753, Okfuskee, in CRSC I, 465 ("firm," "strong"); McIntosh to Glen, 4/3/1754, Kialijee ("Caileges"), in CRSC I, 504 ("confirm," "conclude"). McIntosh wrote that Mortar "went about 10 Days ago to the [Smoky] Mountins" to visit the Cherokees. British reports confirm no attacks between Cherokees and Creeks during the 1753–54 hunting season. In March 1754, John Buckles reported that the two groups hunted in the same "Woods this Winter without doing any Damage to one another"; see Buckles to Glen, 3/15/1754, in CRSC I, 501. On the Lower Creek peace with Cherokees, see "Warriors of Highwassee and Tommothy" to Glen, 4/15/1754, "in the House of Ludvick Grant," in CRSC I, 504–6; and Malatchi to Glen, 5/7/1754, Coweta, in CRSC I, 507.

15. McIntosh to Glen, 4/3/1754, Kialijee ("Caileges"), in CRSC I, 504 ("Satisfaction"); Lachlan McGillivray to Glen, 9/8/1754, New Windsor, in CRSC II, 7 ("joined," "Cherroekees").

16. Document 4, "Private Information of Billy Germany," 8/20/1759, p. 3 (quotes), in Atkin to William Henry Lyttelton, 11/30/1759, box 13, in WHLP. On the uncle–nephew relationship in Creek history, see Charles Hudson, *The Southeastern Indians* (Knoxville: University of Tennessee Press, 1976), 185–196; Ethridge, *Creek Country*, 103–4.

17. Information of George Johnston, 10/2/1754, in CRSC II, 10 (quotes). The context of Johnston's report, submitted to the South Carolina Governor's Council and recorded in the "Book for Indian Affairs," suggests that the three Cherokee emissaries traveled to Okfuskee to confer with Upper Creek headmen (10). On the complex logistics of southern Indian diplomacy, see Piker, *Okfuskee*, 15–52, and O'Brien, *Choctaws*, 54–68.

18. Proceedings, 6/[3]/1753, in CRSC I, 407 (quotes), 410. The secretary incorrectly entered "Sunday, A.M. the 2d Day of June, 1753." The correct date was June 3. On retaliation, see Adair, *History*, 92, 136.

19. Proceedings, 6/[3]/1753, in CRSC I, 407 (quotes); Hahn, *Invention*, 146–47. On Okfuskee Captain's commission and his leadership among the Upper Creeks, see Piker, *Four Deaths*, 156–87.

20. Proceedings, 6/[3]/1753, in CRSC I, 407.

21. Proceedings, 6/4/1753, in CRSC I, 387, 409 ("Shirts," "Women," "Pewther"), 410 ("Relation"), 413 ("therefore," "shall"). While the Lower Creeks attended this conference, the Upper Creeks were especially demanding and "expect more than ordinary Presents" from the governor (410). On Little Tallassee as a Tallapoosa polity in the mid-eighteenth century, see Emistisiguo to Superintendent John Stuart, in vol. 12, EAID, 212 and editor's note, 537n65; and Monica R. Ward, "Little Tallassee: A Creek Indian Colonial Town" (PhD diss., University of North Carolina at Greensboro, 2019), 79–80.

22. In the mid-1750s, British "Idlers" (hunters) were killing and skinning deer and beaver in the "Hunting grounds which they [the Creeks] call their Property"; see Daniel Pepper to Lyttelton, November (?) 1756, box 3, in WHLP. On the Treaty of 1739, also known as the Treaty of Coweta, see Michael D. Green, *The Politics of Indian Removal: Creek Government and Society in Crisis* (Lincoln: University of Nebraska Press, 1982), 25–26; and Hahn, *Invention*, 180, 186. On the Creek–British deerskin trade, see Kathryn E. Holland Braund, *Deerskins and Duffels: The Creek Indian Trade with Anglo-America, 1685–1815* (1993; repr., Lincoln: University of Nebraska Press, 2008), especially 61–80, 121–38.

23. Braund, *Deerskins*, 149, 156–63; Juricek, *Colonial Georgia*, 13–14, 230–303; Bryan C. Rindfleisch, *George Galphin's Intimate Empire: The Creek Indians, Family, and Colonialism in Early America* (Tuscaloosa: University of Alabama Press, 2019), 120–25.

24. Two or three Tallapoosas died in the Ogeechee Incident. For this conflict, see John Reynolds to William Henry Lyttelton, 9/15/1756; Lower Creek headmen to Reynolds, 9/17/1756, in Reynolds to Lyttelton, 10/6/1756; David Douglass to Lower Creeks, 9/13/1756, in White Outerbridge to Lyttelton, 9/14/1756—all in box 2, in WHLP. A talk from Governor Reynolds preceded the Lower Creeks' own. His recipients were "our beloved Friend and Brother Tukulkey" of Coweta and "the rest of our Beloved Men and Warriors of the Creek Nation"; see Reynolds to "Upper [Lower?] Creeks," 9/14/1756, in Reynolds to Lyttelton, Georgia, 9/15/1756, box 2, in WHLP.

25. By early October, most of the fugitives had been apprehended; see Reynolds to Lyttelton, 9/22/1756, Savannah; and Outerbridge to Lyttelton, Fort Augusta, 10/10/1756—both in box 2, in WHLP. For "shall," see Daniel Pepper to Lyttelton, 9/22/1756, James Island, box 2, in WHLP.

26. Pepper to Lyttelton, 11/18/1756, in CRSC II, 254 (quotes). Mary Bosomworth was a "Relation" of "the Wolf King." She was a translator for the British, a relative of powerful Coweta headmen, and wife of the Reverend Thomas Bosomworth. Whether she cooperated with Wolf by attempting to shift blame away from the British in support of an Anglo–Creek alliance is unclear but possible. See journal of Thomas Bosomworth, 9/14/1752, in CRSC I, 289. On Wolf's diplomacy, see Jerome Courtonne, "List of Headmen of the Creeks, giving information re[:] French and British sympathies," October 1758, p. 2, box 8, in WHLP.

27. "The Woolf King" via "Woolf Warriour of the Fushatches" to Lyttelton, "pre" 10/28/1757, box 6 in WHLP ("French"). The Creek headmen in France's "interest"

hailed from Muccolossus, Fusihatchee, and Tuckabatchee. The Treaty of Savannah minutes are enclosed in Georgia governor Henry Ellis to Lyttelton, 11/3/1757, box 6, in WHLP ("Grievances," "antient"). The remainder of article 2 reads, "& peace and good friendship is hereby renew'd & establish'd between the People of the Great King George called White Men, & his beloved Children of both the Creek Nations commonly called the Red Men."

28. Journal of Joseph Wright, entry 8/9/1758, Chehaw, original in Ellis to Lyttelton, 9/8/1758, box 8, in WHLP ("some," "yet"); Superintendent Edmond Atkin, document 7, 9/7/1759, and Atkin to Lyttelton, 11/30/1759, pp. 7–8 ("restore"), box 13, in WHLP; Treaty of Savannah minutes enclosed in Ellis to Lyttelton, 11/3/1757, box 6, in WHLP ("thoroughly").

29. On Wolf's diplomacy after the Ogeechee Incident, see Atkin's correspondence with Lyttelton, such as document 1, 7/3/1759, Camp at "the Springs," pp. 7, 11–12; document 10, 9/28 & 9/29/1759, Tuckabatchee, pp. 1–3, 5, 11; and document 18, 11/16/1759, Okfuskee, p. 1—all in Atkin to Lyttelton, 11/30/1759, box 13, in WHLP. See also Hahn, *Invention*, 258–69, 271, and Piker, *Okfuskee*, 146.

30. Mortar, according to his brother-in-law Gun Merchant, was "the Man, that hath the most Wisdom among us [the Creeks]; & he has also the greatest Influence or Command over our Head Warriours"; see document 17, 11/10/1759, Okchai (?), enclosed in Atkin to Lyttelton, 11/30/1759, Okfuskee, box 13, in WHLP. On Atkin's trade policy, see Juricek, *Colonial Georgia*, 239–46.

31. Document 1, 7/3/1759, Camp at "the Springs," p. 1, enclosed in Atkin to Lyttelton, 11/30/1759, box 13, in WHLP. Wolf Warrior was a "Head Commissioned Warriour" and identified as "Yahahtustunnogy" (1). (This should not be confused with the same war title held by Mortar of Okchai.)

32. Document 1, 7/3/1759, Camp at "the Springs," p. 1 ("There," "old," "Great," "me"), p. 2 ("all," "Towns," "love," "let"), enclosed in Atkin to Lyttelton, 11/30/1759, box 13, in WHLP.

33. Document 1, 7/7/1759, "Camp at Cedar Creek 7 Miles from Talsey or Tuccobatchey," p. 4 ("one"), p. 5 ("Headmen"), enclosed in Atkin to Lyttelton, 11/30/1759, box 13, in WHLP.

34. On Tuckabatchee, see document 1, 7/9/1759, Tuckabatchee, p. 11 ("properest," "most"), enclosed in Atkin to Lyttelton, 11/30/1759, box 13, in WHLP; Adair, *History*, 208–9; Vernon James Knight Jr., *Tukabatchee: Archaeological Investigations at an Historic Creek Town, Elmore County, Alabama, 1984*, Report of Investigations 45 (Tuscaloosa: Alabama State Museum of Natural History, 1985), 179–80; John R. Swanton, *Creek Religion and Medicine* (1928; repr., Lincoln: University of Nebraska Press, 2000), 561; document 2, 7/24/1759, p. 6, enclosed in Atkin to Lyttelton, 11/30/1759, box 13, in WHLP; Piker, *Four Deaths*, 148.

35. Tathlabegey (also spelled Tathlahbegey) hailed from the Lower Creek town of Cusseta. Several micos, including Tuckabatchee's, did not attend the September council. Creek men who did attend came from sixteen "Abeka Towns" and seven "Tallapoosa Towns." Little Tallassee is misidentified as an Abeika town, and some Abeika polities classified as towns were actually talofas, or out-settlements, including Okfuskee's "Suckaspoga." Okfuskee Captain appears as "Tustunnokhahgio Com[missioned]." For the September council, see document 10, 9/28 & 9/29/1759, pp. 1–2 (list of towns, leaders, and Lower Creek assailant), pp. 2–11 (conference minutes), in Atkin to Lyttelton, 11/30/1759,

box 13, in WHLP. On the summertime councils, one of which included "20 women," see document 1, 7/9/1759, Tuckabatchee Square, p. 7–12, 11 ("20") and document 2, 7/24 & 7/25/1759, pp. 1–12—both in Atkin to Lyttelton, 11/30/1759, box 13, in WHLP.

36. Atkin completed his speech on September 29 at Tuckabatchee Half Breed's home. If any headmen conspired with Talhlalegey, they came from Coweta, such as "Ufylegey" or the "Second man," and Cusseta. See document 10, 9/28/1759, p. 2 ("Ufylegey," "Second") & 9/29/1759, p. 7 ("Yard"), p. 11 ("*Answer*"); document 17, 11/10/1759, p. 1 ("*daunted*," "*confounded*")—both enclosed in Atkin to Lyttelton, 11/30/1759, box 13, in WHLP. For the "Hatchet Affair," see Atkin's report to Lyttelton, 11/30/1759, p. 1, box 13, in WHLP; and Juricek, *Colonial Georgia*, 258.

37. On Creek resentment against Atkin, see Ellis to Lyttelton, 10/16/1759, box 12, in WHLP; document 18, 11/16/1759, p. 1, in Atkin to Lyttelton, 11/30/1759, box 13, in WHLP; and Juricek, *Colonial Georgia*, 258. On Mortar's unpopularity, see Hahn, *Invention*, 252.

38. Document 1, 7/7/1759, "Camp at Cedar Creek," p. 4 ("Abehkas"), in Atkin to Lyttelton, 11/30/1759, box 13, in WHLP

39. The Paris Peace significantly altered the imperial jurisdictions of North America and the Caribbean. In exchange for ceding Canada to Britain, France retained its lucrative sugar colonies in Martinique, Guadeloupe, and St. Lucia. Spain ceded Florida to Britain in return for Cuba, which the British navy had captured late in the war. The British divided Florida into East and West Florida. See Alan Taylor, *American Colonies: The Settling of North America* (New York: Penguin Books, 2001), 431–37; Juricek, *Colonial Georgia*, 298–99; and Colin G. Calloway, *The Scratch of a Pen: 1763 and the Transformation of North America* (Oxford: Oxford University Press, 2006), 100–11. For Upper Creek anger at the Paris Peace, see Mortar and Gun Merchant to Georgia governor James Wright, 5/8/1763, in EAID, vol. 11, 352 (quotes). The chief author of this talk was Mortar, who "spoke as follows" (352).

40. For Creek clan moieties, see Hudson, *Southeastern Indians*, 236. For the Bear clan, see John R. Swanton, "Social Organization and Social Usages of the Indians of the Creek Confederacy," in *Forty-Second Annual Report of the Bureau of American Ethnology to the Secretary of the Smithsonian Institution, 1924–1925* (Washington, DC: United States Government Printing Office, 1928), 110–13, (113, for peace responsibility), 145, 149, 154, 164 (for Bear as "almost always White"). "Bear" refers to the grizzly bear or "Whooping Bear" (110). One informant told Swanton in the early 1900s, "The Wolf clan is kindred to the Bear clan, but without the political prestige of the latter" (113).

41. Mortar and Gun Merchant to Wright, 5/8/1763, in EAID, vol. 11, 352 (quotes). On the Master of Breath, see Swanton, *Creek Religion*, 481–82. In addition to defending Creek land, Mortar sought to negotiate the best possible trade settlement for the Abeikas. For a thoughtful analysis of Mortar's agenda in the Creek–British trade after 1763, see Kevin T. Harrell, "The Terrain of Factionalism: How Upper Creek Communities Negotiated the Recourse of Gulf Coast Trade, 1763–1780," *Alabama Review* 68, no. 1 (January 2015): 74–113, here 50–102, 94n48, 112–13.

42. Emistisiguo to Stuart and Wright, 5/20/1764, in EAID, vol. 12, 212 ("As," "we"), 213 ("you"). On Upper Creek trade interests in the mid-1760s and 1770s, see Joshua Piker, "'White & Clean' & Contested: Creek Towns and Trading Paths in the Aftermath of the Seven Years' War," *Ethnohistory* 50, no. 2 (Spring 2003): 315–47. On the Treaty of Augusta, see Hahn, *Invention*, 268.

43. Although Mortar spread his peace talks throughout the "whole Nation," Emistisiguo informed Stuart, his own words suggest he acted on behalf of the Abeika towns and Bear clan. See Mortar and Emistisiguo to Stuart, 7/22/1764, in EAID, vol. 12, 218 (quotes); document 10, 9/28/1759, p. 1 (war title), in Atkin to Lyttelton, 11/30/1759, box 13, in WHLP; and McIntosh to Glen, 4/3/1754, "Caileges" (Kialijee), in CRSC I, 504.

44. The treaty was signed on May 28, 1765; see Pensacola Congress Minutes, 5/28/1765, in EAID, vol. 12, 266–68. Knowing Stuart's designs on Creek lands, Mortar initially refused to attend the Pensacola Congress; see Milo B. Howard Jr. and Robert R. Rea, eds., *The Mémoire Justificatif of the Chevalier Montault de Monberaut* (Tuscaloosa: University of Alabama Press, 1965), 132, 156–59.

45. Pensacola Congress Minutes, 5/30/1765, in EAID, vol. 12, 272 (quotes). The area near the Pensacola Cession pulsed with sacred forces; see Jean-Bernard Bossu, 5/2/1759, "Alabama Territory," letter XVI, in Seymour Feiler, ed., *Jean-Bernard Bossu's Travels in the Interior of North America, 1751–1762* (1768; Norman: University of Oklahoma Press, 1962), 141–51, 149n6.

46. Atkin also reported that Mortar's "own Warriors" abandoned the alliance with the Cherokees and French. See Atkin to Lyttelton, 11/30/1759, p. 3 (quotes), box 13, in WHLP.

Chapter 2

1. On the origins of the Creek-Choctaw War, see Kathryn E. Holland Braund, *Deerskins and Duffels: The Creek Indian Trade with Anglo-America, 1685–1815* (1993; repr., Lincoln: University of Nebraska Press, 2008), 133–34; Greg O'Brien, "Protecting Trade through War: Choctaw Elites and British Occupation of the Floridas," in *Pre-Removal Choctaw History: Exploring New Paths*, ed. Greg O'Brien (1999; repr., Norman: University of Oklahoma Press, 2008): 103–22; and Gregory D. Smithers, *Native Southerners: Indigenous History from Origins to Removal* (Norman: University of Oklahoma Press, 2019), 67–69.

2. For "Cloud," see "A Peace Talk [from] The Creeks to the Chactaws [no.] 8," ca. fall 1770, enclosed in Superintendent John Stuart to Commanding General Thomas Gage, 12/13/1770, TGP. For scholarship that stresses generational tensions between diplomats and warriors, see Gregory Evans Dowd, *A Spirited Resistance: The North American Indian Struggle for Unity, 1745–1815* (Baltimore: Johns Hopkins University Press, 1992), 90–115, 148–66; Colin G. Calloway, *The American Revolution in Indian Country: Crisis and Diversity in Native American Communities* (Cambridge: Cambridge University Press, 1995), 182–212; O'Brien, "Protecting Trade through War"; and O'Brien, *Choctaws in a Revolutionary Age, 1750–1830* (Lincoln: University of Nebraska Press, 2002), 46–48. For a succinct discussion of clan lineage and violence, see Braund, *Deerskins*, 156–59.

O'Brien, "Protecting Trade through War," 108–13, deserves special attention. He argues that the growth of independent trading between Native hunters and British traders after 1763 diminished headmen's ability to distribute goods to their communities. That development undercut headmen and caused generational friction between older, privileged headmen and young hunters and warriors. In response, headmen recouped political power by diverting warriors away from traders and directing them to attack members of the opposing society. Building on O'Brien, my chapter considers why headmen simultaneously conducted diplomacy with and waged war on the Choctaws. The answer is that they fell prey to local priorities, which pulled them into the conflict, undermined peace, and supplemented age as a source of tension with young men.

3. Kinship traditions bent to intertribal affairs as much as Indian–European affairs, the focus of Michelle LeMaster, *Brothers Born of One Mother: British-Native American Relations in the Colonial Southeast* (Charlottesville: University of Virginia Press, 2012), 15–50; and Natalie R. Inman, *Brothers and Friends: Kinship in Early America* (Athens: University of Georgia Press, 2017), especially 2–9, 15–33. On Creek religion, see Charles Hudson, *The Southeastern Indians* (Knoxville: University of Tennessee Press, 1976), especially 317–426; and John R. Swanton, *Creek Religion and Medicine* (1928; repr., Lincoln: University of Nebraska Press, 2000).

4. For an estimate of casualties, see O'Brien, *Choctaws*, 27. For an overview of the Creek-Choctaw War, see John T. Juricek, *Endgame for Empire: British-Creek Relations in Georgia and Vicinity, 1763–1776* (Gainesville: University Press of Florida, 2015), 127–46. Juricek examines the critical years between the Paris Peace and American independence by tracing the evolution of Creek-British relations. Bryan C. Rindfleisch, *George Galphin's Intimate Empire: The Creek Indians, Family, and Colonialism in Early America* (Tuscaloosa: University of Alabama Press, 2019), 149–69, adopts a similar tack, using trader George Galphin's relationship with the Lower Creeks to move the narrative into the revolutionary Native South. While I am influenced by these scholars, my chapter interrogates political relationships *within* Upper Creek communities during an intertribal war.

5. Braund, *Deerskins*, 133–34; Colin G. Calloway, *The Scratch of a Pen: 1763 and the Transformation of North America* (Oxford: Oxford University Press, 2006), 100–11; Smithers, *Native Southerners*, 68–69. After the Paris Peace of 1763, Creeks and other southern Indians sought alternative sources of trade with Spanish officials in New Orleans and Havana. While a thorn in Britain's side, the Spanish never posed a serious challenge to British trade in the late colonial South. See James L. Hill, "'Bring them what they lack': Spanish-Creek Exchange and Alliance Making in a Maritime Borderland, 1763–1783," *Early American Studies: An Interdisciplinary Journal* 12, no. 1 (Winter 2014): 36–67; and Claudio Saunt, *West of the Revolution: An Uncommon History of 1776* (New York: W. W. Norton, 2014), 188–98.

6. On Upper Creek aggression in 1763–66, see John Stuart to Thomas Boone, 10/15/1763, Fort Augusta, and James Colbert, entry 8/3/1763, Copy of Colbert's Journal, enclosed in Stuart to Boone, Arthur Dobbs, and Francis Fauquier, 10/23/1763, Fort Augusta, both in "Minutes of the Southern Congress at Augusta, Georgia," University of North Carolina, http://docsouth.unc.edu/csr/index.html/document/csr11-0084 (accessed June 1, 2020); Elias Legardere to West Florida governor George Johnstone, 3/27/1766, Fort Tombecbé, in BMAM, part 1; Stephen Forrester to Johnstone, 5/25/1766, "Chester-ca-lusfa," in BMAM, part 1. For the 1766–1767 killing cycle, see James Hendrie, interpreting for R. Roi, to Brigadier Taylor, 9/22/1766, Mobile, in BMAM, part 2; Lieutenant John Ritchey to Brigadier Taylor, 1/2/1767, Tombecbé, in BMAM, part 3; and Taylor to Thomas Gage, 3/4/1767, in BMAM, part 4 ("perpetual").

7. Hendrie and Roi to Taylor, 8/29/1766, Mobile, in BMAM, part 1; Taylor to Gage, 10/15/1766, Pensacola, in BMAM, part 2; Emistisiguo to John Stuart, 10/24/1768, in

EAID, vol. 12, 344 ("killing," "draw"); O'Brien, "Protecting Trade through War," 108–13. The late Michael D. Green pointed out that the British welcomed this war because it kept Creek and Choctaw warriors away from vulnerable backcountry settlements. See "The Creek Confederacy in the American Revolution: Cautious Participants," in *Anglo-Spanish Confrontation on the Gulf Coast during the American Revolution*, ed. William S. Coker and Robert R. Rea (Pensacola: Gulf Coast History and Humanities Conference, 1982): 54–75, here 61.

8. Emistisiguo to John Stuart, 10/24/1768, in EAID, vol. 12, 344 ("Towns"); Emistisiguo to John Stuart, 7/12/1769, Augusta, in EAID, vol. 12, 348 (quote reads "the Abekas or Tallipoussas"); Hendrie and Roi to Taylor, 9/22/1766, Mobile, in BMAM, part 2 (Hoithlewaulee/"Cheowalli"); Forrester to Johnstone, 5/25/1766, "Chester-ca-lusfa," in BMAM, part 1 ("Wolf," "100"). On Choctaw societal divisions, see O'Brien, *Choctaws*, 35–36, 135n45. On Muccolossus, see "Travels Through North & South Carolina, Georgia, East & West Florida, the Cherokee Country, the Extensive Territories of the Muscogulges, or Creek Confederacy, and the Country of the Chactaws; Containing an Account of the Soil and Natural Productions of Those Regions, Together with Observations on the Manners of the Indians," in Bartram, 124–25. On Pucantallahassee, see "Journal of the Superintendants Proceedings," enclosed in John Stuart to "Your Lordship's [Wills Hill, Earl of Hillsborough]," 12/28/1768, Charles Town, in CO5, vol. 70, frame 227.

9. Hudson, *Southeastern Indians*, 239; Emistisiguo to John Stuart, 10/24/1768, in EAID, vol. 12, 344 ("Burning"); John Stuart to Lord Hillsborough, 12/28/1768, Charles Town, in CO5, vol. 70, frames 166–67 ("Principal," "Fles'd"); Charles Stuart to John Stuart, 6/12/1770, Pensacola, enclosed in Stuart's dispatch "No. 25," 7/16/1770, in CO5, vol. 75, frame 595 (niece). The Choctaw man who was flayed alive and killed was likely captured sometime before November 16, 1767; see Roderick McIntosh to John Stuart, 11/16/1767, in EAID, vol. 12, 340. Regarding the captive niece, Charles Stuart believed that she would be freed by the "Tuckabatchees." No evidence confirms as much, however, making it likely that she was adopted and remained in town.

10. Hudson, *Southeastern Indians*, 120–83; O'Brien, *Choctaws*, 38; Colonel William Tayler to General Thomas Gage, 9/18/1766, in EAID, vol. 12, 310 ("Black"); "A Peace Talk [from] The Creeks to the Chactaws [no.] 8," ca. fall 1770, enclosed in John Stuart to Gage, 12/13/1770, in TGP ("Cloud").

11. Abeika headmen Gun Merchant of Okchai and Handsome Fellow of Okfuskee supported the initiative; see "A Peace Talk [from] The Creeks to the Chactaws [no.] 8," ca. fall 1770, enclosed in John Stuart to Gage, 12/13/1770, in TGP. On Emistisiguo and Mortar, see Emistisiguo to John Stuart, 10/24/1768, in EAID, vol. 12, 344 and 556n43 (abortive peace attempt); and Emistisiguo in "A Talk from the Creeks to Cha[rles] Stuart Esq in Sep 1770 [no.] 7," enclosed in John Stuart to Gage, 12/13/1770, in TGP ("assured," "Heads"). Deputy Superintendent Charles Stuart, a cousin of John Stuart, served as primary intermediary for the Upper Creeks and Choctaws in 1770.

12. Emistisiguo and Mortar were made "Great Medal Chiefs" at the Pensacola Congress of 1765 along with Deval's Landlord of Pucantallahassee and Okchai's Gun Merchant, who was absent. Wolf of Muccolossus, also absent, later received his medal. See Pensacola Congress Minutes, 6/4/1765, in EAID, vol. 12, 273 and 542n112. On Emistisiguo's and Mortar's expertise, see Emistisiguo to John Stuart, 9/18/1768 and 7/12/1769, in EAID, vol. 12, 343 and 348–49; "Head Men of the Sawanees" (Sawanogi) to lieutenant

governor of West Florida Elias Durnford, 3/4/1770, in EAID, vol. 12, 353 ("Chief"); Emistisiguo to Durnford, 3/4/1770 and Durnford to Upper Creeks, 3/13/1770, in EAID, vol. 12, 351–52 and 354; Pensacola Congress Minutes, 5/30/1765, in EAID, vol. 12, 272; John Stuart to Johnstone, 12/13/1766, Charles Town, in BMAM, part 3.

13. "Head Men of the Sawanees" to Elias Durnford, 2/4/1770, in EAID, vol. 12, 353 ("peace talk"); Charles Stuart to John Stuart, 6/17/1770, Pensacola, in DAR, vol. 2, 109 ("talk," "three," "pipes"); and "Letter from Charles Stuart [to John Stuart] Dated at Pensacola 17th June 1770 Copied 1. 28 Nov: [no.] 3," enclosed in John Stuart to Gage, 12/13/1770, in TGP ("white," "received," "wipe"); Tayler to Gage, 9/18/1766, in EAID, vol. 12, 310. One white wing represented Emistisiguo, the other Mortar.

14. "Emistisiguo to Charles Stuart Esq. a Talk with Peau [few?] Tokens to the Chactaws [no.] 6," ca. September 1770, enclosed in John Stuart to Gage, 12/13/1770, in TGP ("Belt"); Daniel K. Richter, *The Ordeal of the Longhouse: The Peoples of the Iroquois League in the Era of European Colonization* (Chapel Hill: University of North Carolina Press, 1992), 47 (wampum); James Adair, *The History of the American Indians*, ed. Kathryn E. Holland Braund (Tuscaloosa: University of Alabama Press, 2005), 201, 504n169. Adair reported that the southern Indians traditionally created wampum "out of conch-shell, by rubbing them on hard stones, and so they form them according to their liking" (201). By the middle of the eighteenth century, trade beads had replaced shell wampum. On the Upper Creek wampum belt, see "A Talk from the Creeks to Cha. Stuart Esq in Sep 1770 [no.] 7," enclosed in John Stuart to Gage, 12/13/1770, in TGP. I thank Greg O'Brien for insight on the rarity of wampum belt diplomacy in the eighteenth-century Native South.

15. In his description of the wampum belt, Emistisiguo noted that the "White Bead" at one end also designated the Western Division Choctaw town of Congeetoo ("Cungito"), where Deputy Stuart appears to have been instructed to dispatch the belt and message. See "Emistisiguo to Charles Stuart Esq. a Talk with Peau [few?] Tokens to the Chactaws [no.] 6," ca. September 1770, enclosed in John Stuart to Thomas Gage, 12/13/1770, in TGP ("Belt," "Black," "White," "Cungito"); "A Talk from the Creeks to Cha. Stuart Esq in Sep 1770 [no.] 7," enclosed in John Stuart to Gage, 12/13/1770, in TGP; and Mortar in "A Peace Talk [from] The Creeks to the Chactaws [no.] 8," ca. fall 1770, enclosed in John Stuart to Gage, 12/13/1770, in TGP ("came"). On the Western Division town of Congeetoo, where the spiritual leader Taboca lived, see O'Brien, *Choctaws*, 22.

16. "Emistisiguo to Charles Stuart Esq. a Talk with Peau [few?] Tokens to the Chactaws [no.] 6," ca. September 1770, enclosed in John Stuart to Gage, 12/13/1770, in TGP ("Strap," "Clear," "Holaghtaobaye," "take"). For "Holaghtaobaye" as Holacta Hopayi, see EAID, vol. 12, 563n51. In Creek culture, a path also referred to the Spirits' Road (*poya fik-tcàlk innini*), a sacred highway along which departed souls traveled to the afterlife; see Angela Pulley Hudson, *Creek Paths and Federal Roads: Indians, Settlers, and Slaves and the Making of the American South* (Chapel Hill: University of North Carolina Press, 2010), 5–6.

17. "A Peace Talk [from] The Creeks to the Chactaws [no.] 8," ca. fall 1770, enclosed in John Stuart to Gage, 12/13/1770, in TGP (quotes). In addition to Fort Toulouse, the white beads showed "your Town Cungito," or Congeetoo, the Upper Creeks' point town among the Choctaws. On Upper Creek–French connections in the eighteenth century, see Steven C. Hahn, *The Invention of the Creek Nation, 1670–1763* (Lincoln: University of Nebraska Press, 2004), 86–87, 206–7, 226–27.

18. "Abstract of a Letter from Charles Stuart Esq 27 Sept. 1770 [no.] 5," enclosed in John Stuart to Gage, 12/13/1770, in TGP ("Chief," "Scalps"); "A Talk from the Creeks to Cha. Stuart Esq in Sep 1770 [no.] 7," enclosed in John Stuart to Gage, 12/13/1770, in TGP ("going"); "A Peace Talk [from] The Creeks to the Chactaws [no.] 8," ca. fall 1770, enclosed in John Stuart to Gage, 12/13/1770, in TGP ("Sign"). This last document indicates that Gun Merchant of Okchai reprised his role as an intertribal diplomat, presenting the Choctaws via Deputy Stuart with a pouch of tobacco for them to "Smoak."

19. "Emistisiguo to Charles Stuart Esq. a Talk with Peau [few?] Tokens to the Chactaws [no.] 6," ca. September 1770, enclosed in John Stuart to Gage, 12/13/1770, in TGP ("Belt"). For Deputy Stuart, see General Gage to Lord Hillsborough, 7/7/1770, New York, in DAR, vol. 2, 137; Charles Stuart to John Stuart, 12/26/1770, Pensacola, in DAR, vol. 2, 302, 305; and EAID, vol. 12, 563n48.

20. "A Peace Talk [from] The Creeks to the Chactaws [no.] 8," ca. fall 1770, enclosed in John Stuart to Gage, 12/13/1770, in TGP ("sent"). The in-text quote appears to designate both Emistisiguo and Mortar as speakers.

21. Charles Stuart to John Stuart, 12/26/1770, Pensacola, in DAR, vol. 2, 302, 305 (quotes). Emistisiguo was accompanied by Second Man of Little Tallassee, Beaver Tooth King, Little Dick, and unnamed others. Beaver Tooth King was a Tallassee headman; see Pensacola Congress Minutes, 6/4/1765, in EAID, vol. 12, 542n113. Emistisiguo's party was forty miles from Mobile when it learned of the Choctaw attacks and returned home; see Governor Peter Chester to Lord Hillsborough, 3/9/1771, Pensacola, in DAR, vol. 3, 65.

22. Lieutenant General Thomas Gage to Lord Hillsborough, 1/16/1771, New York, in DAR, vol. 3, 30 ("Creek"); Bernard Romans, *A Concise Natural History of East and West Florida*, ed. Kathryn E. Holland Braund (1999; repr., Tuscaloosa: University of Alabama Press, 2014 [1775]), 1, 150–51, 269, 407n250. Throughout 1771, British authorities were also occupied by the fallout of Creeks who killed two settlers. For the Creeks' response to this international incident, see Philemon Kemp to Wright with Talks from Emistisiguo and Gun Merchant, 6/6/1771, Augusta, in DAR, vol. 3, 118–21. The talks were delivered in Okchai on May 1, 1771.

23. What became of the dog is unclear. Later, on October 5, 1771, Romans and his party encountered some "victorious Choctaws, presenting us [with] the fresh scalp of one of his enemies." See Romans, *Concise Natural History*, 7, 74, 150 (figure 14), 151 (Romans's interpretation), 269 ("pine"), 270 ("victorious"), 407n250.

24. Romans, *Concise Natural History*, 150 (figure 14), 151 (quotes), 407n250. On the Deer clan, see John R. Swanton, "Social Organization and Social Usages of the Indians of the Creek Confederacy," in *Forty-Second Annual Report of the Bureau of American Ethnology to the Secretary of the Smithsonian Institution, 1924–1925* (Washington, DC: United States Government Printing Office, 1928), 123–25. Although unlikely, the Lower Creeks may have authored the Creek hieroglyphic, since they made war on the Choctaws in 1770, more than a year before Romans traveled through Choctaw country. On Lower Creek attacks, see "Abstract of a Letter from Charles Stuart Esquire 26 August 1770. [no.] 4," enclosed in John Stuart to Gage, 12/13/1770, in TGP.

25. "A Peace Talk [from] The Creeks to the Chactaws [no.] 8," ca. fall 1770, enclosed in John Stuart to Gage, 12/13/1770, in TGP ("Cloud"); Romans, *Concise Natural History*, 150–51; Agent David Taitt to John Stuart, 10/31/1772, in EAID, vol. 12, 434–35; Taitt to

John Stuart, 11/22/1772, Little Tallassee, enclosed in John Stuart to Earl of Dartmouth (?), 2/25/1773, in CO5/74, frame 775; John Stuart to Earl of Dartmouth, 6/21/1773, Savannah, frame 816; Taitt at Hickory Ground conference, 11/12/1773, in CO5/75, frames 21–22; Taitt to John Stuart, 1/12/1774, Little Tallassee, in CO5/75, frame 37; Taitt to John Stuart, 1/24/1774, Little Tallassee, in CO5/75, frame 44; and Taitt to John Stuart, 10/20/1775, Little Tallassee, in CO5/77, frame 328.

26. Taitt to John Stuart, 10/31/1772, in EAID, vol. 12, 434–35 ("large," "War"); Taitt to Stuart, 11/22/1772, Little Tallassee, enclosed in Stuart to Earl of Dartmouth (?), 2/25/1773, in CO5/74, frame 775 ("gone," "Hunt"); and "Emistisiguo, Beaver tooth King, Half Breed, Nuniss [sic] Friend[,] Speakers" to South Carolina governor Charles Montagu and John Stuart, 10/1/1770, "Great Tallassie" (Tallassee), in EAID, vol. 12, 376 ("daily"). The Alabamas may have participated in at least one raid. In late 1773, fourteen Cherokees visited the Alabama town of Hickory Ground and planned to launch an attack from there on the Choctaws. None other than Mortar was appointed to lead them. See Taitt to John Stuart, 11/12/1773, in EAID, vol. 12, 440.

27. Taitt to John Stuart, 10/20/1775, Little Tallassee, in CO5/77, frame 328 ("burden"). Taitt also wrote that a woman perished during a Choctaw raid on Pucantallahassee, a town frequently at war with the Choctaws, and that Choctaw warriors targeted the Alabama town of Coosada but turned back. For the impact of war on the Tallapoosas, see "David Taitt's Journal to and through the Upper Creek Nation," in DAR, vol. 5, 251–72, here 260 (March 4 entry), 264 (March 23 entry), 268 (April 6 entry); and "Travels Through North & South Carolina," in Bartram, 124. Taitt's journal is enclosed in John Stuart to Lord Hillsborough, 7/19/1772, in DAR, vol. 4, item 512. My sources on Tuckabatchee and Muccolossus are "David Taitt's Journal," in DAR, vol. 5, 268 (April 6 entry); and "Travels Through North & South Carolina," in Bartram, 100–101, 124–25. For both towns as Tallapoosa, see Jerome Courtonne, "List of Headmen of the Creeks, giving information re[:] French and British sympathies," October 1758, p. 2, box 8, in WHLP. For a similar example of ceremonialism in the Abeika towns, see Taitt to John Stuart, 10/20/1775, Little Tallassee, in CO5/77, frame 328. Records on Abeika ceremonial practices during the Creek-Choctaw War are sparse, primarily because British authorities and other colonists traveled to the distant Abeika towns far less than to the Tallapoosa towns, which resided closer to British centers of power.

28. "David Taitt's Journal," in DAR, vol. 5, 268 (April 6 entry). Taitt first observed this dance on April 6, but his entry notes that it began earlier. Evidence suggests that this Choctaw slaying of an important town official was a response to the capture of the "niece to Mingo—Houma—Chito, great Medal Chief of the Little Mucklasses" in Choctaw country. Deputy Charles Stuart "suspect[ed that] the Tuckabatchees" captured her; see his letter to John Stuart, 6/12/1770, Pensacola, enclosed in Stuart's dispatch "No. 25," 7/16/1770, in CO5/71, frame 595. On Mingo Houma Chito, see O'Brien, "Protecting Trade through War," 108, 111. On fire makers in the Native South, see Adair, *History*, 149, and Caleb Swan, "Position and State of Manners and Arts in the Creek, or Muscogee Nation in 1791," in *Information Respecting the History, Condition and Prospects of the Indian Tribes of the United States*, vol. 5, ed. Henry Rowe Schoolcraft (Philadelphia: J. B. Lippincott, 1855): 251–83, here 267–68. On Mad Dog in 1759, see document 2, Tuckabatchee Conference, 7/24/1759, p. 5, enclosed in Edmond Atkin to William Henry Lyttelton, 11/30/1759, box 13, in WHLP.

29. "David Taitt's Journal," in DAR, vol. 5, 268 (April 6 entry). Taitt believed that Mad Dog was "a very artful fellow and is trying to impose on the credulity of his people on purpose to free his sister from her widowhood, who by their laws must remain a widow [for] four years"; see "David Taitt's Journal," in DAR, vol. 5, 269 (April 10 entry). While Taitt may have been correct, Mad Dog's sister unmistakably drew support from her fellow Tuckabatchees, who wished to resurrect their fire maker.

30. "David Taitt's Journal," in DAR, vol. 5, 269 (April 10 entry); Hudson, *Southeastern Indians*, 187; Robbie Ethridge, *Creek Country: The Creek Indians and Their World* (Chapel Hill: University of North Carolina Press, 2003), 74.

31. "David Taitt's Journal," in DAR, vol. 5, 270 (April 17 entry), 271 ("being"), 271 (April 18 entry). One year later, in 1773, Creek headmen joined the Cherokees in ceding land to Georgia in return for the extinguishment of trade debt. This was known as the New Purchase Cession. For years, southern Indian warriors contested the cession and skirmished with Georgia settlers; see Juricek, *Endgame for Empire*, 251–53, and Joshua S. Haynes, *Patrolling the Border: Theft and Violence on the Creek-Georgia Frontier, 1770–1796* (Athens: University of Georgia Press, 2018), 33.

32. "David Taitt's Journal," in DAR, vol. 5, 270 (April 17 entry), 271 ("his"). Not one of the more than fifty dances published in Swanton's *Creek Religion*, 521–34, aimed to restore human life. Nor have I discovered archival evidence from the eighteenth century illuminating such a dance. For one intended to quiet the dead and hasten ghosts to the afterlife, see Speck, "Ceremonial Songs of the Creek and Yuchi Indians," 157–245, here 159, 164, 177–78.

33. "Travels Through North & South Carolina," in Bartram, 124 ("sighs"), 125 ("elegies"). Old Warrior, a brother of "Wolf King," sought retaliation against the Choctaws; see Charles Stuart to John Stuart, 5/17/1766, Pensacola, in CO5/67, frame 491. For other evidence of Muccolossus at war, see Forrester to Johnstone, 5/25/1766, "Chester-calusfa," in BMAM, part 1. Although I could not confirm whether Muccolossus participated in raids on the Choctaws in the 1770s, Bartram's travel account suggests as much.

34. "Travels Through North & South Carolina," in Bartram, 123 ("religious"), 124 ("most," "enemy," "new," "harmony"), 125 (chorus, "solemn"), 261n157; Adair, *History*, 101; Swanton, *Creek Religion*, 521–22. Medicine involved song on many occasions; see David Lewis Jr. and Ann T. Jordan, *Creek Indian Medicine Ways: The Enduring Power of Mvskoke Religion* (Albuquerque: University of New Mexico Press, 2002), 48–55, 70–74. Bartram incorrectly called "Mucclasse" an Alabama town; see Bartram, 108. In fact, Muccolossus was Tallapoosa; see "David Taitt's journal," 4/14/1772, in DAR, vol. 5, 270, and Courtonne, "List of Headmen," October 1758, p. 2, box 8, in WHLP.

35. The Choctaw man possessed a riveting backstory. His mother was Choctaw and a "slave" of the Creeks, while his father was both Creek and European. Bartram believed that he could pass as a "white man" in the region. See "Travels Through North & South Carolina," in Bartram, 97 ("Mustee," "slave"), 100 ("daughter"), 124 ("music," "festival," "white," "having"). According to Hudson, *Southeastern Indians*, 197, marriages in the Native South were "arranged but not forced" and were "as much relationships between kin groups as they were relationships between individuals." On southern Indian marital practices, see Adair, *History*, 175–77. Bartram reported as well that the Muccolossus bride was a "sister" of the resident trader's wife. The British trader was named John Adam Tapley, Wolf's ally, further suggesting that Wolf influenced marriages in

town. Whether that "sister" belonged to Wolf's clan or his wife's is unclear, however; see Braund, *Deerskins*, 78–79, 231n108. Tapley was a controversial figure in Creek country. In 1771, Emistisiguo complained that "there are many White Men in our Nation who follow no other Business but that of Hunting such as Mcfall. Humphry Hubbard, John Stripes and Adam Taply, who declare to our faces they will hunt on our Land, in spite of all opposition or Regulations to the Contrary." One year later, Lower Creeks fumed to Taitt about Tapley, who had been "digging up the Bodies of the Coweta Indians & likewise" committing other "Felonies"; see the Second Pensacola Congress, 10/29/1771 to 10/31/1771, in EAID, vol. 12, 398 ("there") and Taitt to Stuart, 11/22/1772, Little Tallassee, enclosed in John Stuart to Earl of Dartmouth (?), 2/25/1773, in CO5/74, frame 777 ("digging," "Felonies").

36. "Travels Through North & South Carolina," in Bartram, 100, 124.

37. John Stuart to George Germain, 10/26/1776, in CO5/78, frame 521 ("about," "white," "singing"), 522 ("advance," "both," "joined," "house"); "A Peace Talk [from] The Creeks to the Chactaws [no.] 8," ca. fall 1770, enclosed in John Stuart to Gage, 12/13/1770, in TGP ("Cloud"). Both sides affirmed the peace in late July 1777, when seventeen Choctaws visited Little Tallassee, Emistisiguo's town. The headmen likely selected this town since Emistisiguo had been the Choctaws' contact during the peace overtures of 1770. Unfortunately, he died prior to this visit. See Taitt to Stuart, 8/3/1777, CO5/78, frame 699.

Chapter 3

1. "A Talk delivered by the Old Tallasee King's Son [Tame King] at Ogeechee [River]," 6/18/1777, in EAID, vol. 18, 223 ("Three"). For an overview of Creek participation in the War for Independence, see Jim Piecuch, *Three Peoples, One King: Loyalists, Indians, and Slaves in the Revolutionary South, 1775–1782* (Columbia, University of South Carolina Press, 2008), 8, 63–76, 111–17, 150–58, 204–13, 258–65, 332–33; Kathryn E. Holland Braund, "'Like to Have Made a War among Ourselves': The Creek Indians and the Coming of the War of the Revolution," in *Nexus of Empire: Negotiating Loyalty and Identity in the Revolutionary Borderlands, 1760s–1820s*, ed. Gene Allen Smith and Sylvia L. Hilton (Gainesville: University Press of Florida, 2010): 39–62; Angela Pulley Hudson, *Creek Paths and Federal Roads: Indians, Settlers, and Slaves and the Making of the American South* (Chapel Hill: University of North Carolina Press, 2010), 18–26; and Bryan Rindfleisch, "'Our Lands Are Our Life and Breath': Coweta, Cusseta, and the Struggle for Creek Territory and Sovereignty during the American Revolution," *Ethnohistory* 60, no. 4 (Fall 2013): 581–603.

2. For Upper Creek-Cusseta ties, see George Galphin to Georgia governor James Glen, 5/12/1754, Coweta, in CRSC I, 499; Lower Creek headmen to Reynolds, 9/17/1756, in Reynolds to Lyttelton, 10/6/1756, box 2, in WHLP; and Samuel Thomas to Superintendent John Stuart, 9/19/1776, Cusseta, in CO5/78, frame 529. On Cusseta's history, see Steven C. Hahn, "The Cussita Migration Legend: History, Ideology, and the Politics of Mythmaking," in *Light on the Path: The Anthropology and History of the Southeastern Indians*, ed. Thomas J. Pluckhahn and Robbie Ethridge (Tuscaloosa: University of Alabama Press, 2006): 57–93, here 88 ("peace"); Agent James Seagrove to Lower Creeks, 5/13/1793, in ASP/IA, 1:397 ("great"); and Agent Benjamin Hawkins, "A sketch of the Creek Country in the years 1798 and 1799," in LBH, 1:285–327, here 311. For a sustained

analysis of the Creek moiety system, see George E. Lankford, *Looking for Lost Lore: Studies in Folklore, Ethnology, and Iconography* (Tuscaloosa: University of Alabama Press, 2008), 73–96.

3. On the mishmash of peoples in the revolutionary Native South, see Gilbert C. Din, "Spanish Control over a Multiethnic Society: Louisiana, 1763–1803," in *Choice, Persuasion, and Coercion: Social Control on Spain's North American Frontiers*, ed. Jesús F. de la Teja and Ross Frank (Albuquerque: University of New Mexico Press, 2005): 49–76; Piecuch, *Three Peoples, One King*, 14–35; Christina Snyder, "Native Nations in the Age of Revolution," in *The World of the Revolutionary American Republic: Land, Labor, and the Conflict for a Continent*, ed. Andrew Shankman (Routledge, 2014, online publication): 77–94, here 84–90; and Kathleen DuVal, *Independence Lost: Lives on the Edge of the American Revolution* (New York: Random House, 2015), especially 75–218.

4. Alexander McGillivray to Georgia governor John Houstoun, 6/30/1784, p. 2 ("Nation"), in Telamon Cuyler Collection 901, SNAD; "A Talk delivered by [Tame King] at Ogeechee," 6/18/1777, in EAID, vol. 18, 223 ("Three"). On McGillivray's wartime leadership, see the fine analysis in Michael D. Green, "The Creek Confederacy in the American Revolution: Cautious Participants," in *Anglo-Spanish Confrontation on the Gulf Coast during the American Revolution*, ed. William S. Coker and Robert R. Rea (Pensacola: Gulf Coast History and Humanities Conference, 1982): 54–75, here 66–70. McGillivray's opposition to the American rebels is often contrasted with Tame King's seeming cooptation by Georgia's rebel authorities. Some have deemed him "compliant" because he convened treaty councils with Georgia multiple times. Others have argued that Tame King, by consenting to unpopular land cessions, "did not act on behalf of the Creek Nation." Still others suggest that he was a leading member of the "American partisans" in Creek country. These perspectives adopt the nationalist biases of Alexander McGillivray, Tame King's chief opponent, and gloss over political alternatives in Creek country. See Colin G. Calloway, *The American Revolution in Indian Country: Crisis and Diversity in Native American Communities* (Cambridge: Cambridge University Press, 1995), 284 ("compliant"); Claudio Saunt, *A New Order of Things: Property, Power, and the Transformation of the Creek Indians, 1733–1816* (Cambridge: Cambridge University Press, 1999), 79–83; Hudson, *Creek Paths*, 27–33, 30 ("behalf"); and Kevin Kokomoor, *Of One Mind and of One Government: The Rise and Fall of the Creek Nation in the Early Republic* (Lincoln: University of Nebraska Press and American Philosophical Society, 2018), 69–82, 69 ("American"). Joshua S. Haynes, *Patrolling the Border: Theft and Violence on the Creek-Georgia Frontier, 1770–1796* (Athens: University of Georgia Press, 2018), 94–98, is gentler to Tame King and argues that the headman advanced towns' independence during the war. I take that argument one step further by illustrating that Tame King was a spokesperson for provinces, which enveloped towns as well as clans.

5. On the localist shape of politics in the revolutionary Native South, see Natalie R. Inman, *Brothers and Friends: Kinship in Early America* (Athens: University of Georgia Press, 2017), 2–3, 35–54, and Bryan C. Rindfleisch, *George Galphin's Intimate Empire: The Creek Indians, Family, and Colonialism in Early America* (Tuscaloosa: University of Alabama Press, 2019), 170–88. On Tallassee King, see "A Talk delivered by [Tame King] at Ogeechee," 6/18/1777, in EAID, vol. 18, 223 ("Three"), 224 ("Father"), and "A Talk Delivered at Silver Bluff the Third Day of November 1779 to George Galphin Esqr. Commissioner of Indian affairs in Southern Departments by the Tallassee King [actually Tame King]," enclosed in Galphin to General Lincoln, 11/7/1779, in GGL, folder 1, 2.

6. Jack B. Martin and Margaret McKane Mauldin, *A Dictionary of Creek/Muskogee* (Lincoln: University of Nebraska Press, 2000), 153 (*yvmvsē*/tame, *yvmvskętv*/meekness); "Memo. of the [Tame] Kings proposals & Complaints," ca. 1784, Augusta, p. 2 ("weak"), in GA/File II; "A Talk delivered by [Tame King] at Ogeechee" and "A Talk from the Handsome Fellow of the Oakfuskeys," 6/18/1777, in EAID, vol. 18, 224 ("Father"), 225; Robbie Ethridge, *Creek Country: The Creek Indians and Their World* (Chapel Hill: University of North Carolina Press, 2003), 102–4. For "Son," see Information of George Johnston, 10/2/1754, in CRSC II, 10.

7. On the "Middle" Creek towns, see John Reed Swanton, *Early History of the Creek Indians and Their Neighbors*, 216. On Tame King and the Halfway House settlement, see Samuel Thomas to Stuart, 8/16/1778, in CO5/79, frame 78, and "A talk from the kings[,] Beloved men[,] and Warriors of part of the upper Towns present the head men of 13 Towns the Tallesey King [Tame King], or good child of the Halfe way house Speaker" to Daniel McMurphy, agent of the Creek Nation, 6/25/1786, "Aukfuskey [Okfuskee] Towne," p. 1, in Telamon Cuyler Collection 207, SNAD. In April 1772 British agent David Taitt wrote that "Chavacleyhatchie or Halfway House" sat "twenty-five miles ENE" of Tuckabatchee on a "creek called Chavacleyhatchie, being the north branch of Nafabie [Upahee] Creek which empties itself into the Tallapuse River at the Great Tallassies [Tallassee]." He added that this "village ... belongs to the Tallassies" and has "about 20 gun-men and one trader." See "David Taitt's Journal to and through [the] Lower Creek Nation," in DAR vol. 5, 273–82, here 273. See also Ethridge, *Creek Country*, 70–71, 169.

8. George Galphin et al. to Creek headmen, 6/17/1777, in EAID, vol. 18, 222 ("Goods") and "A Talk delivered by [Tame King] at Ogeechee," 6/18/1777, in EAID, vol. 18, 223 ("This"), 224 ("young," "may," "he"). Besides Galphin, the commissioners included "Jon. Bryan, Dan'l McMurphy, John Stewart, R Rae, Stephen Heard, Sam'l Miller" (223). Daniel McMurphy served as Georgia's agent to the Creeks in the 1780s. Tallassee King contacted the rebels two months before the Ogeechee congress; see "A Talk from Indians to Geo. Golphin, one of the Commissioners of Indian Affairs," 4/21/1777, pp. 1–2, in American Philosophical Society, misc. papers, B: F85, vol. 71, fol. 12f. The document is a copy of the original and opens thusly: "A talk from the old talesy King [Tallassee King] to geo galphin Esq. one of the Commissioners of indian's affairs." Thanks to Kathryn Braund for sharing this with me.

9. Rindfleisch, "'Our Lands Are Our Life and Breath,'" 592; Stuart to George Germain, Pensacola, 6/14/1777, CO5/78, frame 633 ("scarcity"); "A Talk delivered by [Tame King] at Ogeechee," 6/18/1777, in EAID, vol. 18, 224 ("loaded"); William McIntosh to Alexander Cameron, 7/6/1777, CO5/78, frame 676 ("quantities"); Samuel Elbert to Creeks, 8/13/1777, in EAID, vol. 18, 261, 585n116.

10. "A Talk delivered by [Tame King] at Ogeechee" and "A Talk from the Handsome Fellow of the Oakfuskeys," 6/18/1777, in EAID, vol. 18, 223 ("Breath," "Master," "Towns," "appointed," "Three"), 224; Rindfleisch, *George Galphin's Intimate Empire*, 174–75. "The greatest part of the Cussitaws [as well as] Utchies and Pallachucla People" attended the Ogeechee meeting or what the British called "Galphins Treaty"; see McIntosh to Cameron, 7/6/1777, in CO5/78, frame 676. On McGillivray's Alabama ancestry, see Linda Langley, "The Tribal Identity of Alexander McGillivray: A Review of the Historical and Ethnographic Data," *Journal of the Louisiana Historical Association* 46, no. 2 (Spring 2005): 231–39.

11. "A Talk delivered by [Tame King] at Ogeechee," 6/18/1777, in EAID, vol. 18, 223 ("Tallapussee"); US Declaration of Independence, 1776 ("merciless"); Haynes, *Patrolling the Border*, 105, 119–24. "Tallapussee" refers to the Tallapoosa River, and "Coosahatchee" means Coosa River. Less clear is the meaning of "Otchsatchee," which barely resembles "Chattahoochee." Joined by several Lower Creek headmen at the Ogeechee congress, however, Tame King could ill afford to omit the Chattahoochee towns from his speech about riverine leadership.

12. "A Talk delivered by [Tame King] at Ogeechee" and "A Talk from the Handsome Fellow of the Oakfuskeys," 6/18/1777, in EAID, vol. 18, 223 (Tame King quotes), 224 (Handsome Fellow quotes). Handsome Fellow's talk confirmed Tame King's remark that Cusseta was the "largest" of the Creek towns (224). So too did a census of the Creek towns conducted by Spanish authorities later in the century. "Casista" (Cusseta) is identified as the most populous, with nine hundred inhabitants. See Pedro Olivier and James Durouzeaux to the Barón de Carondelet, 12/1/1793, "Old Town of Wetonka," in SMV, 4:229–33, here 232. On the Cussetas' attendance at the Ogeechee gathering, see McIntosh to Cameron, 7/6/1777, in CO5/78, frame 676.

13. "A Talk delivered by [Tame King] at Ogeechee," 6/18/1777, in EAID, vol. 18, 223 ("Breath," "Three"); John T. Juricek, *Endgame for Empire: British-Creek Relations in Georgia and Vicinity, 1763–1776* (Gainesville: University Press of Florida, 2015), 244–45, 253–54.

14. Alexander McGillivray to Colonel Stuart, 8/6/1778, Little Tallassee, in CO5/79, frame 41; Piker, *Okfuskee*, 62, 140, 247n12; Stuart to Germain, 3/5/1778, Pensacola, in CO5/79, frames 822–23; McIntosh to Stuart, 4/3/1778, in CO5/79, frame 867; Rindfleisch, "'Our Lands Are Our Life and Breath,'" 593–94; "A Talk from the Young Tallassee King [Tame King] from the Uper and lower Towns, of the Creeks, To George Galphin Esqr. Continental Commissioner[?] of Indian affairs, & Leroy Hammond and Daniel McMurphy Esqr.s Commissioners for the States of So[uth] Carolina and Georgia at Ogeechee," 12/15/1778, enclosed in Galphin to General Benjamin Lincoln, 1/7/1779, in GGL, folder 2, 3 ("ol^d").

15. "A Talk from the Young Tallassee King [Tame King]" to Commissioner Galphin et al., 12/15/1778, enclosed in Galphin to General Lincoln, 1/7/1779, in GGL, folder 2, 1 ("old," "stand," "one"), 2 ("Formerly," "frinds," "be," "still"); Rindfleisch, *George Galphin's Intimate Empire*, 176.

16. "A Talk from the Young Tallassee King [Tame King]" to Commissioner Galphin et al., 12/15/1778, enclosed in Galphin to General Lincoln, 1/7/1779, in GGL, folder 2, 2 (quotes).

17. "A Talk from the Young Tallassee King [Tame King]" to Commissioner Galphin et al., 12/15/1778, enclosed in Galphin to General Lincoln, 1/7/1779, in GGL, folder 2, 3 ("talk," "tis"); document 10, 9/28/1759, p. 1 ("home"), in Edmond Atkin to William Henry Lyttelton, 11/30/1759, box 13, in WHLP; Steven C. Hahn, *The Invention of the Creek Nation, 1670–1763* (Lincoln: University of Nebraska Press, 2004), 271–77. Kathryn Braund points out that Tallassee remained "neutral" for most of the war, indicating that the Tallassees pursued multiple allies to avoid dependence on one, especially Georgia; see Braund, "'Like to Have Made a War among Ourselves,'" 50.

18. Sauwoogelooche, a village offshoot (talofa) of Sauwoogelo, stood by Tame King as well. "A Talk delivered by [Tame King] at Ogeechee," 6/18/1777, in EAID, vol. 18, 223

("Breath"); "A Talk from the Young Tallassee King [Tame King]" to Commissioner Galphin et al., 12/15/1778, enclosed in Galphin to General Lincoln, 1/7/1779, in GGL folder 2, 1 ("Parachuckles," "Hitchatas," "Killigees"), 3 ("great," "headmen," "say," "have"). For towns' provincial affiliations, see Jerome Courtonne, "List of Headmen of the Creeks, giving information re[:] French and British sympathies," October 1758, box 8, in WHLP.

19. Piecuch, *Three Peoples One King*, 124–25, 145–49; Inman, *Brothers and Friends*, 36–37.

20. Tame King said, "Tomathlies, the old fields and Meckasukey send this Twist of Tobacco." Some of these towns, such as Miccosukee, affiliated with the Seminoles, although they remained in contact with the Lower Creeks. The word "fields" is written above a deleted word. See "A Talk from the Young Tallassee King [Tame King]" to Commissioner Galphin et al., 12/15/1778, enclosed in Galphin to General Lincoln, 1/7/1779, in GGL, folder 2, 2 ("Tomathlies," "Muckasukey," "Twist," "friendship," "white"); "Observations on the Creek and Cherokee Indians," in Bartram, 140 ("Ruins"); and Steven J. Peach, "The Failure of Political Centralization: Mad Dog, the Creek Indians, and the Politics of Claiming Power in the American Revolutionary Era," *Native South* 11 (2018): 81–116, here 100–101, 114n29

21. "A Talk Delivered at Silver Bluff the Third Day of November 1779 to George Galphin Esqr. Commissioner of Indian affairs in Southern Departments by the Tallassee King [actually, Tame King]," enclosed in Galphin to General Lincoln, 11/7/1779, in GGL, folder 1, 7 ("white," "Friendship"), 8 ("Father," "headmen," "Delivered," "French"); "A Talk Delivered by George Galphin Esqr. Commissioner of Indian affair[s] to the Tallassee King and a Number of warriors and Beloved Men at Silver Bluff," 11/7/1779, enclosed in Galphin to General Lincoln, 11/7/1779, in GGL, folder 1, 4 ("Every"); Piecuch, *Three Peoples, One King*, 149, 157–58, 210–13; DuVal, *Independence Lost*, 125–27, 147–59; Rindfleisch, *George Galphin's Intimate Empire*, 175–82.

22. "A Talk given by [Tame King on behalf of] the Tallassee King and Sundry Head Men of the Upper and Lower Creek Nation," 5/28/1782, Augusta, p. 1 ("Peace [added: "& quitness"] in the Land"), in Telamon Cuyler Collection 260, SNAD; "Memo. of the [Tame] Kings proposals & Complaints," ca. 1784, p. 4 ("but," "Shall"), in GA/File II. Tame King was indeed in Augusta for the 1782 talk; see the invoice dated June 6, 1782, p. 1, in Telamon Cuyler Collection 839, SNAD. As for the 1784 address, contextual clues suggest a provenance of 1784, when John Houstoun was Georgia's governor. On McGillivray, see Saunt, *New Order*, 62–63, 81–83, and Kokomoor, *Of One Mind*, 81–102.

23. Tame King also requested an audience with US and British diplomats, asking Georgia to pass along "this Talk" to the "great Warriors" in Savannah and Charleston, port cities presently occupied by British forces, and to the Continental Congress in Philadelphia. He referred to George Washington as the "Virginia King." See "A Talk given by [Tame King on behalf of] the Tallasee King," 5/28/1782, p. 1 (quotes), in Telamon Cuyler Collection 260, SNAD.

24. Tame King "says that the French was their old Fathers and that the [added: "Americans"] Spaniards and Dutch have strove to assist them that they might live upon their own Land." See "A Talk given by [Tame King on behalf of] the Tallasee King," 5/28/1782, p. 1 (quotes), in Telamon Cuyler Collection 260, SNAD.

25. "A Talk given by [Tame King on behalf of] the Tallasee King," 5/28/1782, p. 2 ("number," "Head," "nothing"), in Telamon Cuyler Collection 260, SNAD. The complete

list of towns is as follows: "The Cussetaws, The Hichetaws Parachocolau, Hoconey Savoucolo, & Usshatchee, & Savocolouchees," or Sauwoogelooche, the village offshoot of Sauwoogelo, as well as Tallassee. Whether "Usshatchee" was Lower Creek or Seminole is unclear, and it seems unlikely that it was the Tallapoosa town of Fusihatchee. Fat King's talk is enclosed in James Rae to Georgia governor John Martin, 12/28/1782, Augusta, p. 1 ("We"), in Telamon Cuyler Collection 124, SNAD.

26. Treaty of Augusta, 11/1/1783, in EAID, vol. 18, 372, 373 ("Trade"). Fifteen Creek delegates attended the conference: "the Tallesee King [Tame King], Tallesee Warrior, the Fat King, Mad Fish, Topwar King, Alachago, Hitcheto Warrior, Okoney, Okolege, Cuse King, Second Man, Inomatwhata, Inomatawtusnigua, Head Warrior, Gugahacho" (372). "Okoney" did not sign the treaty, but "Cowetaw," whose name does not appear on the list of delegates, apparently did (373). Georgia's role in the negotiations and resulting treaty was no less controversial than that of the Creeks. Georgia settlers had lived on the Oconee lands without Creek permission since the colonial era, and many more invaded the area during the War for Independence. Thus realpolitik brought state commissioners to the treaty table as much as the will to negotiate with Creek leaders. In addition, Georgia undermined the Confederation Congress by arguing that the southern states exercised the legal capacity to make treaties with Native populations in the 1780s. On the Treaty of Augusta, see Saunt, *New Order*, 79 ("small"), 80n60; Hudson, *Creek Paths*, 30–31; Haynes, *Patrolling the Border*, 89–96; Kokomoor, *Of One Mind*, 75–77; and McGillivray to Houstoun, 6/30/1784, Little Tallassee, p. 4 ("S. C. N[.]"), in Telamon Cuyler Collection 901, SNAD.

27. McGillivray to Houstoun, 6/30/1784, p. 2, in Telamon Cuyler Collection 901, SNAD; "Memo. of the [Tame] Kings proposals & Complaints," ca. 1784, p. 2 (quotes), in GA/File II; Treaty of Augusta, 11/1/1783, in EAID, vol. 18, 373.

28. Tame King added that he "never intended" to give up "the forks" where the Oconee and Ocmulgee Rivers converge, indicating that Georgia commissioners had misled the signers. See "Memo. of the [Tame] Kings proposals & Complaints," ca. 1784, p. 1 (quotes), in GA/File II; and "A Talk delivered by [Tame King] at Ogeechee," 6/18/1777, in EAID, vol. 18, 223. See too Kokomoor, *Of One Mind*, 76–81.

29. McGillivray to Houstoun, 6/30/1784, pp. 1–2, in Telamon Cuyler Collection 901, SNAD; Hudson, *Creek Paths*, 29; Haynes, *Patrolling the Border*, 96–98, 107, 110–19; Kokomoor, *Of One Mind*, 81–82, 86, 109.

30. For the impact of the Paris Peace of 1783 on the southern frontier, see David Andrew Nichols, *Red Gentlemen and White Savages: Indians, Federalists, and the Search for Order on the American Frontier* (Charlottesville: University of Virginia Press, 2008), 19–36; DuVal, *Independence Lost*, 229–69.

31. "A talk from . . . the Tallesey King [Tame King], or good child of the Halfe way house Speaker" to McMurphy, 6/25/1786, p. 1, in Telamon Cuyler Collection 207, SNAD. Tame King apprised Georgia authorities of Tallassee King's "feet being grown weak and his breath short." The elder had thus "given him his mouth." Although "the old man was not present[,] it was his talks that was delivered." See "Memo. of the [Tame] Kings proposals & Complaints," ca. 1784, p. 2 ("feet," "old"), in GA/File II. On the Oconee War, see Haynes, *Patrolling the Border*, 96–98, 105–54; Kokomoor, *Of One Mind*, 81–135.

32. "A Talk delivered by the Tallassie King to the Govr & Council," 9/20/1784, "Talk No. II," p. 1 ("good," "never," "expect," "white") and "Tallassie [inserted: "Kings"] Talk delivered to the Govr & Council," 9/22/1784, p. 1 ("big," "friends," "upper," "Stores"),

in GA/File II. There are two versions of the 9/20/1784 talk. "Talk No. II" is the original, which contains several deletions and emendations. "Talk N°. II II," a clean duplicate, is the "Same Talk as No II." The original is a more precise record of Tame King's language. The verbiage of the September talks suggests that Tallassee King had traveled to Augusta, but contextual clues indicate that Tame King delivered these messages on behalf of the elder man, who had become too "weak" and short of "breath" to travel the long distance from Tallassee to Augusta; see "Memo. of the [Tame] Kings proposals & Complaints," ca. 1784, p. 2, in GA/File II. On Galphin's relations with Creeks during the War for Independence, see Rindfleisch, *George Galphin's Intimate World*, 176–82.

33. Some of Houstoun's promises were later codified in the Treaty of Galphinton, signed on November 12, 1785, by Tame King ("Opohelthe Micko") and Fat King ("Inneha Micko"); see EAID, vol. 18, 390–91. Article 2 stipulated that "If any citizen of this state or other person or persons shall attempt to settle or run any of the lands reserved to the Indians for their hunting grounds, such person or persons may be detained until the governor shall demand [punish] him or them" (390). See too Kokomoor, *Of One Mind*, 87–89. For in-text quotes, see "Tallassie [inserted: "Kings"] Talk delivered to the Govr & Council," 9/22/1784, p. 1 ("big"); "A Talk delivered by the Tallassie King to the Govr & Council," 9/20/1784, "Talk No. II," p. 2 ("accused," "witnesses," "hear"); and "a Talk del.^{d} [b]y the Govr & Council to the Tallesse and fat Kings at Augusta," 9/24/1784, p. 3 ("Concern," "prevent," "make")—all in GA/File II. A portion of the text on pages 3 and 4 of the governor's talk bears an *X*, possibly indicating deletion.

34. "A Talk delivered by the Tallassie King to the Govr & Council," 9/20/1784, "Talk No. II," p. 2 ("three," "One"). The Chickasaw headman Payamataha made a postwar alliance with the United States and thus may have participated in Tame King's intertribal networking to bring peace across the region. Yet whether Payamataha and Tame King communicated with one another until the former's death in 1785 is unclear. On Choctaw and Chickasaw diplomacy in the 1780s, see Greg O'Brien, "The Conqueror Meets the Unconquered: Negotiating Cultural Boundaries on the Post-Revolutionary Southern Frontier," *Journal of Southern History* 67, no. 1 (February 2001): 39–72, here 43–45, 49–56, 70–72; James R. Atkinson, *Splendid Land, Splendid People: The Chickasaw Indians to Removal* (Tuscaloosa: University of Alabama Press, 2004), 139–79; and DuVal, *Independence Lost*, 238–45, 304–9.

35. "A Talk delivered by the Tallassie King to the Govr & Council," 9/20/1784, "Talk No. II," p. 2 ("fat," "one"), p. 3 ("string"); "a Talk del.^{d} [b]y the Govr & Council to the Tallesse and fat Kings at Augusta," 9/24/1784, p. 2 ("Tokens," "Wish," "Chickesaws"). US agent Benjamin Hawkins learned from "Tussekiah Micco of Cussetuh" in the 1790s that "The Cussetuhs and Chickasaws consider themselves as people of one fire (*totekitcau humgoce*) from the earliest account of their origin"; see Hawkins, "A sketch of the Creek Country," in LBH, 1:285–327, here 327.

36. "A Talk delivered by the Tallassie King to the Govr & Council," 9/20/1784, "Talk No. II," p. 2, and "Tallassie [inserted: "Kings"] Talk delivered to the Govr & Council," 9/22/1784, p. 2 ("Talk"), in GA/File II; Kokomoor, *Of One Mind*, 69–80, 94.

37. "A talk from the ... Tallesey King [Tame King], or good child of the Halfe way house Speaker" to McMurphy, 6/25/1786, p. 1, in Telamon Cuyler Collection 207, SNAD; Martin and Mauldin, *Dictionary*, 49 (herē), 50 (herkē, herkv), 55 (hopuewv). Tame King's signature on two Creek–Georgian treaties in the mid-1780s is "Opchelthe

Micko" (EAID, vol. 18, 391) and "Opohethle Mico, or Tallisee king" (EAID, vol. 18, 435). "Opohelthe" roughly translates to "good child." For reference to "the good Child King" in 1778, see Samuel Thomas to Stuart, 8/16/1778, in CO5/79, frame 78. Since Tame King would have been too young to assume that title in the 1770s, Tallassee King may have held it and later passed it on to Tame King.

38. "A talk from . . . the Tallesey King [Tame King], or good child of the Halfe way house Speaker" to McMurphy, 6/25/1786, p. 1 ("My," "hope," "will," "I," "path"), in Telamon Cuyler Collection 207, SNAD. For "surrounded" and the possibility that four hundred Creeks attended the "Skalop [Shoulderbone?] Creek" negotiations, see J. Linder to Pedro Favrot, 11/13/1786, "Tinsa [Tensaw district]," in SMV, 3:189. "Jnº. Linder" signed a document named "Orders to Which the Inhabitants of Tinsa Must Conform," 5/27/1792, in SMV, 4:44. The Tensaw district in the lower Mississippi River valley fell under Spanish jurisdiction. For countervailing evidence that two hundred Creeks assembled at Shoulderbone Creek, including women and children, see John Habersham to Edward Telfair, 10/19/1786, Camp Shoulder Bone, box 3, Edward Telfair Papers, Rubenstein. By averaging the totals from the Linder and Habersham letters, I estimate that three hundred Creeks attended Shoulderbone Creek. Fifty-eight delegates signed the treaty; see Haynes, *Patrolling the Border*, 127. For goods distributed to the delegates, see "[Receipt for] rations" signed by Daniel McMurphy, 11/1/1786, pp. 1–2, in Telamon Cuyler Collection 73, and "List of Articles delivered to McMurphy esqʳ," 11/3/1786, pp. 1–2, Telamon Cuyler Collection 229, SNAD. For the Treaty of Shoulderbone Creek, signed on November 3, 1786, see EAID, vol. 18, 433–35. The five hostages were "Cuchas, of the Cussetas"; "Suckawockie, brother to" Cuchas; "Emathlocks, second man of the Broken Arrow"; "Chuuocklie Micko, of the Cowetas"; and "Enautaleche, nephew to the head man of the Swaglos" (EAID, vol. 18, 435). A federal official, James White, ransomed the hostages in spring 1787 (editor's note, EAID, vol. 18, 362, 600n22). For "thundered," see McGillivray to West Florida overnor Arturo O'Neill, 12/3/1786, in EAID, vol. 18, 437.

39. "Treaty with the Creeks, 1790," 8/7/1790, New York City, in IALT, 25–29; Alexander Cornells to James Seagrove, 4/15/1793; James Seagrove to Henry Knox, 4/30/1793, in ASP/IA, 1:384; and "A talk from . . . the Tallesey King [Tame King], or good child of the Halfe way house Speaker" to McMurphy, 6/25/1786, p. 1, in Telamon Cuyler Collection 207, SNAD. For an early study of the treaty, see J. Leitch Wright Jr., "Creek-American Treaty of 1790: Alexander McGillivray and the Diplomacy of the Old Southwest," *Georgia Historical Quarterly* 51, no. 4 (December 1967): 379–400, especially 380–82, 388–94. On the Creek–Georgian treaties of the 1780s, see Haynes, *Patrolling the Border*, 125–29, 135–37, 156–58; Kokomoor, *Of One Mind*, 97–102, 98 ("exercise"), 105–7, 133–35, 340.

40. "A talk from . . . the Tallesey King [Tame King], or good child of the Halfe way house Speaker" to McMurphy, 6/25/1786, p. 1, in Telamon Cuyler Collection 207, SNAD.

Chapter 4

1. On the vectors of war in the late eighteenth-century Native South, see Robbie Ethridge, *Creek Country: The Creek Indians and Their World* (Chapel Hill: University of North Carolina Press, 2003), 137–38, 176, 219–28; James R. Atkinson, *Splendid Land, Splendid People: The Chickasaw Indians to Removal* (Tuscaloosa: University of Alabama Press, 2004), 139–79; Joshua Piker, "Colonists and Creeks: Rethinking the

Pre-Revolutionary Southern Backcountry," *Journal of Southern History* 70, no. 3 (2004): 503–40, here 536–40; Adam Rothman, *Slave Country: American Expansion and the Origins of the Deep South* (Cambridge, MA: Harvard University Press, 2005), 11–13; Angela Pulley Hudson, *Creek Paths and Federal Roads: Indians, Settlers, and Slaves and the Making of the American South* (Chapel Hill: University of North Carolina Press, 2010), 38–46; Kathleen DuVal, *Independence Lost: Lives on the Edge of the American Revolution* (New York: Random House, 2015), 340–46; Joshua S. Haynes, *Patrolling the Border: Theft and Violence on the Creek-Georgia Frontier, 1770–1796* (Athens: University of Georgia Press, 2018), 155–99; Kevin Kokomoor, *Of One Mind and of One Government: The Rise and Fall of the Creek Nation in the Early Republic* (Lincoln: University of Nebraska Press and American Philosophical Society, 2018), 138–213; and Daniel S. Dupre, *Alabama's Frontiers and the Rise of the Old South* (Bloomington: Indiana University Press, 2018), 127–57. Albeit focused on Creek–US relations, Piker argues succinctly that in the second half of the eighteenth century, "Creeks and colonists viewed each other as members of abstract categories—Virginians or Indians—[so that regular contact between the two groups] only contributed to the ever-increasing volume of cross-cultural violence" ("Colonists and Creeks," 540).

2. "Bird [Tail] King, [and] Cussetah King" to Major Henry Gaither, 4/13/1793, Cusseta, in ASP/IA, 1:420 ("three," "talked"), enclosed in Gaither to Secretary of War Henry Knox, 4/19/1793, Fort Fidius, in ASP/IA, 1:419; Deputy Agent Timothy Barnard to Gaither, 6/21/1793, Flint River, in ASP/IA, 1:422 ("resolution").

3. McGillivray died in February 1793. On his final years of leadership, see William S. Coker and Thomas D. Watson, *Indian Traders of the Southeastern Spanish Borderlands: Panton, Leslie & Company and John Forbes & Company, 1783–1847* (Pensacola: University of West Florida Press, 1986), 163–77; DuVal, *Independence Lost*, 324–32, 337. For "three," see "Bird [Tail] King, [and] Cussetah Mico" to Gaither, 4/13/1793, in ASP/IA, 1:420, enclosed in Gaither to Knox, 4/19/1793, Fort Fidius, in ASP/IA, 1:419. On Creek nation-building in the late eighteenth century, see Hudson, *Creek Paths*, 17–19, 86–87; Evan Nooe, "Common Justice: Vengeance and Retribution in Creek Country," *Ethnohistory* 62, no. 2 (April 2015): 241–62; Haynes, *Patrolling the Border*, 178–95, 201; and Kokomoor, *Of One Mind*, 215–16, 231–32. According to Haynes, "Creek people experienced greater coalescence while preserving the privileges of talwa [town] autonomy" in these years (201). To explain the growing coalescence late in the century, this chapter asserts that headmen created policy meant to build unity among and recognize three core rivers/provinces in Creek country.

4. On similar dynamics among the late eighteenth-century Chickasaws, see Natalie R. Inman, *Brothers and Friends: Kinship in Early America* (Athens: University of Georgia Press, 2017), 57–89; and DuVal, *Independence Lost*, 238–45.

5. On the contingency of power in this period, see Coker and Watson, *Indian Traders of the Southeastern Spanish Borderlands*, 157–202; David Andrew Nichols, *Red Gentlemen and White Savages: Indians, Federalists, and the Search for Order on the American Frontier* (Charlottesville: University of Virginia Press, 2008), 151–58, 169–70, 179, 182–83, 188–89; Christina Snyder, "The South," in The Oxford Handbook of American Indian History, ed. Frederick E. Hoxie (New York: Oxford University Press, 2016): 315–33, here 323–24; DuVal, *Independence Lost*, 341–51, 344 ("advanced"); and Dupre, *Alabama's Frontiers* 165–66, 186–88.

6. A Spanish census reported 15,160 Creek and Seminole "souls" in late 1793; see Pedro Olivier and James Durouzeaux to the Barón de Carondelet, 12/1/1793, "Old Town of Wetonka," in SMV, 4:229–33, here 232. Since five hundred Seminoles were counted, I deduct that number from the grand total, thereby yielding a Creek population of 14,660 in late 1793. See too Peter H. Wood, "The Changing Population of the Colonial South: An Overview by Race and Region, 1685–1790," in *Powhatan's Mantle: Indians in the Colonial Southeast*, 2nd ed., ed. Gregory A. Waselkov, Peter H. Wood, and Tom Hatley (Lincoln: University of Nebraska Press, 2006): 57–132, here 58 (figure 1), 60–61 (table 1), 81–87; Hudson, *Creek Paths*, 37–65.

7. On the many dimensions of US southern expansion, see Wood, "Changing Population of the Colonial South," 92, 98–99, 106, 116; Rothman, *Slave Country*, 9–14, 40–42; Hudson, *Creek Paths*, 45–47, 53–56, 80–81; DuVal, *Independence Lost*, 313–20; Inman, *Brothers and Friends*, 77–78. The Chattahoochee River valley was one node among many of cross-cultural contest in the region; see John Bradshaw, deposed by Georgia governor Edward Telfair, 11/22/1790, Augusta, pp. 1–3, in Telamon Cuyler Collection 096, in SNAD; and Nichols, *Red Gentlemen*, 121–23, 183.

8. Haynes, *Patrolling the Border*, 2 ("border"), 158–71; Kokomoor, *Of One Mind*, 142–209; Dupre, *Alabama's Frontiers*, 132–33, 140–53; Bryan C. Rindfleisch, *George Galphin's Intimate Empire: The Creek Indians, Family, and Colonialism in Early America* (Tuscaloosa: University of Alabama Press, 2019), 29, 110. Creek warriors made common cause with Shawnees in Kentucky too; see William Panton to Carondelet, 1/27/1793, Pensacola, in GHQ, 23:3 (September 1939): 300–303, here 301, and James Carey, interpreter for the Cherokees, interviewed by William Blount, governor of the Southwest Territory, 3/20/1793, Knoxville, in ASP/IA, 1:437–39.

9. Nichols, *Red Gentlemen*, 124–27; "Copy of a talk sent to Georgia," 10/4/1793, enclosed in "Copy of a letter from John Golphin to M^r. [William] Panton," 10/16/1793, "Broken Arrows [a Lower Creek town]," in SMV, 4:219 ("you").

10. On Creek–US diplomacy in the early 1790s, see "Talk from the White Lieut[?]. of the Oakfuskeys" to Agent James Seagrove, 8/15/1792, "New York [Nuyaka] in the upper Creeks," in GA/File II, original manuscript; "Bird [Tail] King, [and] Cussetah King" to Gaither, 4/13/1793, in ASP/IA, 1:420, enclosed in Gaither to Knox, 4/19/1793, Fort Fidius, in ASP/IA, 1:419; US Seagrove to Knox, 4/30/1793, St. Marys, in ASP/IA, 1:384; "The Cussetah King, the Mad Dog of the Tuckaubatchee, the White Lieutenant, and myself [John Kinnard of Hitchiti]" to Seagrove, 5/16/1793, Hitchiti, in ASP/IA, 1:388–89, enclosed in Seagrove to Knox, 5/24/1793, St. Marys, in ASP/IA, 1:387–88; Nichols, *Red Gentlemen*, 151–58; Kevin Kokomoor, "Creeks, Federalists, and the Idea of Coexistence in the Early Republic," *Journal of Southern History* 81, no. 4 (November 2015): 803–42, here 815–26; Haynes, *Patrolling the Border*, 173–77, 179–88; and James L. Hill, *Creek Internationalism in an Age of Revolution, 1763–1818* (Lincoln: University of Nebraska Press, 2022), 132–34.

11. Alexander Cornells and "the Upper Creeks" to Seagrove, 4/15/1793, Cusseta, in ASP/IA, 1:384 ("mad"), enclosed in Seagrove to Knox, 4/30/1793, St. Marys, in ASP/IA, 1:384; Gaither to Knox, 4/19/1793, Fort Fidius, in ASP/IA, 1:419; Panton to Carondelet, 4/10/1793, Pensacola, in ETHS 31 (1959): 80 ("fire"), 80n60; "The Cussetah King, the Mad Dog of the Tuckaubatchee, the White Lieutenant, and myself [John Kinnard of Hitchiti]" to Seagrove, 5/16/1793, Hitchiti, in ASP/IA, 1:388 ("friends"), enclosed in Seagrove to Knox, 5/24/1793, St. Marys, in ASP/IA, 1:387–88.

12. On White Lieutenant, see his "Talk" to Agent Seagrove, 8/15/1792, in GA/File II, original manuscript. On the Cusseta meeting and Mad Dog's address to Seagrove, see "At a talk held in the Cussetahs Creek nation, March 22, 1793," in ASP/IA, 1:383. Mad Dog was joined by White Lieutenant of Okfuskee, Alexander Cornells, and headmen from several Lower Creek towns, including Coweta and Hitchiti. On Mad Dog's political and diplomatic training, see Steven J. Peach, "The Failure of Political Centralization: Mad Dog, the Creek Indians, and the Politics of Claiming Power in the American Revolutionary Era," *Native South* 11 (2018): 81–116, here 85–87. See also Kokomoor, *Of One Mind*, 48, 62.

13. Seagrove received the belt addressed to President Washington and forwarded it to Knox. Whether Seagrove received the belt addressed to him and his spouse is unclear. For Mad Dog's second talk to Seagrove, see "the Mad Dog, the White Lieutenant, David Cornell[s], Alexander Cornell[s], Mr. Weatherford, and thirteen other head-men of the Upper Creeks," 4/8/1793, Tuckabatchee, ASP/IA, 1:384, 385 (quotes), enclosed in Seagrove to Knox, 4/30/1793, St. Marys, in ASP/IA, 1:384. "Mr. Weatherford" was Charles Weatherford, a trader and former loyalist who lived among Upper Creeks. In 1779 or early 1780, Weatherford married the Alabama Creek Sehcy III. She later bore a son named William. For the Weatherford family, see Gregory A. Waselkov, *A Conquering Spirit: Fort Mims and the Redstick War of 1813–1814* (Tuscaloosa: University of Alabama Press, 2006), 42.

14. "Bird [Tail] King, [and] Cussetah King" to Gaither, 4/13/1793, Cusseta, in ASP/IA, 1:420 ("three," "have"), enclosed in Gaither to Knox, 4/19/1793, Fort Fidius, in ASP/IA, 1:419; Barnard to Gaither, 5/21/1793, Flint River, ASP/IA, 1:422 ("resolution").

15. Although Creek headmen restrained a war party led by Tame King, this proved an exception to the localist rule. See Barnard to Seagrove, 4/19/1793, Flint River, in ASP/IA, 1:386, and Barnard to Seagrove, 5/12/1793, in ASP/IA, 1:391; Kokomoor, *Of One Mind*, 206–7; Hill, *Creek Internationalism*, 113–14.

16. The five towns in question were Coweta, Broken Arrow, Yuchi, Ouseechee, and Tallassee. See "The Cussetah King, the Mad Dog of the Tuckaubatchee, the White Lieutenant, and myself [John Kinnard of Hitchiti]" to Seagrove, 5/16/1793, Hitchiti, in ASP/IA, 1:388 (quotes), enclosed in Seagrove to Knox, 5/24/1793, St. Marys, in ASP/IA, 1:387–88; and Cornells and "the Upper Creeks" to Seagrove, 4/15/1793, Cusseta, ASP/IA, 1:384 ("mad"), enclosed in Seagrove to Knox, 4/30/1793, St. Marys, in ASP/IA, 1:384. On Kinnard, see George Galphin, deposed by Seagrove, 5/24/1793, Camden County, Georgia, in ASP/IA, 1:389, enclosed in Seagrove to Knox, 5/24/1793, St. Marys, in ASP/IA, 1:387–88; and Kokomoor, *Of One Mind*, 194–95. George Galphin was one of the sons of Metawney and the late deerskin trader of the same name.

17. Seagrove to Knox, 5/24/1793, St. Marys, in ASP/IA, 1:387 ("chastisement," "I," "severe"); "The Mad Dog, of Tuckautbachee," "White Lieutenant, Oakfuskees," "Alexander Cornell[s]," and Charles Weatherford to Seagrove, 6/14/1793, Tuckabatchee, in ASP/IA, 1:396 ("six"); Pedro Olivier to Carondelet, 6/11/1793, "Town of Mongulacha," SMV, 4:167; Barnard to Seagrove, "flint river 20th June 179[3]," p. 1 ("order," "appointed"), copy of letter in GA/File II.

18. Barnard apprised Seagrove that "a number of the heads from the lower creeks . . . agreed to" the death sentences, thereby implying that some objected. See Barnard to Seagrove, "flint river 20th June 179[3]," p. 1, copy of letter in GA/File II; Ethridge, *Creek*

Country, 228–29. Barnard blamed "that old vilian [James] Durouzeaux" for warning the ringleaders of impending doom, stating that Durouzeaux was a double agent who received $300 "pr. year" from Spain to undermine US interests (1). Barnard overlooked the obvious point that the death squad refused to kill those of a different clan. On blood revenge, see John Phillip Reid, *A Law of Blood: The Primitive Law of the Cherokee Nation* (1970; repr., DeKalb: Northern Illinois University Press, 2006), 73–92.

19. Peach, "The Failure of Political Centralization," 81–84; Haynes, *Patrolling the Border*, 172 ("shocking"); Kokomoor, *Of One Mind*, 198–202; Inman, *Brothers and Friends*, 56, 66; Joshua Piker, *The Four Deaths of Acorn Whistler: Telling Stories in Colonial America* (Cambridge, MA: Harvard University Press, 2013), especially 1–33, 78–84, 82 ("more"). Acorn Whistler lived in Little Okfuskee.

20. The Cowetas likely stole the horses that triggered the militia attack. For the Burnt Village affair, see Seagrove to Knox, 10/9/1793, Fort Fidius, in ASP/IA, 1:411 ("plundered," "among," date of raid), 412; Barnard to Seagrove, 10/1/1793, "Oakmulgee," in APS/IA, 1:413; Barnard to Seagrove, 10/17/1793, Flint River, in ASP/IA, 1:415, 416 ("own," "wife"), enclosed in Seagrove to Knox, 10/21/1793, Fort Fidius, in ASP/IA, 1:415; Commandant Enrique White to Carondelet, 10/10/1793, Pensacola, in SMV, 4:216; Barnard to Seagrove, 10/18/1793, Flint River, p. 1 ("have," "fully"), in GA/File II; and Peach, "Failure of Political Centralization," 90–91, 110–11n15. Accounts differ as to the number, gender, and age of the captives. Seagrove's October 9 letter identifies three women and five girls (ASP/IA, 1:411); White reported to Carondelet on October 10 that four women, three girls, and one boy had been kidnapped (SMV, 4:216); and Barnard stated that ten women and children were "lost" (ASP/IA, 1:416).

21. Galphin expected presents from "our friends the Spaniards" as well as Panton. See "Copy of a letter from John Golphin to M^r. [William] Panton," 10/16/1793, Broken Arrow, and the enclosure "Copy of a talk sent to Georgia," 10/4/1793—both in SMV, 4:219 (quotes). On Spain's attempt to counter US expansion by forging alliances with the southern Indians, see DuVal, *Independence Lost*, 309–12, 341–42; and Peach, "Failure of Political Centralization," 99–100. On mixed-race Creeks such as Galphin, who challenged the established leadership in the late eighteenth century, see Bryan C. Rindfleisch, "The Indian Factors: Kinship, Trade, and Authority in the Creek Nation and American South, 1740–1800," *Journal of Early American History* 8 (2018): 1–29, here 4–6, 27–28.

22. Commandant White wrote Carondelet on October 10, "If the war continues, I shall need more powder" for the Creek warriors arriving in Pensacola; see White to Carondelet, 10/10/1793, Pensacola, in SMV, 4:216 ("ask," "government," "If"). Carondelet's name was Francisco Luis Hectór. See too Durouzeaux to Commandant White, 10/18/1793, in SMV, 4:220 ("young," "Very," "The"). Durouzeaux may have written his letter from "Brocon Arow Town" in Lower Creek country (SMV, 4:221). On Creek-settler violence in 1793–94, see Haynes, *Patrolling the Border*, 180–81; Constant Freeman Jr. to Knox, 11/8/1793, Fort Fidius, in ASP/IA, 1:469; and White to Carondelet, 10/10/1793, Pensacola, in SMV, 4:216.

23. On the white and Creek captives, see Louis Leclerc de Milford to Carondelet, 4/14/1794, "Cloaly [Hoithlewaulee]," in SMV, 4:267 ("three"); "A Talk from the Head men of the Cussetas & Cowetas to the Mad dog the Head Warrior & Aleck Cornell of Tuckabatchies & the Tuckabatchie King," 6/27/1794, Cusseta (?), in *GHQ*, 24:2

(June 1940): 150–57, here 155–56; Hallowing King to Commandant White [1793], in SMV, 4:234–35; Blount to Seagrove, 1/9/1794, Knoxville, in TSRO, 323; and Document 117, Blount to Brigadier General James Robertson, 7/21/1794, Knoxville, in AHM 3:4 (October 1898): 354. On the methods and purpose of southern Indian captive-taking, see "Travels Through North & South Carolina, Georgia, East & West Florida, the Cherokee Country, the Extensive Territories of the Muscogulges, or Creek Confederacy, and the Country of the Chactaws; Containing an Account of the Soil and Natural Productions of Those Regions, Together with Observations on the Manners of the Indians," in Bartram, 58, 63, 113–14; and Christina Snyder, *Slavery in Indian Country: The Changing Face of Captivity in Early America* (Cambridge, MA: Harvard University Press, 2010), 13–45.

24. On the Creek-Chickasaw War from Chickasaw perspectives, see Atkinson, *Splendid Land*, 120–79.

25. In 1790 there were sixty-seven thousand white settlers and 13,800 Black people, most of them slaves, in what became Tennessee and Kentucky. On population figures, see Wood, "Changing Population of the Colonial South," 60–61 (table 1), 95, 115–16. On the origins of the Creek-Chickasaw War, see Atkinson, *Splendid Land*, 134–38, 155–58; DuVal, *Independence Lost*, 337, 343–44; James Wilkinson to Estevan Miró, 1/26/1790, Lexington (Kentucky), in ETHS 22 (1950): 137; and Stephen Minor to Manuel Luis Gayoso de Lemos, 12/12/1791, Natchez, in ETHS 26 (1954): 66. For Chickasaw martial power, see David A. Nichols, "The Enterprise of War: The Military Economy of the Chickasaw Indians, 1715– 815," in *The Native South: New Histories and Enduring Legacies*, ed. Tim Alan Garrison and Greg O'Brien (Lincoln: University of Nebraska Press, 2017): 33–46. For Blount's motivations, see Document 139, Blount to Robertson, 12/4/1794, Knoxville, in AHM 3:4 (October 1898): 375–76; Document 184, Blount to Robertson, 1/20/1795, Knoxville, in AHM 4:2 (April 1899): 165–67; and Nichols, *Red Gentlemen*, 155–56, 169. For "our," see Mad Dog to John Forbes, 5/31/1801, Tuckabatchee, in PPLC, p. 1 of original manuscript.

26. Gayoso to Carondelet, 1/8/1793, Natchez, in ETHS 29 (1957): 141 ("announcing"); Spanish Commissary Juan de la Villebeuvre to Carondelet, 2/4/1793, Boukfouka, in ETHS 29 (1957): 148 (assault on the four Creeks); postscript in Commissary Villebeuvre to Carondelet, 2/9/1793, Boukfouka, in ETHS 29 (1957): 154; Panton to Carondelet, 1/2/1793, Pensacola, in PPLC, p. 1 of transcription ("Wackakay"); Cherokee headman Bloody Fellow to Carondelet, 2/11/1793, "In the Village of Tchoukfala," in ETHS 29 (1957): 155 ("Warrior"); "Payemingo" and the Chickasaws to Carondelet, 2/11/1793, "In the Chickasaws," in ETHS 29 (1957): 154 ("we," "receive"); and Commissary Villebeuvre to Carondelet, 2/28(?)/1793, Boukfouka (?), in ETHS 29 (1957): 159 ("three").

27. Mad Dog to Panton, 4/20/1793, Tuckabatchee, in PPLC, p. 1 of transcription ("hard"). Mad Dog's talk was recorded in French, likely by the French-born Louis Leclerc de Milford, who served as an agent for Spain in Upper Creek country at this time. Although this talk has been transcribed and translated into English, I translated a portion of the transcription. The transcription reads, "Le Mad Dog dit qu'il est dur pour un homme rouge qui perd son frère et son neveu de ne pas prendre revanche: personne ne peut me blâmer ni m'en empêcher." My translation reads, "Mad Dog says that it is hard for a red man who loses both his brother and nephew to not take revenge; no person can either blame or prevent me." For the nephew of Wolf's Friend having been "burned,"

see Commissary Villebeuvre to Carondelet, 4/18/1793, Boukfouka, in ETHS 32 (1960): 75. For evidence that the Chickasaws killed two of Mad Dog's relatives sometime in February, see Commissary Villebeuvre to Carondelet, 2/28(?)/1793, Boukfouka (?), in ETHS 29 (1957): 159, 159n80. On torture and retaliation in southern Indian warfare, see "Observations on the Creek and Cherokee Indians," in Bartram, 155 ("ashes"); James Adair, *The History of the American Indians*, ed. Kathryn E. Holland Braund (Tuscaloosa: University of Alabama Press, 2005), 383–85; and John Phillip Reid, *A Law of Blood: The Primitive Law of the Cherokee Nation* (1970; repr., DeKalb: Northern Illinois University Press, 2006), 153–61.

28. Fooy's report is summarized in Commissary Villebeuvre to Gayoso, 5/25/1793, Boukfouka, in ETHS 32 (1960): 90 ("found," "accepted," "some"), 91 ("propose").

29. Commissary Villebeuvre to Gayoso, 5/25/1793, Boukfouka, in ETHS 32 (1960): 91 ("all"); Indian speeches enclosed in Benjamin James to Carondelet (?), 6/1/1793, Long Town, in SMV 4:165 ("belt," "well"), 166 ("I"); Gayoso to Carondelet, 7/25/1793, Walnut Hills, in ETHS 34 (1962): 95 ("Peace"). Benjamin James wrote that the wampum belt came from "Peomingo of the Cowittas" as well as Mad Dog; see his letter to Carondelet (?), 6/1/1793, Long Town, in SMV 4:165. I have been unable to confirm the identity of "Peomingo" of Coweta, a Lower Creek town. On arbitration in southern Indian wars, see Adair, *History*, 376. On Franchimastabé's town, see O'Brien, *Choctaws*, 12. By mediating between the combatants, the Choctaws probably wanted to keep peace with their former Creek enemies and ensure the safety of Choctaws who lived in Chickasaw country. See Commissary Villebeuvre to Carondelet, 2/4/1793, in ETHS 29 (1957): 148.

30. "A Talk From the White Lieutenant of the Oakfuskee and the Mad Dog of Tuckabatchee" to "Tuscabulapo Mingo [a Choctaw headman] of the Macaw Town," 1/19/1794, Tuckabatchee, in SMV, 4:248 ("our," "mischief"), 249 ("Eyes," "Coming"). Seagrove resided in Tuckabatchee at this time and may have shaped the contents of the headmen's talk. Still, his presence merely bolstered the diplomacy of Mad Dog and White Lieutenant. For "Expect," see Wolf's Friend ("Ougelayackabee") to "Chactamathaha Governr. Gayoso at Natchez," 2/22/1794, location (?), in ETHS 38 (1966): 72, 71n11. Although Wolf's Friend decided against sending his talk to Gayoso, Agent Fooy ignored his wishes and sent it anyway.

31. "A Talk From the White Lieutenant of the Oakfuskee and the Mad Dog of Tuckabatchee" to "Tuscabulapo Mingo [a Choctaw headman] of the Macaw Town," 1/19/1794, Tuckabatchee, in SMV, 4:249 ("all").

32. Wolf's Friend to Gayoso, 3/15/1794, Thisatera, in ETHS 38 (1966): 78 ("it"). The Chickasaw headman "heard that the Creeks are on a Good understanding with the Virginuns [Americans]" (78). He may have believed that American officials persuaded Creeks to kill him because of his ties to Spaniards like Gayoso. Whatever the case, his cryptic remark speaks to the fragility of intertribal peace. On Wolf's Friend's town, variously spelled "Thisatera," "Thishatare," and "Tashatulla," see Atkinson, *Splendid Land*, 141.

33. Evidence strongly suggests that the slain Creek was Mad Dog's relative. According to Fooy, "Yffahayo [Mad Dog] and [his] Older brother or Uncle to the Mad dog of the town of Takabathe... was not, as it Seems, Willing to put up With the Manner of the peace Established between them [Upper Creeks and Chickasaws] Without More Satisfaction for Some particular fellow [Mad Dog's kinsman] that Was killed here" in Chickasaw

country. Fooy added that "a bout Seventy" Creek warriors intended to strike Chickasaw country in summer 1794. See Fooy to Gayoso, 7/3/1794, Holkey, in ETHS 40 (1968): 113 ("Yffahayo," "a"). Fooy penned many of his reports from "Holkey," apparently a Choctaw settlement; see Atkinson, *Splendid Land*, 187, 278n4, 297n15. The formation of Mad Dog's war party in early July 1794 implies that his relative had been killed in the previous days or weeks. On Mad Dog's targeting Wolf's Friend, see Wolf's Friend to Gayoso, 7/2/1794, "Thishatare," in ETHS 40 (1968): 110. Only "one Town [Tuckabatchee] [has] lefted up there Wapons against me," Wolf's Friend told the governor.

34. I assume that "Spandahayo" and "Neuhayo" lived in Tuckabatchee since they knew about the war party that Mad Dog assembled in town. See Fooy to Gayoso, 7/3/1794, Holkey, in ETHS 40 (1968): 113 (quotes). By late July, "a Creek [war] party from the village of Fahakio [Mad Dog] was at a place Called Oulque," meaning Holkey; see Commissary Villebeuvre to Gayoso, 7/22/1794, Boukfouka, in ETHS 41 (1969): 101.

35. Document 139, Blount to Robertson, 12/4/1794, Knoxville, in AHM 3:4 (October 1898): 375 ("present," "humble," "give"); General Robertson to John (?) Pitchlynn, 1/22/1795, [Cumberland], in ETHS 42 (1970): 107 ("Killd," "Scalps"); Benjamin James to Commissary Villebeuvre, 2/12/1795, "Choctaw Nation," in ETHS 43 (1971): 103 (location of Chickasaw assault). The métis William Colbert of Long Town called for "open war" with the Creeks in 1795; see Secretary of War Timothy Pickering to Agent David Henley, 8/26/1795, "War Office," in Ayer 926, 1. Pickering failed to discuss Piomingo's thoughts on the renewal of the Creek-Chickasaw War.

36. Benjamin James to Commissary Villebeuvre, 2/12/1795, "Choctaw Nation," in ETHS 43 (1971): 103 ("partys," "Hunting," "returned," "killed," "let"); Fooy to Gayoso, 2/18/1795, Holkey, in ETHS 43 (1971): 107 ("four," "kill"); Joseph Stiggins to Panton, 2/24/1795, "in the Creek Nation," in ETHS 43 (1971): 109; Dog Warrior to Panton, 2/25/1795, Aubecooche (?), in ETHS 43 (1971): 110 ("thought," "don't"). The postscript in Stiggins's letter to Panton suggests that Dog Warrior lived in Aubecooche with his "Nephew," Mackey's friend, who was "Chief of the Abacuchy tribe" (109).

37. Dog Warrior to Panton, 2/25/1795, Aubecooche (?), in ETHS 43 (1971): 109 ("three"); Stiggins to Panton, 2/24/1795, "in the Creek Nation," in ETHS 43 (1971): 109 ("stopped," "thought"). Stiggins reported that Creeks of "Mr. O. Kelleys town" (109) killed the Chickasaw women, a reference to Coosa, where 'John O'Kelley, halfbreed' lived; see Benjamin Hawkins, "Mother Towns of the Upper Creeks, or Muscoguegee," in *Letters of Benjamin Hawkins, 1796–1806*, CWBH, 195. Whether the Coosa widowers killed those responsible for the women's deaths is unclear, but clan custom would not have obligated them to do so. Rather, the Chickasaws who belonged to the clan of the deceased bore responsibility for meting out punishment (on Coosa itself or another Creek town).

38. Commandant White to Carondelet, 3/4/1795, Pensacola, in ETHS 44 (1972): 104 ("belt," "perpetual"), 105 ("ten"). According to White, Mad Dog and the other Creeks departed from the seaport on February 27 "not at all content" with the goods supplied by the commandant (105). White complained that Mad Dog was "the most troublesome Indian with whom I have treated" (105). On Spanish imperial motivations late in the century, see Atkinson, *Splendid Land*, 170–73 and DuVal, *Independence Lost*, 341–42.

39. On Mad Dog's war party, see "Talk . . . from the Cherokees & Creeks" via "Indian Philatuchi" to Carondelet, 10/21/1795, location unknown, in PPLC, p. 2 of original

manuscript in English. The talk reads, "mad dog . . . went out against the Chekesaws and Lost 36 men." Its date suggests that Mad Dog was defeated just days earlier. Philatuchi may have been a Hitchiti headman; see Kokomoor, *Of One Mind*, 60. On Creek war leadership, see Peach, "Failure of Political Centralization," 85–86. In 1793 the Chickasaws received presents from the War Department, including five hundred guns; see Atkinson, *Splendid Land*, 157. For a fixed allotment of presents intended for Chickasaws as well as Choctaws that same year, see "*Estimate of Goods necessary to be furnished the Chickasaw and Chocktaw Indians annually*," enclosed in Blount and General Andrew Pickens to Knox, 8/1/1793, in TSRO, 293. No guns, however, are listed in the "*Estimate*." On the Chickasaws receiving goods piecemeal in late 1794, see Blount to Knox, 9/21/1794, Knoxville (?), in TSRO, 355; Blount to Knox, 11/3/1794, Knoxville, in TSRO, 363–64; and Blount to Knox, 11/10/1794, Knoxville, in TSRO, 368.

40. Creek–Chickasaw hostilities in late spring and early summer 1797 left several dead on each side. See General Robertson to Henley, 6/19/1797, Nashville, and Hawkins to Henley, 6/28/1797, "S.W. Point" (?)—both in unnumbered folder, David Henley Papers, Rubenstein.

41. Hawkins relayed the Chickasaw peace tokens and message to the intended recipients in the Lower Creek town of Coweta on October 27. See Hawkins, "Journal," 10/27/1797, Coweta Square, in LBH, 1:134 ("there"), 135 ("some"), and 10/28/1797, Coweta Square, in LBH, 1:135 ("one," "behave," "Chiefs," "mind"). Invoking kinship metaphor common to southern Indian diplomacy, Tussekiah Mico called "the Abbecoos" the Chickasaws' "older brothers"; see LBH, 1:135. On Tussekiah Mico as a Cusseta, see Hawkins, "A sketch of the Creek Country in the years 1798 and 1799," in LBH, 1:285–327, here 326.

42. Mad Dog's conversation with the Chickasaws is summarized in a talk he addressed to the Seminoles. Richard Thomas, the "Clerk for the Indian Department South of Ohio," sent the talk to the Seminoles via James Burgess. Burgess appears to have been in Spain's employ and located on the Flint River. See Thomas to Burgess, 8/2/1798, Tuckabatchee, in PPLC, p. 1 of original manuscript ("Land," "fast"), 3 ("Clerk").

43. Thomas to Burgess, 8/2/1798, Tuckabatchee, in PPLC, p. 1 of original manuscript (quote).

44. Haynes, *Patrolling the Border*, 203 ("raided," "extorted," "reflected"); Thomas to Burgess, 8/2/1798, Tuckabatchee, in PPLC, p. 1 of original manuscript ("women").

45. White Lieutenant continued to pursue peace with the United States until his death in 1799; see Joshua Piker, *Okfuskee: A Creek Indian Town in Colonial America* (Cambridge, MA: Harvard University Press, 2004), 198–201. Like many headmen, however, he exhausted all options by contacting Governor Carondelet for Spanish support against the Americans, "who are Daily Destroying us." See "A talk from the White Lieut. of the Ocfuskies to his Father the Governor Baron Caron Delite New Orleans," 11/14/1794, in SMV 4:377 ("who"). On the Cussetas' ongoing diplomacy with the United States, see "The [Bird Tail] King & Warior[,] The Big King[,] and The Warrior King" to Panton, 11/20/1794, "Cusittaws Lower Creeks," in SMV 4:377–78. Addressing Panton, these Cusseta headmen "still Consider you our friends and hold you and all other white people [Americans] by the hand" (377). See, too, Kokomoor, *Of One Mind*, 273–78. For "rivers," see "Bird [Tail] King, [and] Cussetah King" to Gaither, 4/13/1793, Cusseta, in ASP/IA, 1:420, enclosed in Gaither to Knox, 4/19/1793, Fort Fidius, in ASP/IA, 1:419.

Chapter 5

1. Singer ("Opayamuko[?]") to Vicente Folch y Juan ("Gov.r of Pensacola"), 8/31/1803, Hickory Ground (?), in PPLC, ɔ. 1 of original manuscript ("no"). Singer put "his mark" to this talk recorded by Daniel McGillivray, a relative of the late Alexander McGillivray. On southern Indian land cessions at the turn of the nineteenth century, see James R. Atkinson, *Splendid Land, Splendid People: The Chickasaw Indians to Removal* (Tuscaloosa: University of Alabama Press, 2004), 194–97; Adam Rothman, *Slave Country: American Expansion and the Origins of the Deep South* (Cambridge, MA: Harvard University Press, 2005), 41–42; Angela Pulley Hudson, *Creek Paths and Federal Roads: Indians, Settlers, and Slaves and the Making of the American South* (Chapel Hill: University of North Carolina Press, 2010), 45–65; and Daniel S. Dupre, *Alabama's Frontiers and the Rise of the Old South* (Bloomington: Indiana University Press, 2018), 189–92.

2. On intertribal alliance-building in the colonial, revolutionary, and early republic Native South, see Steven C. Hahn, *The Invention of the Creek Nation, 1670–1763* (Lincoln: University of Nebraska Press, 2004), 250–52; Gregory A. Waselkov and Ashley A. Dumas, "Archaeological Clues to a Seventeenth-Century Pan-Southeastern Revitalization Movement," paper presented at the Southeastern Archaeological Conference, Mobile, Alabama, 2009; Kathleen DuVal, *Independence Lost: Lives on the Edge of the American Revolution* (New York: Random House, 2015), 295–312, 337–38; Steven J. Peach, "The Failure of Political Centralization: Mad Dog, the Creek Indians, and the Politics of Claiming Power in the American Revolutionary Era," *Native South* 11 (2018): 81–116, here 98–105; Gregory D. Smithers, *Native Southerners: Indigenous History from Origins to Removal* (Norman: University of Oklahoma Press, 2019), 125–30; and Jamie Myers Mize, "'To Conclude on a General Union': Masculinity, the Chickamauga, and Pan-Indian Alliances in the Revolutionary Era," *Ethnohistory* 68, no. 3 (July 2021): 429–48, here 436–41.

3. On the connection between debt and land erosion, see William S. Coker and Thomas D. Watson, *Indian Traders of the Southeastern Spanish Borderlands: Panton, Leslie & Company and John Forbes & Company, 1783–1847* (Pensacola: University of West Florida Press, 1986), 240–72; Kevin Kokomoor, *Of One Mind and of One Government: The Rise and Fall of the Creek Nation in the Early Republic* (Lincoln: University of Nebraska Press and American Philosophical Society, 2018), 272–82; and Dupre, *Alabama's Frontiers*, 189–90.

4. Both McGillivray's and Singer's commitment to intertribal affairs made the Alabamas strong proponents of pan-Indianism in Creek history. Until the 1780s, the Alabamas had been political minorities, arising from an ethno-linguistic identity that differentiated them from other Creeks. While the Abeikas and Tallapoosas spoke Muscogee proper, for instance, the Alabamas spoke a Muscogee dialect that William Bartram called the "Stincard tongue." See "Travels Through North & South Carolina, Georgia, East & West Florida, the Cherokee Country, the Extensive Territories of the Muscogulges, or Creek Confederacy, and the Country of the Chactaws; Containing an Account of the Soil and Natural Productions of Those Regions, Together with Observations on the Manners of the Indians," in Bartram, 108, 260n144. On the Alabama language, see Mary R. Haas, "The Classification of the Muskogean Languages," in *Language, Culture, and Personality: Essays in Memory of Edward Sapir*, ed. Leslie Spier, A. Irving Hallowell, and Stanley S. Newman (1941; repr., Salt Lake City: University

of Utah Press, 1960): 41–56, here 46; Linda Langley, "The Tribal Identity of Alexander McGillivray: A Review of the Historical and Ethnographic Data," *Journal of the Louisiana Historical Association* 46, no. 2 (Spring 2005): 231–39, here 237–39. On the eighteenth- and early nineteenth-century Alabamas, see Gregory A. Waselkov, *A Conquering Spirit: Fort Mims and the Redstick War of 1813–1814* (Tuscaloosa: University of Alabama Press, 2006), 34–48, 53–54; Sheri Marie Shuck-Hall, *Journey to the West: The Alabama and Coushatta Indians* (Norman: University of Oklahoma Press, 2008), 6 ("stayers"), 8 ("with"), 108–36; John T. Juricek, *Colonial Georgia and the Creeks: Anglo-Indian Diplomacy on the Southern Frontier, 1733–1763* (Gainesville: University Press of Florida, 2010), 4, 255; and DuVal, *Independence Lost*, xviii ("Southern"), 256–62, 295–304, 337–38.

5. On kin and other local actors shaping the region's developments in the early nineteenth century, see Waselkov, *Conquering Spirit*, 78–82; Hudson, *Creek Paths*, 67–68, 84–89; Natalie R. Inman, *Brothers and Friends: Kinship in Early America* (Athens: University of Georgia Press, 2017), 92 ("bonding"), 105–6; and Dupre, *Alabama's Frontiers*, 165–66, 198–202. On Creeks guiding intertribal affairs from the bottom up, see the journals of Estevan Folch and John Forbes. These two men attended the 1803 Hickory Ground meeting and recorded its daily goings-on. See Folch, "Journal of a voyage to the Creek Nation from Penzla. [Pensacola] in the year 1803," 5/5/1803 to 6/3/1803, in PPLC, pp. 1–26 of transcription. Forbes's journal is divided into two documents: "A Journal of John Forbes, May [21–27], 1803: The Seizure of William Augustus Bowles," *Florida Historical Quarterly* 9:4 (April 1931): 279–89, and a copy of "Mr. Forbes talks to the Creek chiefs at the Hickory Ground[,] May [and June] 1803 respecting Indian debts," enclosed in unknown author to William Simpson, 6/18/1803, Pensacola, in PPLC, pp. 1–15 of original manuscript. The date range of the latter document is May 27–June 3, 1803.

6. Mad Dog's talk is in Richard Thomas to James Burgess, 8/2/1798, Tuckabatchee, in PPLC, p. 3 of original manuscript ("to").

7. Gilbert C. Din, *War on the Gulf Coast: The Spanish Fight against William Augustus Bowles* (Gainesville: University Press of Florida, 2012), 39–76; David Narrett, *Adventurism and Empire: The Struggle for Mastery in the Louisiana-Florida Borderlands, 1762–1803* (Chapel Hill: University of North Carolina Press, 2015), 211, 215–23; "Travels," in Bartram, 50–55; and Peach, "Failure of Political Centralization," 98–105.

8. Mad Dog failed to explain the meaning of the blue wampum, but it may have been designed to resemble the US flag. See Hawkins, "Journal," 5/27/1798, "In the Evening," Tuckabatchee, in LBH, 1:186 (quotes).

9. For "our," see "Perro Rabioso" (Mad Dog) and "Peck [Aleck?] Cornel[ls]" to Bartolomé Morales, 6/1/1795, Fort Fairfax (GA), translated copy enclosed in Diego de Vegas to the Barón de Carondelet (?), in PPLC, p. 65 [2] of typescript. Vegas was the commandant of San Marcos de Apalache. See also Mad Dog ("Efau haijo") to Agent Benjamin Hawkins, 4/11/1799, Tuckabatchee, in PPLC, p. 1 of original manuscript ("Seminoles"); Thomas to Burgess, 8/2/1798, Tuckabatchee, in PPLC, p. 1 of original manuscript ("it"), 2 ("Nation," "set," "we"); and Hudson, *Creek Paths*, 39–45.

10. Methlogee to James Seagrove, 6/14/1799, Point Peter (GA), p. 1 ("second"), p. 3 (Methlogee's talk), enclosed in Seagrove to Georgia governor James Jackson, 6/17/1799, Point Peter (GA), in Ayer 797. Okaiegigie summarized Seminole attitudes in a talk signed by "Thos. Perryman [Okaiegigie's anglicized name], Uhollimicco, Cutchatustonico,

Oposehajoe, Efahajoe [of Okeha Town], Toatca Tustonica, Opoethlomicco[?], Achalihajoe, Nocushajoe, Hepuckie Ninnawageechy[?], Cuseta epoethlimicco, [and] Jack Meallie," enclosed in "Edw.ᵈ Forrester" to William Panton, 11/14/1796, "Chatahuchy River," in PPLC, p. 1 of typescript (Okaiegigie's talk). There are various emendations made by hand throughout this typescript. Like others in his day, Okaiegigie referred to the Seminoles as the "Lower Towns" and the Creeks as the "Upper Towns." On Okaiegigie as Thomas Perryman, a son of Kenhagee or William (Billy) Perryman, see James L. Hill, *Creek Internationalism in an Age of Revolution, 1763–1818* (Lincoln University of Nebraska Press, 2022), 78, 167, 231n3.

11. On criers, see James Adair, *The History of the American Indians*, ed. Kathryn E. Holland Braund (Tuscaloosa: University of Alabama Press, 2005), 142, and John R. Swanton, *Creek Religion and Medicine* (1928; Lincoln: University of Nebraska Press, 2000), 485. For a "far off king," see Hahn, *Invention*, 199. On the relationship among war, travel, and knowledge, see Greg O'Brien, *Choctaws in a Revolutionary Age, 1750–1830* (Lincoln: University of Nebraska Press, 2002), 52–55. Singer's titles merit extended discussion. In the midst of Creek–Chickasaw negotiations, Hawkins learned from a Lower Creek leader that: "The man who takes this [Creek] talk was appointed as the ambassador of this [Creek] nation, and he was to take talks of this sort and go down and deliver them in the name of his nation; he is Mucclassee Hopoie, Hopoie Micco." For this speech, see Hawkins, "Journal," 10/28/1797, Coweta Square, in LBH, 1:137. Since "Mucclassee Hopoie" and "Hopoie Micco" are titles, it is possible that a headman other than Singer was the "ambassador" in question. Indeed, Hawkins identified "Hopoie Micco of Coweta" in the context of these negotiations (LBH, 1:136). Yet Singer is identified as "Mucclassee Hopoie of Ocheubofau" as well as head of the "pacific mission" in Hawkins to Panton, 7/10/1800, "The neighbourhood of Fort Wilkinson," in LBH, 1:339. Other records confirm Singer and Hopoie Micco as the same person. "Opay Mico, or the Singer" of "Little Tallisee," signed the Treaty of New York in 1790; see IALT, 28. Finally, "Opoey Mico," or Singer of "Hickory Ground," put his mark to the Treaty of Coleraine in 1796; see IALT, 49. The Alabamas had served as diplomatic go-betweens for intertribal combatants in the past; see Greg O'Brien, "Quieting the Ghosts: How the Choctaws and Chickasaws Stopped Fighting," in *The Native South: New Histories and Enduring Legacies*, ed. Tim Alan Garrison and Greg O'Brien (Lincoln: University of Nebraska Press, 2017): 47–69.

12. Hawkins to Panton, 7/10/1800, "The neighbourhood of Fort Wilkinson," in LBH, 1:339; Joshua Piker, *Okfuskee: A Creek Indian Town in Colonial America* (Cambridge, MA: Harvard University Press, 2004), 200; Mad Dog to Seminoles, 6/30/1802, Creek Square at Fort Wilkinson, in ASP/IA, 1:680 ("Aubocoes," "whole," "You," "misled," "it") and "Mooklausau Hopoie [Singer]" to Hawkins, 6/30/1802, Creek Square at Fort Wilkinson, in ASP/IA, 1:580 ("accustomed"), 681. The courier was identified as "Nehethluck Emautlau, of Oketeyocenen" (ASP/IA, 1:680).

13. For the treaty and mark of "Efau Haujo" and "Hopoie Micco," see "A Treaty of Limits between the United States of America and the Creek Nation of Indians," 6/16/1802, in IALT, 58–59. For the treaty minutes, see ASP/IA, 1:668–81; Hudson, *Creek Paths*, 46–48, 52 (map 2). On Seminole connections to the St. Marys, see "Travels," in Bartram, 35–36, and "Observations on the Creek and Cherokee Indians," in Bartram, 153–54. On US–Creek trade relations, see David Andrew Nichols, *Indian Trading*

Factories and the Negotiation of American Empire (Chapel Hill: University of North Carolina Press, 2016), 41–46, 90–91.

14. Thomas to Burgess, 8/2/1798, Tuckabatchee, in PPLC, p. 3 of original manuscript ("Red").

15. Thomas to Burgess, 8/2/1798, Tuckabatchee, in PPLC, p. 2 of original manuscript ("Peace").

16. I have transcribed Mad Dog's talk, addressed to the Seminoles, as follows: "they fower Nations of Reed pepole Ought to be as On, And if Aney of the younger brothers Shold goe Astray we have Aponted the Chickasaws to Set matters to Right, the Cheefs of the fower Nations will Strickley Gard the frontears to Pervent ther young Pepole [warriors] Steling Aney thing belonging to ther nibers [white neighbors], the Chacktaws will[?] Pay Due Attencon[?] from Tom Bigbie to Natchez and the Chickasaws will Gard this[?] frontere[?] and the Cherokees will on ther Part as far as Appalache[?], And the Simanoleys will Gard the fronters[?] towards the[?] Spanenards[?] we have all met And Agree to Burey All . . . [illegible] all Matters with Ower nibars [neighbors]." He used "fower Nations" to group together the Seminoles and Creeks, a tactic designed to regulate Seminole actions. Yet he admitted that the Seminoles possessed their own lands to guard them from American settlers. For these issues and quotes, see Thomas to Burgess, 8/2/1798, Tuckabatchee, in PPLC, p. 2 of original manuscript ("all," "frontears," "Set," "Chacktaws"), 3 ("fower," "On"); Hudson, *Creek Paths*, 48–50.

17. "Efau Haujo [Mad Dog], speaker for the Creek nation" to John Forbes, 5/31/1801, Tuckabatchee, in PPLC, p. 1 of original manuscript ("there," "shall"); "Mucklasauopay or the Singer" to William Panton, 9/28/1799, Hickory Ground, in PPLC, p. 1 of original manuscript ("Woods," "visit"); Coker and Watson, *Indian Traders*, 22–23.

18. "A talk from Mingo Homastubbee of the Choctaws to the Chiefs and Warriors of the Creek nation," 4/10/1802, Choctaw Agency, in PPLC, original manuscript (quotes). In this one-page document, Singer is identified as "Mooklah[?] Hopia of Hickory ground." Mingo Homastubbee was an Eastern Division Choctaw; see O'Brien, *Choctaws*, 102.

19. Mingo Homastubbee's talk, dated October 18[?], 1802, is enclosed in Daniel McGillivray to John Forbes, 12/24/1803, at "Creeks," in PPLC, p. 2 of original manuscript ("papers," "appointed," "into," "received," "Chiefs," "friendly"); "A talk from Mingo Homastubbee of the Choctaws [to] the Creek nation," 4/10/1802, Choctaw Agency, in PPLC, original manuscript ("sincerely," "friendly").

20. "A talk from Mingo Homastubbee [to] the Creek nation," 4/10/1802, Choctaw Agency, in PPLC, original manuscript; Hawkins, "Journal," Coweta Square, 10/28/1797, in LBH, 1:137; Hawkins to Panton, 7/10/1800, "The neighbourhood of Fort Wilkinson," in LBH, 1:339; Folch, "Journal," entry 6/2/1803, Hickory Ground, in PPLC, p. 25 of transcription. According to treaty commissioners James Wilkinson and Benjamin Hawkins, "Since the treaty [of Fort Wilkinson], Efau Haujo [Mad Dog], who was the speaker and first chief of the nation, has abdicated his station to this Hopoie Micco [Singer], and transferred [sic] the seat of the national councils from Tuckaubatchee to Acheaubofau, the town in which his successor resides"; see the commissioners' letter to Secretary of War Henry Dearborn, 7/15/1802, Commissioner's Camp near Fort Wilkinson, in ASP/IA, 1:670. Mad Dog announced his successor on June 30, 1802, referring to him as "Foosahatche Micco" of "Acheaubofau"; see "Efau Haujo" to Hawkins, 6/30/1802, Creek Square at Fort Wilkinson, in ASP/IA, 1:681 ("age").

21. Wilkinson and Hawkins to Dearborn, 7/15/1802, Commissioner's Camp near Fort Wilkinson, in ASP/IA, 1:670 ("transfered"); Folch, "Journal," entry 5/24/1803, Hickory Ground, in PPLC, p. 13 of transcription ("white"); "A talk from Mingo Homastubbee [to] the Creek nation," 4/10/1802, Choctaw Agency, in PPLC, original manuscript ("on").

22. Folch, "Journal," 5/30/1803, in PPLC, pp. 19–20 of transcription; Coker and Watson, *Indian Traders*, 235–45; Gregory D. Smithers, *The Cherokee Diaspora: An Indigenous History of Migration, Resettlement, and Identity* (New Haven, CT: Yale University Press, 2015), 44.

23. Singer to Governor Folch, 8/31/1803, Hickory Ground (?), in PPLC, p. 1 of original manuscript ("four"); Inman, *Brothers and Friends*, 89; Smithers, *Native Southerners*, 133–34.

24. On southern Indian women and hospitality, see Michelle LeMaster, *Brothers Born of One Mother*, 17–23; Piker, *Okfuskee*, 165–66. On Singer's sister and sófki, see Folch, "Journal," in PPLC, p. 6 of transcription (entry 5/15/1803: "top," "smoak," "went," "dish"); Amelia Rector Bell, "Separate People: Speaking of Creek Men and Women," *American Anthropologist* 92, no. 2 (June 1990): 332–45, here 335–36.

25. Folch, "Journal," in PPLC, p. 11 (entry 5/21/1803 "deputies"), p. 14 (entry 5/25/1803: "addresses," "singularly"), and p. 15 (entry 5/25/1803: "actions"; entry 5/26/1803: "young," "different," "preserve") of transcription; John R. Swanton, *Creek Religion and Medicine* (1928; repr., Lincoln: University of Nebraska Press, 2000), 521–22, 527.

26. Folch, "Journal," in PPLC, p. 15 (entry 5/26/1803: "long," "favour"), p. 16 (entry 5/27/1803: "king"), p. 17 (entry 5/28/1803: "white," "spoke," "put"), and p. 18 (entry 5/28/1803: "ceremony") of transcription. Folch mistakenly believed that "two" kings were elected—Mingo Homastubbee and an interpreter of French descent who accompanied the Cherokee delegation. He is known only as Croisiers; see entry 5/24/1803, 9 p.m., on p. 13 and entry 5/28/1803 on p. 17. Forbes confirmed that Mingo Homastubbee was elected to the sole position. See "Journal of John Forbes," *Florida Historical Society Quarterly*, 289 (entry 5/27/1803). On black drink, see Adair, *History*, 81 ("black"), 100–101; and Swanton, *Creek Religion and Medicine*, 538–44.

27. On Fanni Mingos, see Patricia Galloway, "'The Chief Who Is Your Father': Choctaw and French Views of the Diplomatic Relation," in *Powhatan's Mantle: Indians in the Colonial Southeast*, ed. Gregory A. Waselkov, Peter H. Wood, and Tom Hatley (1989; repr., Lincoln: University of Nebraska Press, 2006): 345–70, here 359, 361–64. The Creeks used the term "Fanni Mico" for the same institution, although *fanni* was a Chickasaw and Choctaw term that probably had little meaning in the Creek language; see Piker, *Okfuskee*, 21–28, 214n14.

28. Folch, "Journal," in PPLC, p. 13 (entry 5/24/1803: "be") p. 14 (entry 5/25/1803: "voice," "black"), p. 16 (entry 5/27/1803: "king"), and p. 18 (entry 5/28/1803: "crowd"); Hawkins to Georgia governor John Milledge, 5/30/1803, "Ocheubofau," in LBH 2:453; Coker and Watson, *Indian Traders*, 240–42; Inman, *Brothers and Friends*, 89.

29. Folch, "Journal," in PPLC, pp. 19–20 (entry 5/30/1803: "disagreable"). John Forbes alleged that the southern Indians owed $173,000 on the principal and another $31,000 in interest, generating a grand total of $204,000. See Coker and Watson, *Indian Traders*, 243–48.

30. Singer appears to have been the "Speaker" who replied to Forbes. See Folch, "Journal," in PPLC, pp. 20–21 (entry 5/31/1803: quotes).

31. Folch, "Journal," in PPLC, p. 25 (entry 6/2/1803: quotes); Coker and Watson, *Indian Traders*, 244–45. Folch sensed a Cherokee conspiracy afoot in Hickory Ground possibly because of Doublehead's former status as a Chickamauga. On Doublehead, see Smithers, *Cherokee Diaspora*, 44.

32. Singer to Governor Folch, 8/31/1803, Hickory Ground (?), in PPLC, p. 1 of original manuscript ("resolution," "in," "White"); Folch, "Journal," in PPLC, p. 25 (entry 6/2/1803: "whole").

33. Singer to Governor Folch, 8/31/1803, Hickory Ground (?), in PPLC, p. 1 of original manuscript ("four").

34. [William Simpson] to "[James?] Innerarity," 11/16/1804, "Flint River at [Colonel Hawkins']," in PPLC, p. 1 of "Copy" of original manuscript ("The"); Hudson, *Creek Paths*, 48–65.

35. Simpson to "Innerarity," 11/16/1804, "Flint River," in PPLC, p. 1 of "Copy" of original manuscript (quotes); Coker and Watson, *Indian Traders*, 243–50; Claudio Saunt, *A New Order of Things: Property, Power, and the Transformation of the Creek Indians, 1733–1816* (Cambridge: Cambridge University Press, 1999), 222.

36. Simpson to "Innerarity," 11/16/1804, in PPLC, p. 2 of "Copy" of original manuscript (quotes); Kokomoor, *Of One Mind*, 288–89. Of the Creek Agency treaty, Hawkins wrote, "Hopoie Micco [Singer], the speaker, and select men of the Creek nation" signed "A Treaty concluded between the United States of America and the Creek nation of Indians," 11/3/1804, Creek Agency, in ASP/IA, 1:691.

37. Brigadier General John Clark to Georgia governor George Mathews, 5/19/1794, Hickory Grove, p. 3 ("Cross'd"), p. 4, in Telamon Cuyler Collection 362, SNAD; "Travels," in Bartram, 42 ("sat"); "Journal of the Commissioners who Attended the Running [of] the Line Between The State of Georgia and The Creek Nation of Indians," 2/03/1804, p. 15 ("disposition"), in Telamon Cuyler Collection 086, SNAD; Joshua S. Haynes, *Patrolling the Border: Theft and Violence on the Creek-Georgia Frontier, 1770–1796* (Athens: University of Georgia Press, 2018), 178–99.

38. In descending order, the following headmen signed the Treaty of Washington: Alexander Cornells ("Oche Haujo") of Tuckabatchee, William McIntosh of Coweta, Long Lieutenant ("Tuskenehau Chapco") of Coweta, "Tuskenehau," "Enehau Thlucco," and "Chekopeheke Emanthau." See "Treaty with the Creeks, 1805," 11/14/1805, City of Washington, in IALT, ed. Kappler, 2:86. For "Tuskenehau Chapco" as Long Lieutenant of Coweta, see ASP/IA, 1:676. On the Treaty of Washington, see Hudson, *Creek Paths*, 64, and Kokomoor, *Of One Mind*, 285–90.

39. Singer to Governor Folch, 8/31/1803, Hickory Ground (?), in PPLC, p. 1 of original manuscript ("White"); Kathryn E. Holland Braund, *Deerskins and Duffels: The Creek Indian Trade with Anglo-America, 1685–1815* (1993; repr., Lincoln: University of Nebraska Press, 2008), 150–51; Saunt, *New Order*, 67–135; Hudson, *Creek Paths*, 46–65; Haynes, *Patrolling the Border*, 33–44.

40. Doublehead met the same fate in 1807 after economic considerations prompted him to cede Cherokee land to the United States; see William G. McLoughlin, *Cherokee Renascence in the New Republic* (Princeton, NJ: Princeton University Press, 1986), 92–122. Hawkins reported that Creek headmen "could not agree upon the election of a

speaker for the nation to succeed the late Hopoie Micco who was murdered during the winter by two men of Cussetuh"; see Hawkins to Milledge, 6/9/1806, Creek Agency, in LBH, 2:505. See, too, Hawkins to Jefferson, 9/13/1806, Tuckabatchee, LBH, 2:508; and Simpson to "Innerarity," 11/16/1804, "Flint River," in PPLC, p. 1 of "Copy" of original manuscript ("most"). On Tame King's distrust of Singer as well as Mad Dog, see Daniel McGillivray to William Panton, 10/13/1800, Hickory Ground, in PPLC, p. 1 of original manuscript; and James Durouzeaux to Hawkins, 5/28/1804, Coweta, p. 1, in Telamon Cuyler Collection 220, SNAD.

41. The executions of Acorn Whistler and his nephew in the 1750s were exceptional. By the turn of the nineteenth century, however, Creek-on-Creek violence had escalated, making Singer's assassination part of a growing political trend that created the conditions for the Creek War. See Hahn, *Invention*, 212–14; Joshua Piker, *The Four Deaths of Acorn Whistler: Telling Stories in Colonial America* (Cambridge, MA: Harvard University Press, 2013), 9–28, 134–87; and Kokomoor, *Of One Mind*, 257–65. For at least three Creeks killed by the Cussetas in late 1774, for example, see EAID, vol. 12, 154. For quotes, see Hawkins to Milledge, 6/9/1806, Creek Agency, in LBH, 2:505 ("two") and Hawkins to Dearborn, 1/2/1805, Creek Agency, in LBH, 2:487 ("young," "improvident," "hunting," "old").

Chapter 6

1. My understanding of the two headmen in the prewar era is drawn from "Indian talk" of Tame King ("Hoboheilthlee Micco") to "President [James Madison]," 5/15/1811, Halfway House ("Chatteeck, chu, fau, lee[?]"), frames 554–57, and Big Warrior, "Chief and Warrior of the Creek nation," to "Path maker [Path Killer], Chief of the Cherokee," 5/1[?]/1809, Tuckabatchee, frame 620; both in OSW/LR.

2. The scholarship on the Creek War is vast. Its major themes range from policy and clan law to territoriality and revitalization. A sampling of this literature includes Joel W. Martin, *Sacred Revolt: The Muskogees' Struggle for a New World* (Boston: Beacon Press, 1991), 87–113; Claudio Saunt, *A New Order of Things: Property, Power, and the Transformation of the Creek Indians, 1733–1816* (Cambridge: Cambridge University Press, 1999), 249–72; Karl Davis, "'Remember Fort Mims': Reinterpreting the Origins of the Creek War," *Journal of the Early Republic* 22, no. 4 (Winter 2002): 611–36; Joshua Piker, *Okfuskee: A Creek Indian Town in Colonial America* (Cambridge, MA: Harvard University Press, 2004), 196–204; Adam Rothman, *Slave Country: American Expansion and the Origins of the Deep South* (Cambridge, MA: Harvard University Press, 2005), 119–39; Gregory A. Waselkov, *A Conquering Spirit: Fort Mims and the Redstick War of 1813–1814* (Tuscaloosa: University of Alabama Press, 2006), 32–95; Robert G. Thrower, "Causalities and Consequences of the Creek War: A Modern Creek Perspective," 10–29, and Robert P. Collins, "'A Packet from Canada': Telling Conspiracy Stories on the 1813 Creek Frontier," 53–83, both in *Tohopeka: Rethinking the Creek War and the War of 1812*, ed. Kathryn E. Holland Braund (Tuscaloosa: University of Alabama Press, 2012); Angela Pulley Hudson, *Creek Paths and Federal Roads: Indians, Settlers, and Slaves and the Making of the American South* (Chapel Hill: University of North Carolina Press, 2010), 91–120; Evan Nooe, "Common Justice: Vengeance and Retribution in Creek Country," *Ethnohistory* 62, no. 2 (April 2015): 241–61, here 251–56; and Daniel S. Dupre, *Alabama's Frontiers and the Rise of the Old South* (Bloomington: Indiana University Press, 2018), 211–23.

3. Big Warrior to Path Killer, 5/1[?]/1809, Tuckabatchee, in OSW/LR, frame 620 ("four"). Big Warrior signed his message "BW." The passage containing "the four rivers" quote is as follows: "The small parcel of Lands, and the four rivers we have in our Country, is for us to Live upon. it is our whole dependence; Then There is some of you [inserted: "Two or three of you"] when you meet, you think you making great promises to the white peope; You always ought to look to your old Chiefs for your government."

4. Big Warrior to Path Killer, 5/1[?]/1809, Tuckabatchee, in OSW/LR, frame 620 ("four"). On the multiplicity of peoples in and beyond Creek country whose actions shaped a uniquely rebellious era in the Native South, see Robbie Ethridge, *Creek Country: The Creek Indians and Their World* (Chapel Hill: University of North Carolina Press, 2003), 238–41 and Dupre, *Alabama's Frontiers*, 230–31, 249–50.

5. On the US invasion, see Gregory A. Waselkov and Brian M. Wood, "The Creek War of 1813–1814: Effects on Creek Society and Settlement Pattern," *Journal of Alabama Archaeology* 32, no. 1 (June 1986): 1–24, here 10–15; and Dupre, *Alabama's Frontiers*, 234–43. On Creek history beyond 1815, see John T. Ellisor, *The Second Creek War: Interethnic Conflict and Collusion on a Collapsing Frontier* (Lincoln: University of Nebraska Press, 2010), passim but especially 182–227, 335–416; Denise E. Bates, *The Other Movement: Indian Rights and Civil Rights in the Deep South* (Tuscaloosa: University of Alabama Press, 2012), 22–33, 39–40; Christopher D. Haveman, *Rivers of Sand: Creek Indian Emigration, Relocation, and Ethnic Cleansing in the American South* (Lincoln: University of Nebraska Press, 2016), passim but especially 200–201, 268–69, 294–301; History—Poarch Band of Creek Indians (pci-nsn.gov; accessed March 7, 2021).

6. Big Warrior to Path Killer, 5/1[?]/1809, Tuckabatchee, frames 620–21, and Tame King to President Madison, 5/15/1811, Halfway House, frames 554–57, in both in OSW/LR.

7. Big Warrior to Path Killer, 5/1[?]/1809, Tuckabatchee, in OSW/LR, frame 620 (quotes); "Kanchestaneskee," "Wassasee," "Richard Brown," and "Bear Meat" at "the request of... PathKiller" to Return Meigs, 7/23/1813, "Creek Path," p. 1, in MS2033 Penelope Johnson Allen 0214, SNAD; Hudson, *Creek Paths*, 81–82; Susan M. Abram, "Cherokees in the Creek War: A Band of Brothers," in Braund, *Tohopeka*, 122–45, here 123–24, 129.

8. An anxious Hawkins opined to Eustis that "no good will result to themselves or to the United States by this [Big Warrior's] Union," so "I shall not countenance it." See Hawkins to Eustis, 4/8/1810, Creek Agency, in LBH, 2:562 ("his," "some," "an other," "no," "shall"); Big Warrior to Path Killer, 5/1[?]/1809, Tuckabatchee, in OSW/LR, frame 620 ("square"); "Tus,tun,nug,gee Thlocco [Big Warrior], Speaker of the National Council; his talk [to] Col°. Benjamin Hawkins, Agent for Indian Affairs," 10/29/1812, "Tookaubatchee," p. 1 ("nothing," "We," "have"), p. 3 ("claim"), in GA/File II.

9. Big Warrior to Path Killer, 5/1[?]/1809, Tuckabatchee, in OSW/LR, frame 621 ("for"); Hawkins, "A sketch of the Creek Country in the years 1798 and 1799," in LBH, 1:285–327, here 318 ("Eagle"); "Kanchestaneskee" et al. to Return Meigs, 7/23/1813, "Creek Path," p. 1, in MS2033 Penelope Johnson Allen 0214, SNAD.

10. Tame King to Madison, 5/15/1811, Halfway House, frames 554 ("you," "chiefs," "I"), 555 ("speaker"), in OSW/LR. Tame King also addressed President Madison in Hawkins to Eustis, 10/10/1809, Creek Agency, in LBH, 2:556, 557n1.

11. Tame King to President Madison, 5/15/1811, Halfway House, frame 554 ("large," "chiefs"), in OSW/LR.

12. On the council's executions, see Assistant Agent Nimrod Doyell to Hawkins, 5/3/1813, Creek Agency, in ASP/IA, 1:843–44; Kokomoor, *Of One Mind*, 337 ("Creek," "as").

13. Big Warrior and Alexander Cornells to Hawkins, 4/26/1813, Tuckabatchee, in ASP/IA, 1:843 (quotes), enclosed (?) in Doyell to Hawkins, 5/3/1813, Creek Agency, in ASP/IA, 1:843–44; Kokomoor, *Of One Mind*, 331–40.

14. Doyell to Hawkins, 5/3/1813, Creek Agency, in ASP/IA, 1:844 ("chiefs," "uncles"). The nephews in question were executed in the Abeika towns of Imookfau and "Kinhijee" (Kialijee).

15. Hawkins to Secretary of War John Armstrong Jr., 7/28/1813, Creek Agency, in LBH, 2:652 ("killed," "destroyed"); Hawkins to Armstrong, 6/28/1813, Creek Agency, in LBH, 2:643 ("driven"); Saunt, *New Order*, 255–62, 257n40; Piker, *Okfuskee*, 201–2.

16. On "Chatteeck, chu, fau, lee," see Tame King to President Madison, 5/15/1811, Halfway House, frame 554, in OSW/LR.

17. Hawkins to Eustis, 2/14/1810, Creek Agency, in LBH, 2:561, and Hawkins to Captain Edmund P. Gaines, 10/25/1810, "Chattucchufaule," in LBH, 2:575. On "Chaglahache or Middle Town," see the Spanish census of Creek country enclosed in Pedro Olivier to the Barón de Carondelet, 12/1/1793, "Old Town of Wetonka," in SMV, 4:229–33, here 231. For Creek terms, see Jack B. Martin and Margaret McKane Mauldin, *A Dictionary of Creek/Muskogee* (Lincoln: University of Nebraska Press, 2000), 15–16. For "magic," see "Talosee Fixico, a runner from Tuckaubatchee" to Hawkins, 7/5/1813, Creek Agency, in ASP/IA, 1:847.

18. Alexander Cornells to Hawkins, 6/22/1813, Creek Agency, in ASP/IA, 1:846 (quotes). On madness as a spiritual ailment, see James Adair, *The History of the American Indians*, ed. Kathryn E. Holland Braund (Tuscaloosa: University of Alabama Press, 2005), 191.

19. Cornells to Hawkins, 6/22/1813, in ASP/IA, 1:846 (quotes).

20. Cornells to Hawkins, 6/23/1813, in ASP/IA, 1:846 (quotes). On Cusseta-Yuchi ties, see Hawkins, 'sketch of the Creek Country," in LBH, 1:313; and document 10, 9/28/1759, p. 2, in Atkin to Lyttelton, 11/30/1759, box 13, in WHLP. For "some Uchees . . . on the way to join the prophets party," see Hawkins to Armstrong, 10/11/1813, Creek Agency, in LBH, 2:672.

21. Cornells to Hawkins, 6/23/1813, in ASP/IA, 1:846; "Talosee Fixico" to Hawkins, 7/5/1813, in ASP/IA, 1:847 ("to"); Hawkins "*A demand on the Fanatical Chiefs and associates of an explanation of their conduct. To Creek Chiefs who have taken the talks of the prophets,*" 7/6/1813, Creek Agency, in Hawkins to Armstrong, 7/13/1813, Creek Agency, in LBH, 2:647. The Spanish census of Creek country in 1793 identified "Casista" (Cusseta) as the largest town, with nearly one-thousand inhabitants; see Olivier to Carondelet, 12/1/1793, in SMV, 4:232.

22. "Talosee Fixico" to Hawkins, 7/5/1813, in ASP/IA, 1:847 (quotes); Michael D. Green, *The Politics of Indian Removal: Creek Government and Society in Crisis* (Lincoln: University of Nebraska Press, 1982), 25–26 (treaty).

23. Cornells to Hawkins, 6/22/1813, Creek Agency, in ASP/IA, 1:846 ("nearest"); Hawkins to Mitchell, 7/7/1813, Creek Agency, in LBH, 2:644 ("attack," "seem,"

three-hundred and twenty); Hawkins to Mitchell, 7/22/1813, "Capt. Carr's, Ocmulgee," in LBH, 2:648 (week, "one," thirteen); Hawkins to Armstrong, 7/26/1813, Creek Agency, in LBH, 2:648 (Coweta); Hawkins to Armstrong, 7/28/1813, Creek Agency, in LBH, 2:651–52; Saunt, *New Order*, 256.

24. Kathryn E. Holland Braund, "Reflections on 'Shee Coocys' and the Motherless Child: Creek Women in a Time of War," *Alabama Review* 64, no. 4 (October 2011): 255–84, here 263, 265 (quote), 283–84. On Creek and métis women in the Tensaw district, see Waselkov, *Conquering Spirit*, 47–55.

25. Charles Hudson, *The Southeastern Indians* (Knoxville: University of Tennessee Press, 1976), 264–69; John R. Swanton, *Creek Religion and Medicine* (1928; repr., Lincoln: University of Nebraska Press, 2000), 528, 597–98, 614; Kathryn E. Holland Braund, "Guardians of Tradition and Handmaidens to Change: Women's Roles in Creek Economic and Social Life during the Eighteenth Century," *American Indian Quarterly* 14, no. 3 (Summer 1990): 239–58; Piker, *Okfuskee*, 166–68; Michelle LeMaster, *Brothers Born of One Mother: British-Native American Relations in the Colonial Southeast* (Charlottesville: University of Virginia Press, 2012), 15–50; Braund, "Reflections on 'Shee Coocys,'" 255–84; Malinda Maynor Lowery, "Kinship and Capitalism in the Choctaw and Chickasaw Nations," in *The Native South: New Histories and Enduring Legacies*, edited by Tim Alan Garrison and Greg O'Brien (Lincoln: University of Nebraska Press, 2017): 200–19.

26. I was unable to determine the fate of the second brother. Doyell to Hawkins, 5/3[?]/1813, Creek Agency, in ASP/IA, 1:843 (quotes). One passage reads thusly: the executioners "found one of the murderers, and his brother, who defended themselves, and made battle until they [one brother?] were killed; the other made his escape. As there were but two guilty in the town, brothers, and one killed helping his brother, the warriors were told by the king, the debt was satisfied. The one who thus escaped could speak English pretty well. This fellow got his gun and set out the morning after, to kill white people" (844).

27. This could have been one of the women who had earlier hidden canoes from the Redsticks in Hoithlewaulee. See Big Warrior to Hawkins, 8/4/1813, "William McIntosh[']s," 9 p.m., p. 1 (quotes), copy of original in GA/File II. Big Warrior had fled Tuckabatchee by this point and held council among the Lower Creeks, where this woman may have traveled. On Redstick disunity, see Collins, "'A Packet from Canada,'" 53–83. On the new settlements formed by Redsticks, see Braund, "Reflections on 'Shee Coocys,'" 273–74.

28. Reed's wife supplied accurate information about the Redsticks, which suggests that she was not a Redstick spy. See Big Warrior to Hawkins, 8/4/1813, "William McIntosh[']s," 9 p.m., p. 1 ("Hardy"), copy of original in GA/File II. On Reed, see Hawkins, "Journal," 2/2/1797, in LBH, 1:41, and Hawkins to Edward Price, 2/10/1797, "Flint River," in LBH, 1:67. In his letter to Price, a factor at Colerain Station, Hawkins wrote of "Hardy Reed, of Coweta" (67), although editor C. L. Grant refers to Reed as a "trader to the Upper Creeks" (67n2).

29. Hoithleponiyau's report to Hawkins is as follows: "1st they were to put to death all who assisted the Chiefs to give satisfaction for the murders at Ohio. 2nd all the old Chiefs friendly to peace and those who refused to join the prophets, by this means to unite the nation in one opinion then wait for Tecumseh," the Shawnee war leader who

led a pan-Indian confederacy with his younger brother, Tenskwatawa, in the Ohio. See Hoithleponiyau to Hawkins, 3/14[?]/1813, "Extracts of Occurrences in the Agency for Indian Affairs," in Hawkins to Mitchell, 8/17/1813, Creek Agency (?), in LBH 2:655 (quotes; additional quotation marks deleted).

30. Hoithleponiyau to Hawkins, 8/14[?]/1813, "Extracts of Occurrences," in Hawkins to Mitchell, 8/17/1813, Creek Agency, in LBH, 2:655; Alejandra Dubcovsky, *Informed Power: Communication in the Early American South* (Cambridge, MA: Harvard University Press, 2016), 3–8.

31. Hoithleponiyau to Hawkins, 8/14[?]/1813, "Extracts of Occurrences," in Hawkins to Mitchell, 8/17/1813, in LBH, 2:655 ("near"). Molton of Coosada appears in the colonial-era records and so must have been an elder man by 1813. He was also known as Topalga, which may have been his war title. On the British making Topalga a small medal chief following the Treaty of Pensacola in 1765, see EAID, vol. 12, 273.

32. In his foundational study of the Redstick movement, religious studies scholar Joel Martin argues that Redstick women served as *hōmpita haya*, or "food preparers"; see Martin, *Sacred Revolt*, 145. Yet I struggled to locate evidence confirming this and other examples about Redstick women. Apart from the women who informed on the Redsticks, neither Americans nor Creeks knew about daily life among the Redsticks. For "two," see Hawkins to Armstrong, 9/13/1813, Creek Agency, in LBH, 2:660.

33. On the Pensacola embassy and Burnt Corn Creek, see John Innerarity to James Innerarity, 7/27/1813, Pensacola, pp. 1–6, extract of letter in GA/File II; Collins, "'A Packet from Canada,'" 63, 68-69; Martin, *Sacred Revolt*, 150–52; Big Warrior to Hawkins, 8/4/1813, "William Mc Intosh[']s," 9 p.m., p. 1, copy of original in GA/File II. On the Tensaw métis, see Waselkov, *Conquering Spirit*, 47–48, 55. According to Waselkov, the Creek settlement at the Tensaw moved away from the "traditional" town plan of the "nucleated village with adjacent communal fields." Instead, Tensaw plantations were "dispersed very widely," featuring livestock and Black slaves. No extant evidence demonstrates that this was a talwa, since it had no mico, council, square ground, or rotunda. Yet the Tensaw métis community resembled a talofa, a "daughter community to the Alabama talwas" (all quotes 48).

34. Thrower, "Causalities,' 16 ("sorrows"); Waselkov, *Conquering Spirit*, 127–38; Dupre, *Alabama's Frontiers*, 209–10, 228–29.

35. Waselkov and Wood, "Creek War," 6; Davis, "'Remember Fort Mims,'" 633–34; Waselkov, *Conquering Spirit*, 153–54, 177–202, 210–12; Dupre, *Alabama's Frontiers*, 237.

36. At least nine towns and one talofa pledged peace with the United States after Fort Mims. For "[Coweta?] Tallahassee [a talofa]," Coweta, Tuckabatchee, and Cusseta, see Hawkins to Mitchell, 9/6/1813, Creek Agency, in LBH, 2:660. For Ouseechee, Fish Ponds, Wewocau, Kialijee, and "Hoolchoie [Okchai]," see Hawkins to Armstrong, 9/13/1813, Creek Agency, in LBH, 2:660. For Eufaula and confirmation of Fish Ponds and Kialijee, see Hawkins to Brigadier General John B. Floyd, 9/30/1813, Creek Agency, in LBH, 2:669, 663n2. A Kialijee courier informed Big Warrior in early October 1813 that the "red club men" saturated the "Tallisee [River] down" to the Alabamas. For this courier, see "The Big Warrior and all of the friend Chiefs to Colonel Benjamin Hawkins agent of the Creek Nation," 10/4/1813, Coweta, p 1, copy of original in GA/File II. The talk from "Hoboheilthle Haujo of Thiotlogulgar [Fish Ponds]" is in Hawkins to General Floyd, 10/4/1813, Creek Agency, in LBH, 2:670 ("towns").

37. To quantify the affected polities, I use Waselkov and Wood, "Creek War." In their article, see 12–13 (table 1: map references 10–26 for destroyed towns and villages); 14 (table 1: map references 49–60 for abandoned towns and villages). See also 10 ("total"), 12 ("adjoining"), and 20. On the invasion, see Martin, *Sacred Revolt*, 158–63; Dupre, *Alabama's Frontiers*, 237.

38. Thrower, "Causalities," 22–23; Waselkov and Wood, "Creek War," 12–13 (table 1: map references 28–48 for additional destroyed polities); Martin, *Sacred Revolt*, 162–63; Hawkins to Armstrong, 7/19/1814, Creek Agency, in LBH, 2:689 ("conquered").

39. Article 7 promised food and clothing to Creeks "reduced to extreme want." See "Treaty with the Creeks," signed August 9, 1814, in IALT, 2:107 ("unprovoked," "conformity," "inhuman," "sanguinary," "conquest"), 109 ("reduced"), 109–10 (thirty-three signers). William McIntosh of Coweta signed "for" three headmen (110). See too Hudson, *Creek Paths*, 116 (map 3), 117; Braund, "Introduction," in Braund, ed., *Tohopeka*, 6; and Waselkov, "Fort Jackson and the Aftermath," in Braund, ed., *Tohopeka*, 158–69, here 164 (figure 8.1).

40. Hawkins to Jackson, 8/6/1814, Fort Jackson, in LBH, 2:691–93, 692 ("line"); Big Warrior to Hawkins, 9/18/1815, "Journal of Occurrences at the Convention of the Creeks at Tookaubatche commencing," in LBH, 2:753–61, here 754 ("our," "whole," "woods"); Rothman, *Slave Country*, 138; Waselkov, "Fort Jackson," in Braund, ed., *Tohopeka*, 162.

41. Big Warrior's invocation of the Redsticks' "towns" and "relations" is in Hawkins to George Graham, 4/23/1816, "Camp on Tallapoosa near F. Jackson," in LBH 2:783.

42. Saunt, *New Order*, 270–72, 289–90; Rothman, *Slave Country*, 135–39, 217–24; Dupre, *Alabama's Frontiers*, 241–43, 251–52.

43. Big Warrior to Path Killer, 5/1[?]/1809, Tuckabatchee, in OSW/LR, frame 620 ("four").

Conclusion

1. Big Warrior to Path Killer, 5/1[?]/1809, in OSW/LR, frame 620 ("four"); "Bird [Tail] King, [and] Cussetah King" to Major Henry Gaither, 4/13/1793, in ASP/IA, 1:420 ("three"), enclosed in Gaither to Knox, 4/19/1793, Fort Fidius, in ASP/IA, 1:419; "A Talk delivered by [Tame King] at Ogeechee," 6/18/1777, in EAID, vol. 18, 223.

2. Raymond D. Fogelson, "The Ethnohistory of Events and Non-Events," *Ethnohistory* 36 no. 2 (Spring 1989): 133–47, here 134–35; Claudio Saunt, "The Native South: An Account of Recent Historiography," *Native South* 1 (2008): 45–60, here 45–49.

3. Vernon James Knight, "Puzzles of Creek Social Organization in the Eighteenth and Nineteenth Centuries," *Ethnohistory* 65, no. 3 (July 2018): 373–89.

4. These Creeks were the fifth and final voluntary emigration party leaving their ancestral homeland on their own terms. Thousands more Creeks followed as imprisoned and coerced migrants. Altogether, federal, state, commercial, and settler forces were responsible for the removal of some twenty-three thousand Creeks to Indian Territory. See *"Journal of Occurrences* on the route of a Party of Emigrating Creek Indians, kept by Lieut. Edw Deas [Lieutenant Edward Deas] Disbursing Agent in the Creek Emigration," "Excerpt from the Autobiography of John Hewitt Jones," and editorial information in Christopher D. Haveman, ed., *Bending Their Way Onward: Creek Indian Removal in Documents* (Lincoln: University of Nebraska Press, 2018), 121, 128–36, 137

(December 6, 1835: 511 Creeks), 141–42 (December 25, 1835: two keel boats), 146 (January 11, 1836: one keel boat was damaged and abandoned), 147 (January 13, 1836: "sand-bar"; January 15, 1836: "Sand-Bar"), 148 (January 19, 1836: "another"), 149 (January 20, 1836: "This"; January 22, 1836: sandbar), 151 (February 2, 1836: Fort Gibson), 174 ("on"), 694n19, 697n46; John T. Ellisor, *The Second Creek War: Interethnic Conflict and Collusion on a Collapsing Frontier* (Lincoln: University of Nebraska Press, 2010), passim but especially 182–227, 335–416; Christopher D. Haveman, *Rivers of Sand: Creek Indian Emigration, Relocation, and Ethnic Cleansing in the American South* (Lincoln: University of Nebraska Press, 2016), 3 (twenty-three thousand), 9, 175–233. I acknowledge my debt to Haveman for the apt phrase "rivers of sand."

Bibliography

Unpublished Primary Sources

Bowen, Emanuel. *A New Map of Georgia, with Part of Carolina, Florida and Louisiana.* 1748. Historic Map File, hmf0117. Georgia Department of Archives and History, Morrow.

British Museum Additional Manuscripts, no. 21671. Parts 1-4. Library of Congress. Photostats.

David M. Rubenstein Rare Book and Manuscript Library. Duke University, Durham, NC.

George Galphin Letters, 1778-80. Edward E. Ayer Manuscript Collection. MS 313 Newberry Library, Chicago.

Indians—Creeks—Affairs, 1783-1836. File II. Reference Services. RG 4-2-46. Georgia Department of Archives and History, Morrow.

Indians—Benjamin Hawkins Letters, 1812. File II. Reference Services. RG 4-2-46. Georgia Department of Archives and History, Morrow.

Indians—Creeks—Big Warrior, 1813. File II. Reference Services. RG 4-2-46. Georgia Department of Archives and History, Morrow.

Indians—Creeks—Talks, 1781-85. File II. Reference Services. RG 4-2-46. Georgia Department of Archives and History, Morrow.

The Indian Trade in the Southeastern Spanish Borderlands: Papers of Panton, Leslie and Company. University of West Florida. Microfilm and Gale: Archives Unbound.

James Seagrove Correspondence, 1799. Edward E. Ayer Manuscript Collection. MS 797. Newberry Library, Chicago.

Letters Received by the Office of the Secretary of War Relating to Indian Affairs, 1800-23. National Archives Microfilm Publications, roll 1 (1800-16), folder 1811, microcopy 271. National Archives and Records Service, Washington, DC, 1959.

Records of the British Colonial Office. Class 5 Files. Part 1, Westward Expansion, 1700-1783. Edited by Randolph Boehm. University Publications of America, Frederick, MD, 1983.

Southeastern Native American Documents, 1730-1842. Digital Library of Georgia. http://dlg.galileo.usg.edu.

Thomas Gage Papers, 1754-1807. American Series. William L. Clements Library, University of Michigan, Ann Arbor.

Timothy Pickering Correspondence, 1795-98. Edward E. Ayer Manuscript Collection. MS 926. Newberry Library, Chicago.

William Henry Lyttelton Papers, 1755–61. Series I: Correspondence and Documents. William L. Clements Library, University of Michigan, Ann Arbor.

Published Primary Sources

Adair, James. *The History of the American Indians*. Edited by Kathryn E. Holland Braund. Tuscaloosa: University of Alabama Press, 2009.

Calloway, Colin G., ed. *Revolution and Confederation*. Vol. 18 of *Early American Indian Documents: Treaties and Laws, 1607–1789*. Edited by Alden T. Vaughan. Bethesda: University Publications of America, 1994.

Carter, Clarence Edwin, ed. *The Territory South of the River Ohio, 1790–1796*. Vol. 4 of *The Territorial Papers of the United States*. Washington, DC: Government Printing Office, 1936.

Corbitt, D. C. "Papers Relating to the Georgia-Florida Frontier, 1784–1800." *Georgia Historical Quarterly* nos. 19–25 (1935–41).

Corbitt, D. C., and Roberta Corbitt, eds. "Papers from the Spanish Archives Relating to Tennessee and the Old Southwest, 1783–1800." East Tennessee Historical Society Publications 9–49 (1937–77).

Cumming, William P. *The Southeast in Early Maps*. Edited by Louis De Vorsey Jr. 3rd ed. Chapel Hill: University of North Carolina Press, 1998.

Davies, K. G. *Documents of the American Revolution, 1770–1783*. Vols. 2–3. Shannon: Irish University Press, 1972–73.

———. *Documents of the American Revolution, 1770–1783*. Vol. 5. Dublin: Irish University Press, 1974.

Foster, Thomas, ed. *The Collected Works of Benjamin Hawkins, 1796–1810*. Tuscaloosa: University of Alabama Press, 2003.

Garrett, W. R., ed. "Correspondence of Gen. James Robertson." *American Historical Magazine* 3, no. 4 (October 1898): 348–94.

———. "Correspondence of Gen. James Robertson." *American Historical Magazine* 4, no. 2 (April 1899): 163–92.

Grantham, Bill. *Creation Myths and Legends of the Creek Indians*. Gainesville: University Press of Florida, 2002.

Grant, C. L., ed. *Letters, Journals and Writings of Benjamin Hawkins*. 2 vols. Savannah: Beehive Press, 1980.

Howard, Milo B., and Robert R. Rea. *The Mémoire Justificatif of the Chevalier Montault de Monberaut*. Tuscaloosa: University of Alabama Press, 1965.

Juricek, John T., ed. *Georgia Treaties, 1733–1763*. Vol. 11 of *Early American Indian Documents: Treaties and Laws, 1607–1789*. Edited by Alden T. Vaughan. Frederick, MD: University Publications of America, 1989.

———, ed. *Georgia and Florida Treaties, 1763–1776*. Vol. 12 of *Early American Indian Documents: Treaties and Laws, 1607–1789*. Edited by Alden T. Vaughan. Bethesda: University Publications of America, 2002.

Kappler, Charles J., ed. *Indian Affairs: Laws and Treaties*. Vol. 2. Washington, DC: Government Printing Office, 1904.

Kinnaird, Lawrence, ed. *Spain in the Mississippi Valley, 1765–1794, Part II: Post War Decade, 1782–1791*. Vol. 3. Washington, DC: Government Printing Office, 1946.

———, ed. *Spain in the Mississippi Valley, 1765–1794, Part III: Problems of Frontier Defense, 1792–1794*. Vol. 4. Washington, DC: Government Printing Office, 1946.

Lowrie, Walter, and Matthew St. Clair Clarke, eds. *American State Papers: Class II, Indian Affairs*. 2 vols. Washington, DC: Gales and Seaton, 1832–34.

Martin, Jack B., and Margaret McKane Mauldin, *A Dictionary of Creek/Muskogee, with Notes on the Florida and Oklahoma Seminole Dialects of Creek*. Lincoln: University of Nebraska Press, 2000.

McDowell, William L., ed. *Colonial Records of South Carolina: Documents Relating to Indian Affairs, May 21, 1750–August 7, 1754*. 1958. Reprint, Columbia: South Carolina Department of Archives and History, 1992.

———, ed. *Colonial Records of South Carolina: Documents Relating to Indian Affairs, 1754–1765*. 1970. Reprint, Columbia: South Carolina Department of Archives and History, 1992.

Romans, Bernard. *A Concise Natural History of East and West Florida*. 1775. Edited by Kathryn E. Holland Braund. Reprint, Tuscaloosa: University of Alabama Press, 2014.

Speck, Frank Gouldsmith, "Ceremonial Songs of the Creek and Yuchi Indians." Transcribed by Jacob D. Sapir. Anthropological Publications 1, no. 2 (1911): 157–245. University Museum, University of Pennsylvania.

Swan, Caleb. "Position and State of Manners and Arts in the Creek, or Muscogee Nation in 1791." In *Information Respecting the History, Condition and Prospects of the Indian Tribes of the United States*, edited by Henry Rowe Schoolcraft, 251–83. Vol. 5. Philadelphia: J. B. Lippincott, 1855.

Swanton, John R. *Creek Religion and Medicine*. 1928. Reprint, Lincoln University of Nebraska Press, 2000.

———. *Early History of the Creek Indians and Their Neighbors*. Bureau of American Ethnology Bulletin 73. Washington, DC: Government Printing Office, 1922.

———. *Myths and Tales of the Southeastern Indians*. 1929. Reprint, Norman: University of Oklahoma Press, 1995.

———. "Social Organization and Social Usages of the Indians of the Creek Confederacy." In *Forty-Second Annual Report of the Bureau of American Ethnology to the Secretary of the Smithsonian Institution, 1924–1925*. Washington, DC: United States Government Printing Office, 1928.

Waselkov, Gregory A., and Kathryn E. Holland Braund, eds. *William Bartram on the Southeastern Indians*. Lincoln: University of Nebraska Press, 1995.

Secondary Sources

Barr, Juliana. *Peace Came in the Form of a Woman: Indians and Spaniards in the Texas Borderlands*. Chapel Hill: University of North Carolina Press, 2007.

Barr, Juliana, and Edward Countryman, eds. *Contested Spaces of Early America*. Philadelphia: University of Pennsylvania Press, 2014.

Bates, Denise E. *The Other Movement: Indian Rights and Civil Rights in the Deep South*. Tuscaloosa: University of Alabama Press, 2012.

Bell, Amelia Rector. "Separate People: Speaking of Creek Men and Women." *American Anthropologist* 92, no. 2 (June 1990): 332–45.

Boulware, Tyler. *Deconstructing the Cherokee Nation: Town, Region, and Nation among Eighteenth-Century Cherokees*. Gainesville: University Press of Florida, 2011.

Braund, Kathryn E. Holland. *Deerskins and Duffels: The Creek Indian Trade with Anglo America, 1685–1815*. 1993. Reprint, Lincoln: University of Nebraska Press, 2008.

———. "Guardians of Tradition and Handmaidens to Change: Women's Roles in Creek Economic and Social Life during the Eighteenth Century." *American Indian Quarterly* 14, no. 3 (Summer 1990): 239–58.

———. "'Like to Have Made a War among Ourselves': The Creek Indians and the Coming of the War of the Revolution." In *Nexus of Empire: Negotiating Loyalty and Identity in the Revolutionary Borderlands, 1760s–1820s*, edited by Gene Allen Smith and Sylvia L. Hilton, pp. 39–62. Gainesville: University Press of Florida, 2010.

———. "Reflections on 'Shee Coocys' and the Motherless Child: Creek Women in a Time of War." *Alabama Review* 64, no. 4 (October 2011): 255–84.

Calloway, Colin G. *The American Revolution in Indian Country: Crisis and Diversity in Native American Communities*. Cambridge: Cambridge University Press, 1995.

———. *The Scratch of a Pen: 1763 and the Transformation of North America*. Oxford: Oxford University Press, 2006.

Champagne, Duane. *Social Order and Political Change: Constitutional Governments among the Cherokee, the Choctaw, the Chickasaw, and the Creek*. Stanford, CA: Stanford University Press, 1992.

Chaudhuri, Jean, and Joyotpaul Chaudhuri. *A Sacred Path: The Way of the Muscogee Creeks*. Los Angeles: UCLA American Indian Studies Center, 2001.

Collins, Robert P. "'A Packet from Canada': Telling Conspiracy Stories on the 1813 Creek Frontier." In *Tohopeka: Rethinking the Creek War and the War of 1812*, edited by Kathryn E. Holland Braund, pp. 53–83. Tuscaloosa: University of Alabama Press, 2012.

Corkran, David H. *The Creek Frontier: 1540–1783*. Norman: University of Oklahoma Press, 1967.

de la Teja, Jesús F., and Ross Frank, eds. *Choice, Persuasion, and Coercion: Social Control on Spain's North American Frontiers*. Albuquerque: University of New Mexico Press, 2005.

Davis, Karl. "'Remember Fort Mims': Reinterpreting the Origins of the Creek War." *Journal of the Early Republic* 22, no. 4 (Winter 2002): 611–36.

Din, Gilbert C. *War on the Gulf Coast: The Spanish Fight against William Augustus Bowles*. Gainesville: University Press of Florida, 2012.

Dowd, Gregory Evans. *A Spirited Resistance: The North American Indian Struggle for Unity, 1745–1815*. Baltimore: Johns Hopkins University Press, 1993.

Dubcovsky, Alejandra. *Informed Power: Communication in the Early American South*. Cambridge, MA: Harvard University Press, 2016.

Dupre, Daniel S. *Alabama's Frontiers and the Rise of the Old South*. Bloomington: Indiana University Press, 2018.

Ethridge, Robbie. *From Chicaza to Chickasaw: The European Invasion and the Transformation of the Mississippian World, 1540–1715*. Chapel Hill: University of North Carolina Press, 2010.

———. *Creek Country: The Creek Indians and Their World*. Chapel Hill: University of North Carolina Press, 2003.

———. "The Origins and Coalescence of the Creek (Muscogee) Confederacy: A New Synthesis." In *Studies in Eighteenth-Century Culture* 52 (2023): 113–31.
Ellisor, John T. *The Second Creek War: Interethnic Conflict and Collusion on a Collapsing Frontier.* Lincoln: University of Nebraska Press, 2010.
Fogelson, Raymond D. "The Ethnohistory of Events and Non-Events." *Ethnohistory* 36, no. 2 (Spring 1989): 133–47.
Galloway, Patricia "'The Chief Who Is Your Father': Choctaw and French Views of the Diplomatic Relation." In *Powhatan's Mantle: Indians in the Colonial Southeast*, edited by Gregory A. Waselkov, Peter H. Wood, and Tom Hatley, pp. 345–70. Rev. ed. Lincoln: University of Nebraska Press, 2006.
Garrison, Tim Alan and O'Brien, Greg, eds. *The Native South: New Histories and Enduring Legacies.* Lincoln: University of Nebraska Press, 2017.
Green, Michael D. "The Creek Confederacy in the American Revolution: Cautious Participants." In *Anglo-Spanish Confrontation on the Gulf Coast during the American Revolution*, edited by William S. Coker and Robert R. Rea, pp. 54–75. Pensacola: Gulf Coast History and Humanities Conference, 1982.
———. *The Politics of Indian Removal: Creek Government and Society in Crisis.* Lincoln: University of Nebraska Press, 1982.
Haas, Mary R. "The Classification of the Muskogean Languages." In *Language, Culture, and Personality: Essays in Memory of Edward Sapir*, edited by Leslie Spier, A. Irving Hallowell, and Stanley S. Newman, pp. 41–56. 1941. Reprint, Salt Lake City: University of Utah Press, 1960.
———. "Creek Inter-Town Relations." In *A Creek Source Book*, edited by William C. Sturtevant, pp. 479–89. New York: Garland Publishing, 1987.
Hahn, Steven C. *The Invention of the Creek Nation, 1670–1763.* Lincoln: University of Nebraska Press, 2004.
———. "The Cussita Migration Legend: History, Ideology, and the Politics of Mythmaking." In *Light on the Path: The Anthropology and History of the Southeastern Indians*, edited by Thomas J. Pluckhahn and Robbie Ethridge, pp. 57–93. Tuscaloosa: University of Alabama Press, 2006.
Hall, Joseph M. *Zamumo's Gifts: Indian-European Exchange in the Colonial Southeast.* Philadelphia: University of Pennsylvania Press, 2009.
Harrell, Kevin T. "The Terrain of Factionalism: How Upper Creek Communities Negotiated the Recourse of Gulf Coast Trade, 1763–1780." *Alabama Review* 68, no. 1 (January 2015): 74–113.
Hatley, Tom. "Cherokee Women Farmers Held Their Ground." In *Powhatan's Mantle: Indians in the Colonial Southeast*, edited by Peter H. Wood, Gregory A. Waselkov, and Tom Hatley, pp. 305–35. Rev. ed. Lincoln: University of Nebraska Press, 2006.
Haveman, Christopher D., ed. *Bending Their Way Onward: Creek Indian Removal in Documents.* Lincoln: University of Nebraska Press, 2018.
———. *Rivers of Sand: Creek Indian Emigration, Relocation, and Ethnic Cleansing in the American South.* Lincoln: University of Nebraska Press, 2016.
Haynes, Joshua S. *Patrolling the Border: Theft and Violence on the Creek-Georgia Frontier, 1770–1796.* Athens: University of Georgia Press, 2013.

Hill, James L. "'Bring Them What They Lack': Spanish-Creek Exchange and Alliance Making in a Maritime Borderland, 1763–1783." *Early American Studies: An Interdisciplinary Journal* 12, no. 1 (Winter 2014): 36–67.

———. *Creek Internationalism in an Age of Revolution, 1763–1818*. Lincoln: University of Nebraska Press, 2022.

Hudson, Angela Pulley. *Creek Paths and Federal Roads: Indians, Settlers, and Slaves and the Making of the American South*. Chapel Hill: University of North Carolina Press, 2010.

Hudson, Charles M. *The Southeastern Indians*. Knoxville: University of Tennessee Press, 1976.

Inman, Natalie R. *Brothers and Friends: Kinship in Early America*. Athens: University of Georgia Press, 2017.

Jackson, Harvey H. *Rivers of History: Life on the Coosa, Tallapoosa, Cahaba, and Alabama*. Tuscaloosa: University of Alabama Press, 1995.

Juricek, John T. *Colonial Georgia and the Creeks: Anglo-Indian Diplomacy on the Southern Frontier, 1733–1763*. Gainesville: University Press of Florida, 2010.

———. *Endgame for Empire: British-Creek Relations in Georgia and Vicinity, 1763–1776*. Gainesville: University Press of Florida, 2015.

Kan, Sergei A., and Pauline Turner Strong, eds. *New Perspectives on Native North America: Cultures, Histories, and Representations*. Lincoln: University of Nebraska Press, 2006.

Kidwell, Clara Sue, and Alan Velie. *Native American Studies*. Lincoln: University of Nebraska Press, 2005.

Kilpatrick, Jack F., and Anna G. Kilpatrick. "Muskogean Charm Songs among the Oklahoma Cherokees." Smithsonian Contributions to Anthropology 2, no. 3 Washington, DC: Smithsonian Press, 1967.

Knight, Vernon James. "Puzzles of Creek Social Organization in the Eighteenth and Nineteenth Centuries." In *Ethnohistory* 65, no. 3 (July 2018): 373–89.

Kokomoor, Kevin. "Creeks, Federalists, and the Idea of Coexistence in the Early Republic." *Journal of Southern History* 81, no. 4 (November 2015): 803–42.

———. *Of One Mind and of One Government: The Rise and Fall of the Creek Nation in the Early Republic*. Lincoln: University of Nebraska Press and American Philosophical Society, 2018.

Langley, Linda. "The Tribal Identity of Alexander McGillivray: A Review of the Historical and Ethnographic Data." *Journal of the Louisiana Historical Association* 46, no. 2 (Spring 2005): 231–39.

Lankford, George E. *Looking for Lost Lore: Studies in Folklore, Ethnology, and Iconography*. Tuscaloosa: University of Alabama Press, 2008.

Lee, Wayne. "Peace Chiefs and Blood Revenge: Patterns of Restraint in Native American Warfare, 1500–1800." *Journal of Military History* 71, no. 3 (July 2007): 701–41.

LeMaster, Michelle. *Brothers Born of One Mother: British-Native American Relations in the Colonial Southeast*. Charlottesville: University of Virginia Press, 2012.

Lewis, David, and Ann T. Jordan. *Creek Indian Medicine Ways: The Enduring Power of Mvskoke Religion*. Albuquerque: University of New Mexico Press, 2002.

Martin, Joel W. *Sacred Revolt: The Muskogees' Struggle for a New World*. Boston: Beacon Press, 1991.

McLoughlin, William M. *Cherokee Renascence in the New Republic*. Princeton, NJ: Princeton University Press, 1986.

Mize, Jamie Myers. "'To Conclude on a General Union': Masculinity, the Chickamauga, and Pan-Indian Alliances in the Revolutionary Era," *Ethnohistory* 68, no. 3 (July 2021): 425-48.
Morris, Michael P. *George Galphin and the Transformation of the Georgia-South Carolina Backcountry*. Lanham, MD: Lexington, 2015.
Morrison, Kenneth M. *The Solidarity of Kin: Ethnohistory, Religious Studies, and the Algonkian-French Religious Encounter*. Albany: State University of New York Press, 2002.
Nabokov, Peter. *A Forest of Time: American Indian Ways of History*. Cambridge: Cambridge University Press, 2002.
Narrett, David. *Adventurism and Empire: The Struggle for Mastery in the Louisiana-Florida Borderlands, 1762-1803*. Chapel Hill: University of North Carolina Press, 2015.
Nichols, David Andrew. *Engines of Diplomacy: Indian Trading Factories and the Negotiation of American Empire*. Chapel Hill: University of North Carolina Press, 2016.
———. *Red Gentlemen and White Savages: Indians, Federalists, and the Search for Order on the American Frontier*. Charlottesville: University of Virginia Press, 2008.
Nooe, Evan. "Common Justice: Vengeance and Retribution in Creek Country." *Ethnohistory* 62, no. 2 (April 2015): 241-61.
O'Brien, Greg. *Choctaws in a Revolutionary Age, 1750-1830*. Lincoln: University of Nebraska Press, 2002.
———. "The Conqueror Meets the Unconquered: Negotiating Cultural Boundaries on the Post-Revolutionary Southern Frontier." *Journal of Southern History* 67, no. 1 (February 2001): 39-72.
———. "Protecting Trade through War: Choctaw Elites and British Occupation of the Floridas." In *Pre-Removal Choctaw History: Exploring New Paths*, edited by Greg O'Brien, pp. 103-22. 1999. Reprint, Norman: University of Oklahoma Press, 2008.
Oatis, Steven J. *A Colonial Complex: South Carolina's Frontiers in the Era of the Yamasee War, 1680-1730*. Lincoln: University of Nebraska Press, 2004.
Peach, Steven J. "The Failure of Political Centralization: Mad Dog, the Creek Indians, and the Politics of Claiming Power in the American Revolutionary Era," *Native South* 11 (2018) 81-116.
Perdue, Theda. "Writing the Ethnohistory of Native Women." In *Rethinking American Indian History*, edited by Donald L. Fixico, pp. 73-86. Albuquerque: University of New Mexico Press, 1997.
Piecuch, Jim. *Three Peoples, One King: Loyalists, Indians, and Slaves in the Revolutionary South, 1775-1782*. Columbia: University of South Carolina Press, 2008.
Piker, Joshua. "Colonists and Creeks: Rethinking the Pre-Revolutionary Southern Backcountry." *Journal of Southern History* 70, no. 3 (2004): 503-40.
———. *The Four Deaths of Acorn Whistler: Telling Stories in Colonial America*. Cambridge, MA: Harvard University Press, 2013.
———. *Okfuskee: A Creek Indian Town in Colonial America*. Cambridge, MA: Harvard University Press, 2004.
———. "'White & Clean' & Contested: Creek Towns and Trading Paths in the Aftermath of the Seven Years' War." *Ethnohistory* 50, no. 2 (Spring 2003): 315-47.

Ramsey, William L. *The Yamasee War: A Study of Culture, Economy, and Conflict in the Colonial South*. Lincoln: University of Nebraska Press, 2008.

Reid, John Phillip. *A Law of Blood: The Primitive Law of the Cherokee Nation*. 1970. Reprint, DeKalb: Northern Illinois University Press, 2006.

Rindfleisch, Bryan C. "Cherokee Kings and Creek Kings: Intra-Indigenous Connections and Interactions in the Eighteenth-Century American South." *Journal of Southern History* 85, no. 4 (November 2019): 769–802.

———. *George Galphin's Intimate Empire: The Creek Indians, Family, and Colonialism in Early America*. Tuscaloosa: University of Alabama Press, 2019.

———. "The Indian Factors: Kinship, Trade, and Authority in the Creek Nation and American South, 1740–1800." *Journal of Early American History* 8 (2018): 1–29.

———. "'Our Lands Are Our Life and Breath': Coweta, Cusseta, and the Struggle for Creek Territory and Sovereignty during the American Revolution." *Ethnohistory* 60, no. 4 (Fall 2013): 581–603.

———. "The 'Owner of the Town Ground, Who Overrules All When on the Spot': Escotchaby of Coweta and the Politics of Personal Networking in Creek Country, 1740–1780." *Native South* 9 (2016): 54–88.

Rothman, Adam. *Slave Country: American Expansion and the Origins of the Deep South*. Cambridge, MA: Harvard University Press, 2005.

Saunt, Claudio. "The Native South: An Account of Recent Historiography." *Native South* 1 (2008): 45–60.

———. *A New Order of Things: Property, Power, and the Transformation of the Creek Indians, 1733–1816*. Cambridge: Cambridge University Press, 1999.

———. *West of the Revolution: An Uncommon History of 1776*. New York: W. W. Norton, 2014.

Shankman, Andrew, ed. *The World of the Revolutionary American Republic: Land, Labor, and the Conflict for a Continent*. New York: Routledge, 2014. Online publication.

Shuck-Hall, Sheri Marie. *Journey to the West: The Alabama and Coushatta Indians*. Norman: University of Oklahoma Press, 2008.

Smithers, Gregory D. *The Cherokee Diaspora: An Indigenous History of Migration, Resettlement, and Identity*. New Haven, CT: Yale University Press, 2015.

———. *Native Southerners: Indigenous History from Origins to Removal*. Norman: University of Oklahoma Press, 2019.

Taylor, Alan. *American Colonies: The Settling of North America*. New York: Penguin Books, 2001.

———. *The Civil War of 1812: American Citizens, British Subjects, Irish Rebels, and Indian Allies*. New York: Alfred A. Knopf, 2010.

Thrower, Robert G. "Causalities and Consequences of the Creek War: A Modern Creek Perspective." In *Tohopeka: Rethinking the Creek War and the War of 1812*, edited by Kathryn E. Holland Braund, pp. 10–29. Tuscaloosa: University of Alabama Press, 2012.

Urban, Greg. "The Social Organization of the Southeast." In *North American Indian Anthropology: Essays on Society and Culture*, edited by Raymond J. DeMallie and Alfonso Ortiz, pp. 172–93. Norman: University of Oklahoma Press, 1994.

Waselkov, Gregory A. *A Conquering Spirit: Fort Mims and the Redstick War of 1813–1814*. Tuscaloosa: University of Alabama Press, 2006.

Waselkov, Gregory A., and Ashley A. Dumas. "Archaeological Clues to a Seventeenth-Century Pan-Southeastern Revitalization Movement." Paper presented at the Southeastern Archaeological Conference, Mobile, 2009.

Waselkov, Gregory A., and Brian M. Wood. "The Creek War of 1813–1814: Effects on Creek Society and Settlement Pattern." *Journal of Alabama Archaeology* 32, no. 1 (June 1986):1–24.

Waselkov, Gregory A., and Marvin T. Smith. "Upper Creek Archaeology." In *Indians of the Greater Southeast: Historical Archaeology and Ethnohistory*, edited by Bonnie G. McEwan, pp. 242–64. Gainesville: University Press of Florida, 2000.

Wright, J. Leitch. "Creek-American Treaty of 1790: Alexander McGillivray and the Diplomacy of the Old Southwest." *Georgia Historical Quarterly* 51, no. 4 (December 1967): 379–400.

———. *Creeks and Seminoles: The Destruction and Regeneration of the Muscogulge People*. Lincoln: University of Nebraska Press, 1986.

———. *William Augustus Bowles, Director General of the Creek Nation*. 1967. Reprint, Athens: University of Georgia Press, 2010.

Unpublished Secondary Sources

Fletcher, Debra Lynne. "They Lived; They Fought: The Creek-Choctaw War, 1763–1776." Master's thesis. Auburn University, 1983.

Ward, Monica R. "Little Tallassee: A Creek Indian Colonial Town." PhD diss. University of North Carolina, Greensboro, 2019.

Index

Italicized references indicate illustrations.

Abeikas. *See under* Creeks, Abeika province
Acorn Whistler, 92, 195n41
Adair, James, 2–3, 10, 23, 25, 154n3, 169n14
Alabama (state), 144, 148
Alabama River. *See* rivers
Alabamas. *See* Creeks, Alabama province
American War for Independence, 63–64, 88, 107, 109, 133; Creek-Choctaw War and, 43, 58, 147; French participation in, 71; impact on Creek country, 67, 70–71, *81*, 178n26; Spanish participation in, 72; United States victory, 72, 76
Arkansas River. *See* rivers
assassination: of Doublehead (Cherokee leader), 194n40; of Singer of Hickory Ground, 124. *See also* southern Indians
Atchau Haujo of Coweta, 134
Atkin, Edmond, 4, 21–22, 33, 34–37, 70, 166n46; Hatchet Affair, 36–37, 165n36

Barnard, Timothy, 87–88, 90, 183n18
Bartram, William, 3, 10, 56–57, 96, 123, 172nn34–35, 189n4
Battle of Tohopeka (Horseshoe Bend), 143
Big Warrior of Tuckabatchee, 1; Creek War and, 126–27, 134–35, 137, *138*, 142; Hickory Ground council and, 116, 119–20; intertribal alliance by, 126,
128–32, 134; localism and, 127, 129; on riverine power, 1, 5, 7, 146; Treaty of Fort Jackson (1814) and, 143–44
Bird Tail King of Cusseta, 16, 87–88, *89*, 90
Black Warrior River. *See* rivers
Blount, William, 95, 98, 99–101, 187n39
Bosomworth, Mary, 163n26
Bowen, Emanuel, *13*, 14, 66
Bowles, William Augustus, 109–10; at Hickory Ground, 119–20; Seminoles and, 112
Braund, Kathryn E. Holland, 136, 175n8, 176n17
British Empire, 5, 23, 35, 47, 58, 72 107, 118, 147, 165n39; Southern Indian Department and, 21, 37; trade and, 30–31, 40, 42, 44–47, 70. *See also* Creeks; Creek-British relations; *names of specific treaties*
Burnt Corn Creek violence, 140–41; Creek War (1813–14) and, 141

captive bondage: and Black slavery in British colonies, 39; and Black slavery in United States, 85–86, 127, 141, 144, 185n25; and Black slaves' participation in the American War for Independence, 64; and Indian slave trade, 12, 22, 154n3; and Native tradition of captive exchange, 26–27, 94, 162n13; and Native tradition of captive-taking, 14, 23, 42, 45, 86,

213

captive bondage (*continued*)
96, 147, 168n9, 172n35, 184n23; and origins of United States interstate slave trade, 123, 144; and Tensaw métis and ownership of Black chattel slaves, 141, 199n33; and white American captive-taking in Burnt Village affair, 92–94
Carlos III, 101
Charles Town, Carolina, 2, 12; as Charleston, South Carolina, 69; and Creek-British deerskin trade, 5–6
Charles Town conference (1753), 26–30, 162n12
Chattahoochee, as Lower Creek province. *See* Bird Tail King of Cusseta; Creeks, Lower Creek province
Chattahoochee River. *See* rivers
Chaudhuri, Jean, 8
Chavacleyhatchie Creek, 66
Cherokees, 1, 5, 9, 14, 23–31, 34, 83, 111, 128, 147, 162n14, 162n17, 171n26; Chickamauga division, 86, 194n31; Creek War (1813–14) and, 143; intertribal peace efforts and, 113–17, 192n16, 193n26; land cessions and, 172n31; Lower Cherokee division, 22, 24, 34, 161n8; towns of, 22, 24–25, 128, 161n9. *See also* Creek-Cherokee War; Doublehead; southern Indians
Chickasaws, 10, 14, 64, 83, 95, 118, 159n23, 179n34, 185n27, 186n29, 186n33, 193n27; intertribal peace efforts and, 111–15, 117, 188n41, 192n16; and relationship with Lower Creek town of Cusseta, 78, 102, 179n35; towns of 95, 97, 98, 186n32, 187n35; United States and, 187n39; Upper Creek diplomacy and, 5, 78–79, 102, 147, 161n8; William Blount and, 99–101; women, 100, 187n37. *See also* Creek-Chickasaw War; southern Indians
children, 3, 21, 73, 80, 86, 92–93, 135, 163n27, 184n20. *See also under* Creeks

Choctaws, 14, 42, *52*, 64, 118, 147, 159n23, 166n2, 193n27; Georgia and, 79; intertribal alliance and, 78–79, 111, 113–14, 128, 192n16, 193n26; leaders of, 49, 169n15; music and, 56–58; raids by, 42, 44–45, 50–51, 53–54, 170n23, 171n27, 172n33; towns of, 42, 169n15, 169n17; United States and, 187n39; Upper Creek diplomacy and, 5, 46–50, 58, 97–98, 114–18, 168n11, 169n15, 169n17, 170n18, 173n37, 186n29, 192n18. *See also* Creek-Choctaw War; Mingo Homastubbee; southern Indians
Clark, John, 122
Coffee, John, 142–43
communication, 46, 48, 52, 88, 108, 113, 139–40, 153n1. *See also* Dubcovsky, Alejandra; Creeks, talks
Congeetoo (Choctaw town), 169n15. *See also* Creek-Choctaw War; Emistisiguo
Coosa River. *See* rivers
Cornells, Alexander (Tuckabatchee leader), 87, 91, 119, 133, 135, 153n1
cotton, 86, 127, 144
Courtonne, Jerome, on Creek towns, 159n24, 172n34, 176n18
Creeks, Abeika province, political culture of: ix, 5–7, 146; and collaboration with the Lower Creeks, 27, 63–64, 78, 88, 90–91, 93, 176n12, 183n12; and collaboration with the Tallapoosas, 21–22, 26–27, 30, 34, 39, 42, 46–47, 63, 66, 68, 78–80, 94, 97–98, 112, 147; communities of, 12, *13*, 159n24; Creek War (1813–14) and, 131–32, 140, 142–43, 197n14; diplomacy with the British and, 34–37, 162n12, 164n35, 165n41, 166n43; diplomacy with the Cherokees and, 23–27, 161n8; diplomacy with the Chickasaws and, 97–98, 102; diplomacy with the Choctaws and, 42, 46–50, 168n11; diplomacy with the United States/Georgia, 63, 66, 68, 78–80, 142;

influence of local actors/peoples in, 28–30, 36, 38, 40–41, 53–54, 90, 100, 131; in intertribal affairs, 9; pacific mission to the Seminoles and, 112; riverine leadership and, ix, 10–11, 21–22, 35, 42, 50; shared history and language with the Tallapoosas, 11–14, 189n4; Three Rivers Resolution and, 83–84, 87–88, 95. *See also names of specific conflicts and leaders*

Creeks, Abeika province, towns of: Aubecooche, 12–13, 24, 100, 131, 187n36; Breed Camp, 24, 161n8; Coosa, 13, 24–25, 100, 187n37; Fish Ponds, 142; Hillabee, 142–43; Kialijee, 71, 197n14, 199n36; Nauchee, 25–26, 161n9; Nuyaka, 182n10; Okchai, 12–13, 22–24, 26–27, 41, 56, 142, 170n22, 199n36; Okfuskee, 6, 12–13, 16, 22, 24–29, 63–64, 67–68, 77–80, 92–93, 101, 131, 154n3, 159n24, 161n4, 162n14, 162n17; Pucantallahassee, 26–27, 45, 171n27; Tullushatchee, 142; Upper Eufaula, 26; Wewocau, 140, 142; Woccoccoie, 95

Creeks, Alabama province, political culture of: 5–6, 146; as advocates of southern Indian union, 108–09, 189n4; Alabama "stayers" and, 108; and Alexander McGillivray of Little Tallassee and opposition to the United States, 64, 74–75, 175n10; and collaboration with Mad Dog of Tuckabatchee, 109–13, 113–16, 192n20; communities of, 13, 14; Creek War and, 131–32, 132, 139–40, 142; diplomacy with the British and, 36; as go-betweens in intertribal war, 191n11; and impact of Singer of Hickory Ground, 107–9, 112, 113–16, 116–21, 121–25; language of, 159n23, 189n4; and legacy of alliance with the French, 49; and political parity in Creek country, 108–9, 147; and subordination to Abeika and Tallapoosa leadership during the Creek-Choctaw War, 42, 47, 49–50, 171n26; women and, 139–40. *See also Hickory Ground council of 1803; names of specific conflicts and leaders*

Creeks, Alabama province, towns of: Coosada/Koasati, 14, 49–50, 171n27, 199n31; Ecunchate/Holy Ground, 142; Hickory Ground, 107, 115–23, 128, 171n26, 192n20; Tuskegee, 112

Creeks, clans: 8–10; Bear clan, 8, 38–41, 47, 165n40, 166n43; Deer clan, 8, 51, 52, 53, 170n24; Eagle clan, 1, 8, 129; interclan networking and, 130; political impact of, 51, 52, 53, 92, 129; Wolf clan, 165n40

Creeks, diplomacy: and attempt to recruit American women as diplomats, 88; as gendered, 116–17; as hospitality, 117, 136; as multilateralism, 69–70, 72; as reflected in titles, 79, 112; with the British, 21–22, 28–30, 34, 38–41, 47, 168n12; with the Cherokees, 22–27, 115–18; with the Chickasaws, 83–84, 96–98, 102; with the Choctaws, 42–43, 48–50, 114–15; with the French, 34, 49, 73; with the Seminoles, 109–12; with the Spanish, 73, 100–101, 187n38; with the United Provinces/Dutch Empire, 73; with the United States, 64–66, 74, 81, 82, 83, 86–90, 97, 109–10, 114, 123, 126, 131, 136–37, 138, 139–40, 142, 147, 188n45, 199n36. *See also names of specific conflicts, leaders, and treaties*

Creeks, kinship: 9–10, 158nn17–19; blood revenge and role of, 91–92; clan lineages, 4–5, 8–10, 158n18; "crying blood," 25, 94, 100, 101, 161n10; Deer clan, 8, 51–53; Eagle clan, 1, 8, 129; Hathagalgi and, 38; *huti*, 8; matrilineal kinship reckoning, 8–10, 28, 55, 65, 117, 158n17; nephews and role of, 28, 69, 131; retaliation and role of, 25, 31–32, 51, 92, 95–96, 98–99; siblings, 55–56; uncles, 28

216 | Index

Creeks, local actors/peoples: children, 7, 30, 45–46, 96, 103, 119, 129, 146–47, 180n38; elders, 7, 35, 65, 69–72, 79, 129, 147, 178n31; warriors, 7, 28–31, 35–37, 43, 45–46, 50–54, 79, 86–87, 90–94, 103, 110, 117–18, 125, 127–32, 145–46; women, 7, 36–37, 41, 45–46, 54–57, 92–93, 103, 117, 119, 127, 136–37, *138*, 139–40, 145, 147, 157n15, 180n38, 184n20, 198n27, 199n32

Creeks, Lower Creek province, political culture of: 5–6, 14, 22, 34, 36, 59, 109, 146, 148, 154n3, 162n12, 167n4, 172n35, 183n18; American War for Independence and, 66–68, 70–71, 73–75, 78–79, 176n11; assassination of Singer and, 124; conflict with US settlers and, 86–87, 93, 103, 122; Creek-Cherokee War and, 23–24, 162n14; Creek-Chickasaw War and, 102; Creek-Choctaw War and, 170n24; Creek policy and, 83–84, 88, *89*, 90, 91; Creek War (1813–14) and, 132–34, 142–43, 198n27; Edmond Atkin and, 36; Forbes Purchase (1804) and, 121–23; kinship and, 158n18; Ogeechee Incident and, 31–33; peace mission to Seminoles and, 112; Three Rivers Resolution and, 83–84, 86–87, *89*, 90; Treaty of Augusta (1763) and, 39; Treaty of Washington (1805) and, 123. *See also names of specific conflicts and leaders*

Creeks, Lower Creek province, towns of: Apalachicola, 70, 74, 119, 120–21; Broken Arrow, 183n16; Coweta, 5, 10, 32, 86, 123, 134–35, 142, 156n9, 160n25, 162n12, 165n36, 183n12, 183n16, 184n20, 188n41; Cusseta, 16, 18, 63–64, 68, 82, 85–91, 102, 125, 134–35, 176n12, 197n21; Hitchiti, 70, 74, 91, 183n12, 187n39; Oconee, 74; Ouseechee, 183n16; Sauwoogelo, 70, 74, 176n18, 177n25; Yuchi, 70, 134, 183n16Creeks, politics: big house (*cukofv rakko*) and, 133; in historical scholarship, 4–5, 154n8; localism and, 4–5, 28, 33, 37–38, 40–43, 50, 54, 65, 72, 84, 90, 102–3, 109, 116–17, 119, 127, 131, 135, 136–40, 147–48; nationhood and, 22, 75, 128; National Council and, 7, 17, 64, 83, 107, 116, 126, 130, 133; out-settlements (*talofas*) and, 14, 66, 92, 132, 142–43, 164n35, 176n18, 199n33, 199n36; towns (*talwas*) and, 12, 142–43

Creeks, power: as relational, 10–11, 158n20; as riverine concept, 1–11, 22, 50, 63, 67–68, 83–84, 127, 132, 135–36, 146, 153n2, 154n8, 156n9, 176n11. *See also* Creeks, diplomacy

Creeks, provinces: 1–2, 4–6; in policy, 83–84; as political entities, 4–6, 7, 22–23, 64–65, 68, 83–84, 90, 108, 131–32, 135, 140, 146, 174n4, 181n3

Creeks, removal: Indian Removal Act (1830), 145; forcible removal, 147; voluntary removal, 148, 200n4

Creeks, talks: 1, 7, 146, 153n1; between Creeks and Seminoles, 109–110, 190n10, 192n16; British authorities and, 32, 38–39, 45, 163n24, 165n39, 166n43; in context of southern Indian coalition, 114–16, 118, 120, 128–29, 188n42, 192n16; during Creek-Cherokee War, 24, 26, 29; during Creek-Chickasaw War, 95, 97–98, 103, 112, 185n27, 191n11; addressed to Choctaws, 42, 47, 50; involving Tame King of Tallassee/Halfway House, 66, 70, 72–74, 77–80, 130, 133, 176n12, 177n23, 178nn31–32; kinship and, 28, 103, 130; as political discussion, 84, 88; as reliable source of Creek thought, 7; US authorities and, 87–88, 93, 183n12, 186n30. *See also* communication; *names of specific conflicts, leaders, and treaties*

Creeks, Tallapoosa province, political culture of: ix, 1, 5–7, 146; the American War for Independence and diplomacy by, 63–64 66–67, 69–72, 73, 75, 77–80, 81; and ceremony during the Creek-Choctaw War, 54–58, 171n27; and collaboration with the Abeikas, 21–22, 26–27, 30, 34, 39, 42, 46–47, 63, 66, 68, 78–80, 86–87, 94, 97–98, 112, 147; and collaboration with the Alabamas, especially Singer of Hickory Ground, 107–8, 109–11, 113–16; and collaboration with the Lower Creeks, 74, 87, 90–91, 133–34, 148; communities of, 12, 13, 14, 159n24, 164n35; Creek War (1813–14) and, 126–27, 131–32, 135, 142–43; and defeat by the Chickasaws, 101; diplomacy with the British and, 34–37, 39–40, 44–45, 164n35; diplomacy with the Cherokees and, 23, 26–27, 162n12; diplomacy with the Chickasaws and, 96–98, 102; diplomacy with the Choctaws and, 42, 46–50; diplomacy with the Spanish, 100–101; intertribal relations of, 8–9; local actors/peoples and, 28, 30, 33, 53, 54, 96, 98–99, 103, 116, 129; as Middle Creeks, 13, 14, 66, 132–33; Ogeechee Incident and, 32–34, 163n24; opposition to Georgia by, 87; riverine leadership and, 10–11, 34, 46–47, 50, 54–65, 68, 83–84, 127; shared history and language with the Abeikas, 11–14, 189n4; southern Indian union and, 102, 107–8, 109–11, 113–16, 117–20, 128–29; Three Rivers Resolution and, 83, 86, 88, 90, 97; women and, 57–58, 137, 138, 139, 140. *See also names of specific conflicts and leaders*

Creeks, Tallapoosa province, towns of: Autossee, 26, 71, 112, 131, 142; Cooloome, 26; Fusihatchee, 34, 163n27, 178n25; Hoithlewaulee, 45, 137–39, 198n27; Little Tallassee, 26, 44–45, 163n21, 164n35 173n37; Muccolossus, 26, 34, 45, 54, 56–58, 112, 139, 163n27, 172n33–34; Sawanogi, 26; Tallassee, 12, 14, 26, 63–65, 68–70, 73, 77–78, 175n7, 176n17, 177n25, 183n16; Tuckabatchee, 1, 12, 14, 16, 26, 35–37, 46, 54–56, 58, 70, 88, 91, 97–99, 101, 110, 116, 129, 134–35, 142, 163n27, 175n7, 186n30, 186n33, 187n34, 192n20, 198n27

Creeks, *talofas* (out-settlements/villages): Halfway House, 14, 66, 132–33, 135; Little Okfuskee/Burnt Village, 92–94; Sauwoogelooche, 176n18, 177n25

Creeks, trade: with British colonists, 2, 5, 30–31, 40, 42, 44–48, 70, 172n35; Creeks on British goods, 30–31; debt from, 108, 119, 121–24, 172n31, 193n29; with French colonists, 21, 42, 44; with merchant houses, 93, 108, 114, 119–20; with Spanish colonists, 44, 93–94, 140, 167n5; Treaty of Paris and, 42, 46, 167n5; US commerce among Upper Creeks, 85–86, 138–39

Creeks, traditions: bathing ritual, 2–3; ceremonial ground (*cuko rakko*), 133; dances, 43, 54–56, 58, 117, 171n28, 172n32; farming, 8, 67, 85–86, 109, 117, 127; foodways, 117, 136; Green Corn Ceremony or Busk, 3, 36, 54, 55, 57, 154n4; hunting, 31, 114–15, 163n22; language, 3–4, 12, 189n4; marriage, 3, 57–58, 136–37, 139, 172n35; Master of Breath, 38–39; medicine/physic, 39, 54–55; métis, 141; migration, 3, 148, 154n3, 200n4; moiety system, 36; mound-building, 3, 71; purification ceremony, 3; Tie-Snake, 4; torture, 23, 45–46, 96, 185n27

Creeks, Upper Creeks: 5–6; as foundation of historical narrative, 13–14, 147. *See also names of specific leaders, conflicts, and treaties*

Creeks, water: association with women, 8; in Muscogee language, 3–4; spiritual properties of, 3–4, 8

Creek–British relations, 5, 21–22, 28–29, 31–37, 38–40, 47, 65, 92, 107, 118, 147, 161n4, 163n22, 163n26, 165n41, 170n22, 199n31; Creek memory and, 69; during the American War for Independence, 64, 69, 88; during Creek-Choctaw War, 43–45, 49, 53, 54, 58, 166n2, 167n7; genesis of the Seminoles and, 109. *See also names of specific conflicts, leaders, and treaties*

Creek-Cherokee War, 9, 113, 147; British interest in, 26–27, 161n6; cause and conclusion of, 22, 27–28; local actors/peoples and 28–31; Lower Creeks and, 22–23, 27; provincial leadership during, 21–22, 26; Upper Creek diplomacy and, 24–28. *See also names of specific leaders*

Creek-Chickasaw War, 9, 83–84, 95–96, 101, 113, 147, 185n27, 186n33, 188nn40–41; conclusion of, 102–03; Creek policy and, 94–95, 97; Cusseta and, 83, *89*, 85, 102; kinship and, 96, 98, 100; local actors/peoples and, 96, 98–100, 103; origins of, 95; Spanish interest in, 101; Upper Creek diplomacy and, 96–98; US interest in, 83, 99, 187n39. *See also names of specific leaders*

Creek-Choctaw War, 9, 42, 44–46, 50–54, 113, 147, 171nn26–27; Alabamas and, 171n26; British interest in, ; ceremonial traditions and, 43, 54, 56–57; conclusion of, 58, 64; Creek pictograph and, *52*, 170nn23–24; Cusseta and, 64; Deer clan warriors and, 51, *52*, 53–54; local actors/peoples and, 54–58; second phase of, 53; Upper Creek diplomacy and, 42, 46–50. *See also names of specific leaders*

Creek–Georgia alliance, 64–68, 72–80, *81*, 82, 135, 174n4, 175n8, 178n26, 178n28. *See also* Galphin, George; Tallassee King (Tallassee Mico) of Tallassee; Tame King of Tallassee/Halfway House; Treaty of Augusta (1763); Treaty of Augusta (1783)

Creek–Seminole relations, 109–13, 121–22. *See also names of specific leaders*; Seminoles; southern Indians

Creek–US relations, 5, 147, 188n45, 196n8; in diplomacy, 73, *81*, 86, *89*, 90, 96, 114; during Creek War, 136–40, 199n36; land cessions and, 107–8, 121–22; Seminoles and, 109–13; in war, 77, 83, 126, 130, 141–43. *See also* Creek War (1813–14); *names of specific treaties*; Oconee War; Three Rivers Resolution

Creek War (1813–14), 9; causes of, 126–27, 130–31, 195n2, 197n14; contingency and, 127–30, 196n3; Creek diplomacy with the US during, 126, 128–29, 132, 137, 142 199n36; paradox of provincial leadership and, 132–35; Redstick violence during, 126, 131–32, 135, 137, 141, 198nn26–29; US conquest of Creeks resulting from, 142–44; women and, 136–40, 198n28, 199n32. *See also* Burnt Corn Creek violence; *names of specific leaders*; Treaty of Fort Jackson (1814)

Creek War (1836), 148

creeks: Chavacleyhatchie, 66, 132, 175n7; Shoulderbone, 80; Upahee, 175n7. *See also* rivers

Cumberland River. *See* rivers

Cussetah Micco of Cusseta, 133–34

Cussetuh Tuskeinchau of Okfuskee, 112

Deas, Edward, 148

de Soto, Hernando, 11–12. *See also* Spanish Empire

Deval's Landlord of Pucantallahassee, 27, 30, 168n12. *See also* Creek-Choctaw War

diplomacy. *See under* Creeks, talks; *names of specific conflicts, leaders, and treaties*

Dog Warrior of Aubecooche, 100

Doublehead (Cherokee leader), 115–18, 120, 194n31, 194n40

Doyell, Nimrod, 131, 137
Dubcovsky, Alejandra, 139
Dupre, Daniel S., 11
Durouzeaux, James, 94, 183n18
Dutch Empire, 73–74, 177n24
DuVal, Kathleen, 84–85

Emistisiguo of Little Tallassee, 39, 147: British intermediaries and, 47, 173n37; death of, 173n37; diplomacy with the British, 39–41, 166n43, 168n12, 172n35; diplomacy with the Choctaws, 46–50, 51–52, 169n15, 173n37; raids on the Choctaws by, 50, 53–54
ethno-ethnohistorical method, 6–7, 156n12. *See also* Fogelson, Raymond D.
Ethridge, Robbie, 12
Eustis, William, 129

Fanni Mingo ("squirrel king"), 118–20, 193n27. *See also* Choctaws; Hickory Ground council of 1803; Mingo Homastubbee
Fat King of Cusseta, 70–71, 73–75, 78–80, 84. *See also* American War for Independence; Tame King of Tallassee/Halfway House; Treaty of Augusta (1783)
Floridas: in American War for Independence, 64; as area of multinational contest, 86, 109–10; British East and West Florida, 3, 40, 50; and Redstick migration to, 128; Spanish East and West Florida, 72, 93, 120; Treaty of Fort Jackson (1814) and, 143; Treaty of Paris (1763) and, 165n39; Treaty of Paris (1783) and, 76
Fogelson, Raymond D., 6
Folch, Estevan, 117–18, 119–20
Folch y Juan, Vicente, 120
Fooy, Benjamin, 96, 100, 186n30, 186n33
Forbes, John, 108, 116, 117–20, 190n5, 193n26, 193n29. *See also* John Forbes & Company (JFC)

Forbes Purchase (1804), 121–23. *See also* John Forbes & Company (JFC); Seminoles
Fort Gibson, 148
Fort Jackson, 143. *See also* Treaty of Fort Jackson (1814)
Fort Mims, 141
Fort Mims Massacre, 141–42
Fort Toulouse ("Alabama Fort"), 49, 169n17
Fort Wilkinson, Georgia, 113. *See also* Treaty of Fort Wilkinson (1802)
Franchimastabé of West Yazoo (Choctaw leader), 97, 186n29
French and Indian War (1754–60), 21, 31, 33–34, 38, 41. *See also* Seven Years' War (1756–63)
French Empire, 12, 33; and alliance with Alabamas, 49; in American War for Independence, 64, 69–73; British traders and, 30, 42, 44; in Seven Years' War, 34, 38, 165n39; and trade with Creeks, 21
Fushatchee Micco of Okfuskee, 112

Gage, Thomas, 51
Gaither, Henry, 83, 88
Galphin, George, 10, 23, 25, 65, 66, 69, 71–72, 77, 86
Gálvez, Bernard de, 72
Gayoso de Lemos, Manuel, 98
Georgia: American War for Independence and, 63; controversial treaty tactics and, 75–76, 80, 178n26, 178n28; Creek ancestors' migration to, 3; and Creek diplomacy to stay Georgia's expansion, 64–65, 66–68, 69–72, 73–76, 77–80, 81, 174n4; Creek violence against, 80, 82, 86–87, 93–94, 103; Ogeechee Incident and, 31–33; original boundary between Creeks and, 135; population of, 85; settler incursion on Creek lands and, 38–39, 92, 122–23, 135, 144. *See also* Creek-Georgia alliance; Galphin, George; Tallassee King (Tallassee

220 | Index

Georgia (*continued*)
  Mico) of Tallassee; Tame King of Tallassee/Halfway House
Glen, James, 25, 30; as intermediary in Creek-Cherokee War, 25–26, 29
"good child," in Creek culture and language, 79–80
Gun Merchant of Okchai, 24; and diplomacy with Cherokees, 24, 26–27, 29; and diplomacy with Choctaws, 168n11, 170n18; Hatchet Affair and, 37; on Mortar of Okchai, 164n30

Hahn, Steven C., 154n8
Handsome Fellow of Okfuskee: diplomacy with the Americans and, 66, 68, 176n12; diplomacy with the Cherokees and, 29; diplomacy with the Choctaws and, 168n11; death of, 69; as son of Red Coat King of Okfuskee, 29
Harrell, Kevin T., 165n41
Hawkins, Benjamin, 102; Creek criticism of, 120–21, 124, 126–27; Creek War (1813–14) and, 130–31, 135, 137, 142; and criticism of William Augustus Bowles, 110; and role in land cessions, 113, 122–23, 144; and partnership with John Forbes 108, 119; as US agent to the southern Indians, 110, 121–22, 188n41, 191n11, 196n8. *See also* Creek War (1813–14); *names of specific leaders and treaties*
Haynes, Joshua, 86, 154n8, 174n4, 181n3
Hectór, Francisco Luis (Barón de Carondelet), 93, 96, 184n22, 188n45
Hickory Ground council of 1803, 116–21; and impact on Big Warrior of Tuckabatchee, 128–29; and resulting noncession compact, 107, 120, 122–24
Hilton, Sylvia, 11
historical narratives: indigenous thought and, 6–7, 14, 147; theories of, 14
Hiwassee (Cherokee town), 24–25, 161n9. *See also* Cherokees; The Raven of Hiwassee

Hoboheilthle Haujo of Fish Ponds, 142
Hoithleponiyau, 139, 198n29
Holacta Hopayi/Holaghtaobaye (Choctaw leader), 49
Hopoie Yauholo of Tuskegee, 112
Houstoun, John, 74, 77–79, 177n22. *See also* Georgia; Tame King of Tallassee/Halfway House

Inman, Natalie, 8, 158n18
intertribal history. *See names of specific conflicts, groups, and leaders; southern Indians*

Jackson, Andrew, 142–44
James, Benjamin, 99–100, 186n29
Jefferson, Thomas, 123. *See also* US Declaration of Independence
John Forbes & Company (JFC), 108, *111*, 114, 119–22. *See also* Forbes, John; Forbes Purchase (1804); Panton, Leslie & Company (PLC); Panton, William
Johnston, George, 28, 162n14, 162n17
Johnstone, George, 40
Jones, John Hewitt, 148

Kinnard, John (Hitchiti leader), 91
kinship. *See under* Creeks, kinship
Knox, Henry, 80, 86–87, 126–27
Kokomoor, Kevin, 130, 154n8, 156n13, 187n39

leadership. *See names of specific conflicts and leaders*
LeMaster, Michelle, 8, 161n5, 167n3
local actors/peoples. *See* Creeks, local actors/peoples
Long Lieutenant of Coweta, 194n38
Long Lieutenant of Tallassee, 4
Louisiana, 12, 93
Lyttelton, William Henry, 32

Macon, Georgia, 71
Mad Dog of Tuckabatchee: Creek hunting and, 95; description of, 36, 158n20, 172n29, 192n20; diplomacy

by, 86, 88, 90, 93–94, 96–97, 102–3, 147, 183n12, 190n8; leadership of, 54–56, 135; loss of family and retaliation by, 96, 98–99, 185n27, 186n33, 187n34; and relationship with Spanish, 100–101, 187n38; southern Indian coalition and, 102, 107–8, 109–13, 113–116, 140, 146, 192n16; speech at Hickory Ground, 117–18; war party by, 101, 187n39
Madison, James, 129–30
Malatchi of Coweta, 162n12
Manrique, González, 140
Mathews, George, 94
McGillivray, Alexander (Little Tallassee leader), 67, 175n10; death of, 84, 181n3; description of leadership, 64–65, 73; and opposition to Tame King of Tallassee/Halfway House, 74–76, 174n4; and southern Indian coalition, 108, 189n4
McGillivray, Lachlan, 24, 162n14
McIntosh, William (Coweta leader), 123
McMurphy, Daniel, 79–80, 175n8
McQueen, Peter, 137, 140
Methlogee of Miccosukee, 111, 119, 121. *See also* Seminoles
Mingo Homastubbee (Choctaw leader), 114–16, 117–19, 121, 192n18, 193n26. *See also* Choctaws; Fanni Mingo
Mississippian era, 12
Mississippi Territory, 123, 141–42
Mortar of Okchai, 27, 84, 144, 147; and alliance with French and Lower Cherokees, 34, 37, 166n46; and diplomacy with the British, 38–41, 165n41, 166n43, 168n12; diplomacy with Cherokees and, 27, 162n14; diplomacy with Choctaws and, 47–50, 162n14, 169n13; Gun Merchant of Okchai on, 164n30; and kinship connections, 38, 40–41, 75; nephew of, 28; and opposition to land cessions, 38; and raids on Choctaws, 53–54, 148, 171n26
Mucklasso Mingo (Chickasaw leader), 97

Nabokov, Peter, 14. *See also* historical narratives
Native North America, 1–2, 158n20; as reshaped by treaties, 38, 46, 49, 76, 165n39
Neuhayo of Tuckabatchee, 99
New Purchase Cession (1773), 172n31

O'Brien, Greg, 166n2, 169n14
Ocmulgee Old Fields, 3, 71, 123
Ocmulgee River. *See* rivers
Oconee Cession, 74–76, 77–80, 82. *See also* Treaty of Augusta (1783); Treaty of New York (1790)
Oconee River. *See* rivers
Oconee War, 77, 79–80, 83
Ogeechee Incident (1756), 32–34, 163n24
Ogeechee River. *See* rivers
Okeelysa (nephew of Mortar), 28
Okfuskee Captain of Okfuskee, ix, 11, 84, 135, 144, 146; diplomacy with the British and, 21–22, 25–26, 29–30, 35–37, 164n35; influence of local actors/peoples on, 29; riverine leadership and, 21–22, 147

pan-Indianism. *See names of specific conflicts, groups, and leaders*; southern Indians
Panton, Leslie & Company (PLC), 93, 95, 99–100, 108, 112, 114
Panton, William, 93, 96, 100, 114, 188n45
Paris Peace. *See* Treaty of Paris (1763)
Path Killer of Little Turkey's Town, 1, 7, 128, 146
Pearl River. *See* rivers
Pensacola, 40; as base for Panton, Leslie & Company (PLC), later John Forbes & Company (JFC), 93, 119; Creek-Choctaw War and, 45, 47, 53, 53; as space for diplomacy, 40, 93, 101, 137, 140, 168n12, 184n22, 199n31; Spanish repossession of, 64; vicinity of as sacred, 166n45
Pepper, Daniel, 32, 163n22
pictograph ("hieroglyphick painting"), 51, 52, 53, 170nn23–24

Piker, Joshua, 6–7, 8, 92, 154n8, 180n1
Pinckney, William, 161n6
Piomingo of Long Town (Chickasaw leader), 95, 97–98, 187n35
Poarch Band of Creek Indians, 128, 141
posts on Gulf Coastal Plain: Baton Rouge, 64; Manchac, 64; Mobile, 45, 50–51, 64, 128, 170n21; Natchez, 64, 98, 114; St. Marks, 72, 112
power. *See under* Creeks, power
provinces. *See under* Creeks—*names of specific provinces*

Raven, The, of Hiwassee, 24–25, 161n9. *See also* Cherokees
Red Coat King of Okfuskee, 66; diplomacy with the Cherokees and, 26–29, 162n13
Reed, Hardy, 137, *138*, 139, 198n28
Reid, John Phillip, 25
Revolutionary War. *See* American War for Independence
Reynolds, John, 32
Rindfleisch, Bryan, 8, 10–11, 154n8, 157n16, 158n18, 184n21
riverine power. *See under* Creeks, power
rivers: Alabama, 2, 14, 39–40, 45, 49, 107, 143; Apalachee, 114; Arkansas, 148; Black Warrior, 115; Chattahoochee, 2, 4, 36, 63, 83, 86, 92, 131, 147, 154n3, 176n11, 182n7; Coosa, 1–2, 12–13, 23–24, 36, 39, 49, 53–54, 68, 83, 100, 107, 128, 131, 142–43, 176n11; Cumberland, 85–86, 95, 99; environment and, 137, 143; Muscogee language and, 3–4; Ocmulgee, 2–3, 71, 76, 122–23, 154n3, 178n28; Oconee, 2, 31–32, 63, 74–78, 80, 85–87, 103, 113, 122, 154n3, 178n26, 178n28; Ogeechee, 31–32, 66–71, 135; Pearl, 27; political geography and, 4, 114; St. Marys, 86–87, 90, 113; Tallapoosa, 2, 12–13, 23–24, 36, 39, 45, 49, 54, 56–57, 66, 68, 83, 107, 137, 139–40, 143, 154n3, 175n7, 176n11; Tallaseehatchee 4; Tennessee, 83, 85–86, 95, 99–100, 114; Tombigbee, 45, 95, 103, 114
Robertson, James, 99
Romans, Bernard, 51, *52*, 53, 170nn23–24

Saunt, Claudio, 7, 154n8
Seagrove, James: Burnt Village affair and, 93–94, 184n20; and death of brother and political fallout, 90–92; diplomacy with Creek headmen and, 87–88, 183n13, 186n30; Seminoles and, 111
Seminoles, 3, 109, 182n6; land cessions and, 113, 121; leaders of, 111, 119–20; and relationship with Lower Creeks, 71, 86, 121, 177n20; and relationship with Upper Creeks and, 5, 14, 109–13, 117, 147, 188n42, 192n16; and resistance to Creek interventionism, 111–12, 190n10; resistance to US expansion and, 128, 190n10; towns of, 71, 111, 177n20; trade debt and, 119, 122–23; William Augustus Bowles and, 109–10, 112, 119
Semothle (Seminole leader), 120. *See also* Seminoles
settler incursion: by the British 31–32, 38–39, 107, 109, 163n22; by the Spanish, 11–12, 154n3; by the United States, 71, 77–78, 85–87, 103, 108, 113–15, 122, 144, 147
Seven Years' War (1756–63), 11, 21, 23, 43, 165n39. *See also* French and Indian War (1754–60)
Shawnees: as allies of southern Indians in 1790s, 182n8; as intermediaries during Creek-Cherokee War, 24, 161n8; and role in Creek War (1813–14), 198n29
Simpson, William, 121–22
Singer of Hickory Ground, 107, *111*, 146, 189n1; Alabama "stayers" and, 108–9; death of, 121, 124, 126, 131, 195n41; on Forbes Purchase, 121–22;

and influence in Creek country, 121, 124; and partnership with Mad Dog of Tuckabatchee, 112, 140, 192n20; and role in conclusion of Creek-Chickasaw War, 112, 191n11; and role in Hickory Ground council and resulting non-cession compact, 107, 120, 122–24; sister of, 117; southern Indian union and, 109, 112, 113–16, 189n4; titles and, 112, 191n11, 192n18; Treaty of the Creek Agency (1804) and, 122, 194n36; Treaty of Fort Wilkinson (1802) and, 113
sister of Singer of Hickory Ground: political impact on Hickory Ground council, 117
slavery. *See* captive bondage
Smith, Gene, 11
sófki, 117
southern Indians: and alliance-building among, 8–9, 14, 27, 48, 53, 78–79, 97–98, 102, 107–8, 109–12, 113–16, 128–29, 146–47; and call for intertribal history of Native South, 8–9, 156n13; and concept of four mothers, 116–17; and concept of four nations, 114, 128, 192n16; musical traditions and, 56–57; and non-cession compact, 107, 120, 122–24; Southern Confederacy and, 108; wars among, 9, 23–28, 42–46, 50–54, 56, 83, 95–96, 98–102, 143, 147–48. *See also specific conflicts, groups, and leaders*
Southwest Territory (Tennessee), 83, 85–86, 95, 99
Spandahayo of Tuckabatchee, 99
Spanish Empire, 11–12, 64, 100–101. *See also* Creeks, trade
Stiggins, Joseph, 100
St. Marys River. *See* rivers
Stono Rebellion (1739), 22
Stuart, Charles, 47–51, 53, 168n9, 168n11, 169n15
Stuart, John, 39–41, 45, 47, 51, 53, 58, 64, 67, 69, 166n44

Swanton, John R., 38, 158n17, 160n25, 165n40

Taitt, David, 53, 54–56, 171–72nn27–29, 175n7
talks. *See under* Creeks, talks
Tallapoosa River. *See* rivers
Tallapoosas. *See* Creeks, Tallapoosa province
Tallaseehatchee River. *See* rivers
Tallassee King (Tallassee Mico) of Tallassee, 65–66, 69–72, 74, 77, 80, 82
Tame King of Tallassee/Halfway House, 63, *81*, 174n4; and critic of Singer, 124; and death of, 143–44; and diplomacy with Europeans, 72, 176n17, 177nn23–24; and diplomacy with Georgia, 66–68, 69–72, 72–76, 77–80, 178n28, 179n37; as "good child," 77, 79–80; intertribal alliance by, 78–79, 107, 179n34; and opposition to US expansion, 80, 82, 83, 87, 126, 129–30, 183n15; partnership with Cusseta leadership by, 70–71, 73–75, 78–80, 133–34, 147–48; partnership with Lower Creek and Seminole towns by, 71, 177n20; political capital at Halfway House and, 66, 132–33; as a Redstick leader, 126, 132–36; and reliance on Tallassee King, 65, 66, 69–72, 77, 79, 175n8, 178nn31–32, 179n37; as a riverine leader, 64–65, 84, 127, 144, 146, 176n11. *See also* Creeks, talks; Creek–Georgia alliance; Treaty of Augusta (1783)
Tathlabegey of Cusseta, 36–37, 164n35
Telfair, Edward, 86, 93
Tennessee, 83, 86, 95, 102, 114, 128, 142, 185n25. *See also* Southwest Territory (Tennessee)
Tensaw, 141, 180n38, 199n33
Thisatera (Chickasaw town), 98, 186n32
Thompson, Alice, 94

Three Rivers Resolution, 83–84; challenges to by local actors/peoples, 90–94, 99–102; formation of, 88, 90, 96–98; intervention by Cusseta to support, *89*, 90, 102; origins of, 85–88. *See also specific conflicts and leaders*
Thrower, Robert G., 141
Tohopeka (Horseshoe Bend), 143
Tombigbee River. *See* rivers
trade. *See* Creeks, trade; Creek-British relations
Treaty of 1739 (Treaty of Coweta), 31, 135, 163n22
Treaty of Augusta (1763), 39–40
Treaty of Augusta (1783), 74–76, 77–79, 178n26
Treaty of Fort Jackson (1814), 143–44
Treaty of Fort Wilkinson (1802), 113, 121, 192n20
Treaty of Galphinton (1785), 179n33
Treaty of New York (1790), 80, 82, 87–88, 191n11
Treaty of Paris (1763), 38–39, 42, 44, 46, 49, 73, 165n39, 167n5
Treaty of Paris (1783), 73, 76, *81*, 178n30
Treaty of Pensacola (1765), 40–41, 199n31
Treaty of Savannah (1757), 33, 163n27
Treaty of Shoulderbone Creek (1786), 80, 180n38
Treaty of the Creek Agency (1804), 122–24, 194n36
Treaty of Washington (1805), 123–24, 129, 194n38
Tuckabatchee Half Breed of Tuckabatchee, 36
Tugalo (Lower Cherokee town), 22
Tuskeenohau of Cusseta, 134
Tussekiah Mico of Cusseta, 102
Tustunnuggee Hopoie of Tuckabatchee, 133

United States, 5; Cherokees and, 1, 194n40; Chickasaws and, 179n34; expansion into Deep South, 67–68, 107–9, 120, 122–23, 140–45; as an expansionist colonial power, 65, 73, 84–85; "expansion with honor" policy and, 86; "plan of civilization" policy and, 126–27; population statistics, 85. *See also* Creeks, diplomacy; *names of specific conflicts and leaders*
Upper Creeks. *See* Creeks, Upper Creek province
US Declaration of Independence, on Indigenous peoples, 67–68

Villebeuvre, Juan de la, 96, 99, 185n27, 186n29, 187n34

wampum, 48; Creek/Muscogean adaptation of, 48, 50, 169n14; in diplomacy with the Spanish, 101; in diplomacy with the United States, 88, 110, 190n8; in intertribal diplomacy, 48–49, 97, 108, 118, 169n15, 186n29. *See also* Creeks, diplomacy
war. *See names of specific conflicts, groups, leaders, and treaties*
War for Independence. *See* American War for Independence
War of 1812, 11, 126. *See also* Creek War (1813–14)
War of the Austrian Succession (1739–1748), 22–23
Washington, George, 87, 96; Creek diplomacy and, 88, 183n13; Creek honorific as "Virginia King," 177n23; presidential administration and policy of, 86, 91
water. *See under* Creeks, water; rivers
Weatherford, Charles, 183n13
Weatherford, William, 141
West Yazoo (Choctaw town), 97
White, Enrique, 93, 101, 184n22, 187n38. *See also* Mad Dog of Tuckabatchee
White Lieutenant of Okfuskee, 69; Creek-Chickasaw War and, 100–101; death of, 112; and diplomacy with the Spanish, 188n45; and diplomacy

with the United States, 85–88, 90, 92, 94, 112, 183n12, 188n45; Three Rivers Resolution and, 97
Wolf, Eric, 10, 158n20
Wolf of Muccolossus, 26; Creek-Cherokee War and, 26, 152n12; Creek-Choctaw War and, 45, 56–58; and diplomacy with the British, 32–34, 37, 163n26, 168n12, 172n35; and opposition from below, 33–34; relatives of, 30, 56, 163n26, 172n33; on Tuckabatchee as a meeting ground, 36

Wolf's Friend of Thisatera (Chickasaw leader), 96–99, 185n27, 186n30, 186nn32–33
Wolf Warrior of Fusihatchee, 34–37, 164n31
women, 3, 8, 10, 21, 25, 30, 51, 86, 88, 94, 96, 100, 135, 171n27. *See also under* Creeks, kinship
Wright, James, 38
Wright, Joseph, 33

Yamasee War (1715–1718), 22
Yaufkee Emautlau of Autossee, 112

www.ingramcontent.com/pod-product-compliance
Lightning Source LLC
Chambersburg PA
CBHW032213230426
43672CB00011B/2545